A SOUTHERN ILLINOIS ALBUM

I0809953

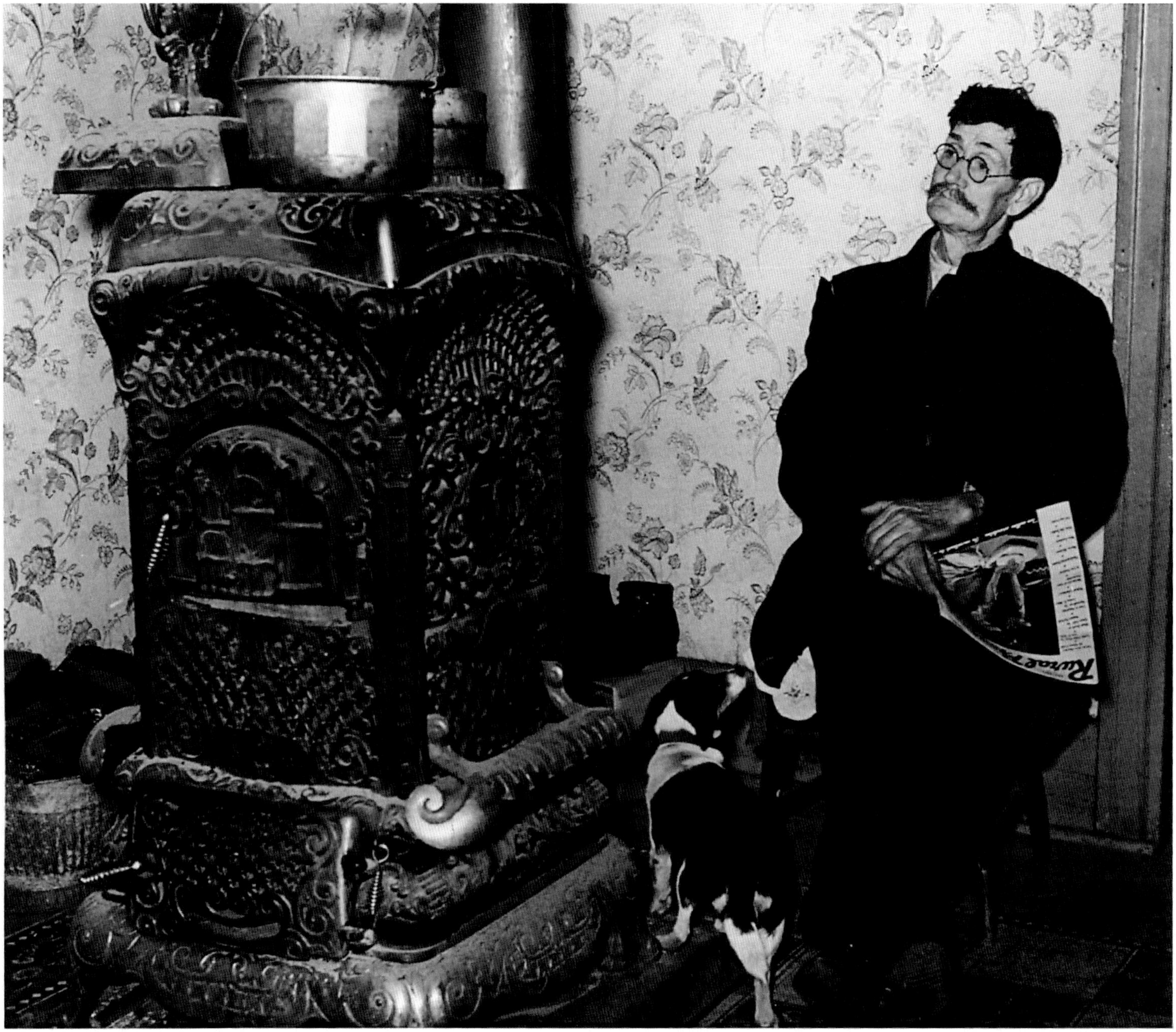

A SOUTHERN ILLINOIS ALBUM

Farm Security Administration Photographs, 1936–1943

HERBERT K. RUSSELL

with a foreword by F. JACK HURLEY

SOUTHERN ILLINOIS UNIVERSITY PRESS

Carbondale

Southern Illinois University Press
Mail Code 6806; Southern Illinois University;
Morris Library, 605 Agriculture Dr.,
Carbondale, IL 62901
siupress.com

Copyright © 1990 by the Board of Trustees, Southern Illinois University
All rights reserved
Printed in the United States of America
Production supervised by Natalia Nadraga

First printed December 1989.

Library of Congress Cataloging-in-Publication Data

Russell, Herbert K.
A southern Illinois album.

(Shawnee books)
1. Illinois—Description and travel—1865–1950—Views.
2. Illinois—Rural conditions—Pictorial works.
I. United States. Farm Security Administration.
II. Title.
F542.R87 1990 997.3'042 89-6241
ISBN 0-8093-1588-2
ISBN 0-8093-1589-0 (pbk.)

Printed on recycled paper

The manufacturer's authorized representative in the EU for product safety: Mare Nostrum Group B.V., Mauritskade 21D, 1091 GC Amsterdam, The Netherlands. gpsr@mare-nostrum.co.uk

SIU
Southern Illinois University System

CONTENTS

FOREWORD

THIS IS AN ALBUM of photographs that were taken nearly fifty years ago by photographers working for a federal agency, the Farm Security Administration. Herbert Russell gives a good, brief explanation of the agency itself and the photographers who were, from time to time, in its service. But because these pictures were taken a long time ago, in a very different era than our own, and because we tend today to live in an image-saturated world that discourages close visual analysis, I want to look closely at a selected few of the pictures that Herb Russell has chosen. There is a tremendous bank of information contained in this collection and I hope that I can help you, the viewer, unlock that bank for yourself.

Herb Russell has chosen to arrange these photographs in a way that Roy Stryker, the director of the photographic arm of the FSA, would have liked very much. "Farming and Farm Towns," "Miners and Mineral Wealth," "Life on the River and Shore," "Recreation and Religion," and "Signs of the Times" reflect the way Roy's mind worked and the way the great file in Washington was, and is, organized. Roy Stryker was a social scientist, not an artist, and his interests reflected this background. He was far more interested in creating a permanent document of American life at a given point in time than he was in creating art (if, in fact, he knew what the word meant). Some of the people who worked for the photographic project of the FSA were artists in the deepest sense of the word, but even they had to learn to confine their needs to make personal statements within the overall needs of the organization.

Now let us look at some of the individual pictures in the specific sections of this book. Let us look at them in the context of today and also let us try to understand the original context in which they were made. The first picture in the section called "Farming and Farm Towns" is actually part of a series that also originally included the last picture in the section. John Vachon was visiting Crawford County in May of 1940. As part of his instructions from Roy Stryker, he probably carried a note to the effect, "Get some pictures of tomato agriculture, if you can. We need them for the file." John found his farmer planting young tomato seedlings and went to work. The first shot shows the overall context. The farmer drives his team across the photograph from right to left, riding a piece of equipment that includes a small disc plow in the front, a tank that probably holds liquid fertilizer, with two small (and in this picture rather insignificant) figures riding low to the ground behind. We sense the flatness of the country, the stretch of land away to the horizon, the size of the field, the heat of the sun directly overhead (note the position of the shadows directly beneath the horses). The purpose of the picture is clearly to put the farmer and his equipment and his helpers into their correct relationship to the land, and it succeeds on that level. It was never intended to be an emotion-charged photograph. It was intended to be a photograph of tomato planting. Vachon's second shot, and the last picture in the series on farming and farm towns, was taken the same day and involves the same people, but in this case we have a different kind of image. Here Vachon has shifted to the back of the equipment and much closer. Now the picture is about the emotional experience of planting seedlings all day in the sun. Now we see the patience in the bend of the farmer's back and head, we see the two little girls perched very low behind so that they can drop the individual plants into the ground and cover them up. This is a picture about hard work, done by a family working together. You could hardly say that these people are having "fun," but they are getting a job done and taking satisfaction in it. Which of these two pictures is "better"? Most of us today would probably unhesitatingly choose the second. We like our pictures to contain some emotion. Stryker and, I think, Vachon, would have argued that both pictures are valid, one for its informational content and the other for its emotional content.

Many of the photographs originally were taken for specific special purposes. We look at Arthur Rothstein's picture, "Rural land. Saline County," or Russell Lee's "Soil erosion on land that has been cleared of timber" and we say to ourselves, "What terrible roads they had back then," or "Isn't that an awful-looking field?" At the time, however, Rothstein's picture was intended to be shoved under the nose of a legislator in order to convince him or her that no one should have to live on such a road. Lee's picture of soil erosion was just the sort of image that the government could use in a pamphlet to try to convince farmers to use their land more carefully. These were working pictures. Again, they were never intended to be art. They were intended to make a point and they did their job well. In doing that job, they also became a part of the permanent record so that we can today look back and be glad that most of us do not have to contend with such roads and that most of us know how to avoid such fields.

Some of the pictures that we now look upon as images of nostalgia were originally intended as sources of reassurance, both that rural life was still alive and well and that the FSA was doing everything it could to help. By the late 1930s Americans had been hearing for years about the disastrous state of rural America. In fact, for many farmers, things were getting a bit better by the late years of the Great Depression. The FSA was helping with its programs of small loans to farmers and it wanted the general public to know what was going on. Look at the picture by Arthur Rothstein on page 8. An FSA rehabilitation client named Opal Shaw, and his wife, are holding jars of canned goods that they have produced. They are smiling. Their farm is not an affluent one, the barn behind them is weathered and rough, but Opal and wife look healthy and warm in the January light and those jars signify security. A similarly conceived picture appears on page 12. Here John Vachon has allowed a family of FSA rehabilitation borrowers to define security visually as a huge pile of stovewood and an impressive stepladder of children, seven in all. My personal favorite, however, is Vachon's "FSA tenant purchase borrower and his family. Crawford County. May, 1940" (page 15). Here we have it all. Father reading an informative news journal, *Poultry Keeper*, while mother sews and the two sturdy, barefoot boys play on the living-room linoleum. Signs of affluence abound. The linoleum itself is one, as is the wallpaper. More important are the pump organ and the radio. These people are doing well by 1940 standards and part of the reason is the fact that they have gotten help from the FSA. Were pictures of this sort propaganda? In a way, yes. They were used to show both rural and urban viewers that the agency was doing good work. They were not, however, faked. The man and his wife did exist. That was their home and those were their children. The possessions were theirs and they had gotten help from the government. If the children were cleaner than usual and the room a bit more orderly than might have been the case on more casual occasions, this probably reflects the desire of the housewife to put her best foot forward as much as the desire of the government agency to show off the results of the programs to best advantage.

Some pictures show more than they were intended to. Consider the image on page 21, which shows an FSA rehabilitation supervisor with a client. Here Arthur Rothstein has caught a young, almost dangerously earnest rehabilitation supervisor in conference with a much-older, ill-shaven farmer. The supervisor's clothes, his leather jacket and his clean shirt and tie, his wire-rimmed glasses, and even his cigarette signal education and privilege. On his lap are the forms that tell us that this is government at work. Near his head is a printed sign exhorting all to incorporate "seed disinfectants at planting time." He is flanked by an impressive filing cabinet. His body language combines a certain earnestness of purpose with the relaxed sense that he is in command. He leans back in his chair. The farmer does not have such luxuries. He is the applicant. He sits forward in his chair, hands gripping the felt hat that is his one sign of respectability. His blue work shirt is buttoned at the neck but there is no tie to dress it, not that a tie would dress a work shirt and bib overalls very much. Stolid and decent, the farmer seems to represent the small independent yeoman that Jefferson had hoped would always dominate American life. Jefferson's yeoman sits with his hat in hands waiting for a decision from the kid with the degree from Ag School and the government job. It is an image that was prophetic in 1939 and it still has power to disturb us today.

The section of the book entitled "Miners and Mineral Wealth" is Arthur Rothstein's and it should be. Arthur loved industrial subjects and did them well. Like any boy who came from a Jewish upbringing in New York in the late 1920s and early 1930s, Arthur believed in the strength of the working class. His core assumptions included the ideas that work is good, that the toughest, dirtiest work is honorable, and that the family is the center of the workingman's life. To be out of work was the ultimate tragedy. At this stage of his life, Arthur tended to mistrust bosses and big corporations and the pictures reflect this attitude as well.

Rothstein's picture "Coal miner and daughter" is a wonderful, tender picture of the pride of a father in his beautiful little girl, but it is also a hymn in praise of the working class. The man's hands are working hands. His cap is a workman's cap, his clothes and boots are built for work. It is a positive, upbeat image. On the same trip, however, and in the same town, Bush, Arthur Rothstein found two much sadder images of men who were out of work, with time heavy on their hands. "Unemployed mine worker. Bush. January, 1939" is actually one of Rothstein's better-known pictures. It has had considerable use and for obvious reasons. It is a picture that stays in the mind. The resignation and confusion on the face of the man, the indrawn way he sits on the chair near the massive but outdated cast-iron stove, and the solicitous concern of the beagle dog make the picture an icon of unemployment. The other image, entitled "Unemployed coal miner. Bush. January, 1939" uses many of the same elements. A man waits with his elbow on the kitchen table. There is very little food on the table and an old kerosene lamp ties the room to past technology in the same way that the cast-iron stove does in the other picture. There is even a solicitous dog, though in this case we have to be satisfied with a picture on the wall calendar. It is not an image with the immediate impact of its earlier cousin, yet there are disturbing details, especially the small pile of shotgun shells on the table behind the lamp. Is the man going hunting for rabbits to feed his family, or for bosses, or strike-breakers?

As a young man, Arthur Rothstein believed in organized labor. His picture of an "Officer of the United Mine Workers of America. Herrin. January, 1939" reflects this attitude. Here is a portrait of strength, force, and integrity. This fellow looks straight, but *tough*—just the sort you want handling negotiations—if you are in the union. Mining in all its processes fascinated Rothstein and he took the risks to go right down into the mines, firing off flashbulbs in a potentially explosive atmosphere in order to get the pictures of men setting roof braces and loading the cars. Seeing these pictures of men with their bent bodies and kindly, work-worn faces, one can, perhaps, more easily acknowledge the need for safer conditions and better wages. Certainly that was part of what Arthur Rothstein intended us to see.

These photographs of mines, miners, and mining, and subsequent pictures of life on and near the river, as well as pictures of recreation and religion and even signboards, raise an interesting question. These photographers were supposed to be taking pictures that related to a federal farm program. What were they doing down in mines, or riding on riverboats, or looking at signs? The answer lies in Roy Stryker's broad conception of the job that the photographic arm of the FSA was supposed to do. In a 1939 interview Stryker told his friend Jim McCamy that he had from the first assumed that his group's primary function was to record and defend the work of the agency, but once that was done, he felt that they were free to record the whole milieu in which the agency's work went on. Now, *milieu* is a very broad word. The milieu of the FSA was American life and culture. In short, Stryker and his photographers took the pictures that their agency needed for its own use, but they also used the time and film that the government made available to do what they loved best, to create as complete a document as possible of American life and culture in the late depression years. There was nothing underhanded about this. In fact, it was widely acknowledged and applauded. We today can be thankful that the New Deal was tolerant of such a broad-based experiment because otherwise we would have far less visual information about the way our grandparents lived.

To return to our perusal of the pictures, the section entitled "Life on the River and Shore" might well have contained a subtitle, "the 1937 flood." That flood was a bad one and it received widespread coverage in the national and international news media. Stryker saw no point in using his photographers to take the same pictures everyone else was getting—floating animals, inundated houses, and shivering families. Instead, he asked them to look for photographs that would symbolize the aftermath of the flooding. Russell Lee's picture of overturned houses in Shawneetown, page 67, is just such a picture, as are several others. This was part of the milieu, or context, that farming and the FSA had to operate in in 1937, and so, of course, it was considered a good and valid picture. Looking at these aftermath pictures today, we are struck by the mud, the depressing rows of tents that people had to stay in for weeks, and the crowded conditions, yet Lee's picture, "Part of a flood refugee family in a tent" also reminds us that much was saved and that, somehow, life went on with even the occasional light moment.

Light moments also seem to dominate the section on recreation and religion. It is good to see these pictures included for our impressions of the 1930s are too often based on Lange's photograph of the migrant mother, reproduced in this book's Preface, or Steinbeck's *Grapes of Wrath*. People have to get together, for recreation, or for entertainment or for worship, or whatever. From time to time, normal, healthy people must see each other and rub elbows, even if there is a depression or the beginnings of a war on. I am glad that Arthur Rothstein managed to get into the Oke Doke dance hall in Williamson County in January of 1939. Those two pictures were not easy for a Jewish kid with a New York accent that stood out a mile to get, yet he got in and got them. The clannishness of the men standing near the oil-drum stove is a document of the highest order as is the self-conscious respectability of the dancing couple in the second photograph.

"Signs of the Times" provides us with a number of thought-provoking images that fittingly end this *Southern Illinois Album*. All the FSA photographers loved signs and looked for them at every opportunity. Signs could be humorous as the one advertising "Dr. Spring's office" (page 105), or they could indicate the cost of living, as in the store window that announces sausage at three pounds for 25 cents and oleomargarine for 9½ cents a pound (page 108). Some signs of the times were not signs at all. A factory with many of the windows broken out, indicating abandonment, was all too often a sign of the times, and one that we recognize all too easily today. The incorporation of tin advertising signs into a shanty, as in the picture by Arthur Rothstein on page 102, was certainly a sign of the times, and signs were also used to paper the insides of the more humble houses in order to keep out wind and cold. Some signs of the times are more obvious to us today than they were to contemporaries. I doubt, for example, if Arthur Rothstein thought of his picture of a Sinclair gasoline station attendant cleaning an automobile's windshield as anything unusual. Indeed, this was a document of the mundane and ordinary. Show it to your children to prove to them that gasoline stations actually used to offer service!

The passage of time has a wonderful and mysterious effect on the photographs. Changes in clothing styles, car bodies, tastes in furniture, and standards of living all become sharper with time. So much has changed in the past fifty years, yet much has remained the same in Southern Illinois and elsewhere in this country. Certainly modern standards of living are higher, but in other respects there are powerful similarities. People still consider their families important. They still worry about security, although they may not define security as a very large woodpile and seven children. They still fight the snow in the wintertime and some still fight the mud in spring. They still prefer to work and hate to be out of work. They still get together for recreation and for church and, from time to time, the river still threatens them. Perhaps that is why these pictures still hit us so strongly. The time is a long time ago. The people look just a little different, as do the cars, the houses, and the agricultural equipment. Yet underneath the superficial differences we are reminded that these people are us and their problems are not unrecognizably different from our own. We look at these pictures of hard times and hard-won gains and think, could we do as well? Could we cope? And somehow we are reassured. These people are us. They came through it. If we had to, we could too.

F. Jack Hurley

PREFACE

THE PHOTOGRAPHS IN THIS BOOK owe their existence to an idea by one of President Franklin D. Roosevelt's advisers—to document the problems of rural life in the Great Depression and thereby show the need for FDR's social programs. Toward these ends, government-hired photographers were sent all over the United States in the mid-1930s, particularly to those regions where the depression hit the hardest: to the Dust Bowl states of the Great Plains, to migrant labor camps in Michigan and California, to mining towns in West Virginia, to worn-out farms in Georgia, and to Southern Illinois.

A dozen staff photographers and several part-time personnel snapped over a quarter of a million pictures between 1935 and 1943. In so doing, they produced one of the largest photo collections in American history. The pictures turned out to be unusually effective when printed in the popular media (which published them for free), and in the end they helped FDR achieve the social legislation he desired for America's rural areas.

But the photographs were ultimately to have a more far-reaching effect than originally planned. What began as political propaganda with an expected short life soon came to be regarded as Ameri-

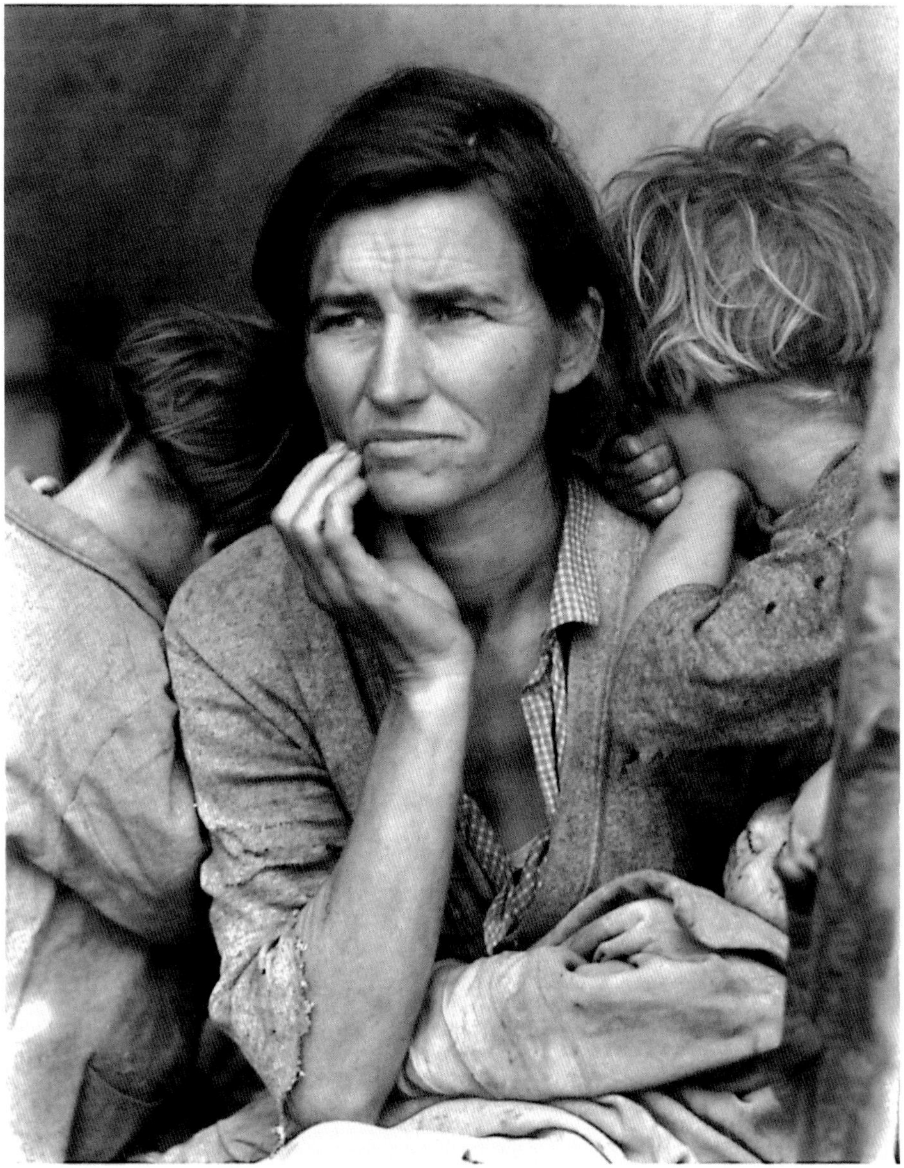

This photograph of a thirty-two-year-old migrant mother of seven stranded at dusk in the California fruit belt near Nipomo is probably the best known of the thousands of pictures taken by FSA photographers. The photograph was taken by Dorothea Lange in 1936.

cana of a more enduring type. Today, many of the pictures are viewed as valuable historical documents, or as art—or as both. Typical of the latter is the picture that is probably the best known of the 270,000 images, the Dorothea Lange photograph of a migrant mother.

Taken near Nipomo, California, in March 1936, Lange's picture shows thirty-two-year-old Florence Thompson in a tent by the side of the road on the evening of the day in which she had sold the tires from her car to buy food. As Thompson looked uneasily down the road (there was no work in Nipomo), two of her seven children turned away from the dust of the road and the camera while a third, too young to worry, slept. Lange quickly took five pictures and then departed. Although she failed to learn Thompson's name, Lange succeeded in acquiring something else; as has been remarked more than once, she captured "the face of the Great Depression."

Not one of the pictures in this book is as well known as this—indeed, few have ever been printed in book form—but most of them have one element in common with Lange's picture: these too are the faces of the Great Depression, not as the world has seen them, but as they were viewed in the coal-mining towns of Herrin, West Frankfort, and Zeigler; in the river communities of Shawneetown, Cairo, and Grayville; in farming regions near McLeansboro, Newton, and Harrisburg; and in two dozen other Southern Illinois county seats, hamlets, and landings.

The historical background of this extraordinary archive is fascinating. In May 1935, Roosevelt's assistant secretary of agriculture, Rexford G. Tugwell, guided into existence a New Deal program administered by a new organization called the Resettlement Administration (RA) to help low-income farmers and farm laborers improve their lives through land conservation, low-interest loans, and relocation to more productive surroundings. The organization and program were successful and two years later were absorbed by the Department of Agriculture under a new name—the Farm Security Administration (FSA).

To direct the FSA's Historical Section, or publications unit, Tugwell chose Roy Stryker, a former acquaintance from Columbia University, whom he induced to take the position at $5,600 per year and with a job description broad enough to include whatever Stryker wanted it to:

> Direct the activities of investigators, photographers, economists, sociologists and statisticians engaged in the accumulation and compilation of reports . . . , photographic material, vital statistics, agricultural surveys, maps, and sketches necessary to make accurate descriptions of the various . . . phases of the Resettlement Administration, particularly with regard to the historical, sociological and economic aspects of the several programs and their accomplishments.

Because Stryker knew the value of photographs from his college-teaching days, he decided to rely on these to get his message across. As a result of that decision, he set out to acquire an appropriate staff, and in so doing recruited individuals who would later distinguish themselves as some of the most gifted photographers of the twentieth century.

To staff his unit Stryker first hired his former student photographer at Columbia University, Arthur Rothstein, a recent chemistry graduate who set up the Farm Security Administration darkroom and then went on the road (in 1935) as a full-time photographer. Rothstein is particularly important to this discussion, not only because he took one of the best-known FSA photographs (of the Dust Bowl), but also because he visited Illinois in 1939 and 1940 and left behind the FSA's largest pictorial record of Southern Illinois in the Great Depression. When Rothstein eventually left the FSA in 1940, he served as a picture editor in the Office of War Information (1941–43) and then in the Army Signal Corps (1943–46) before beginning a twenty-five-year career as director of photography for *Look* magazine. He subsequently served in a similar capacity at *Parade*. By the close of his long life

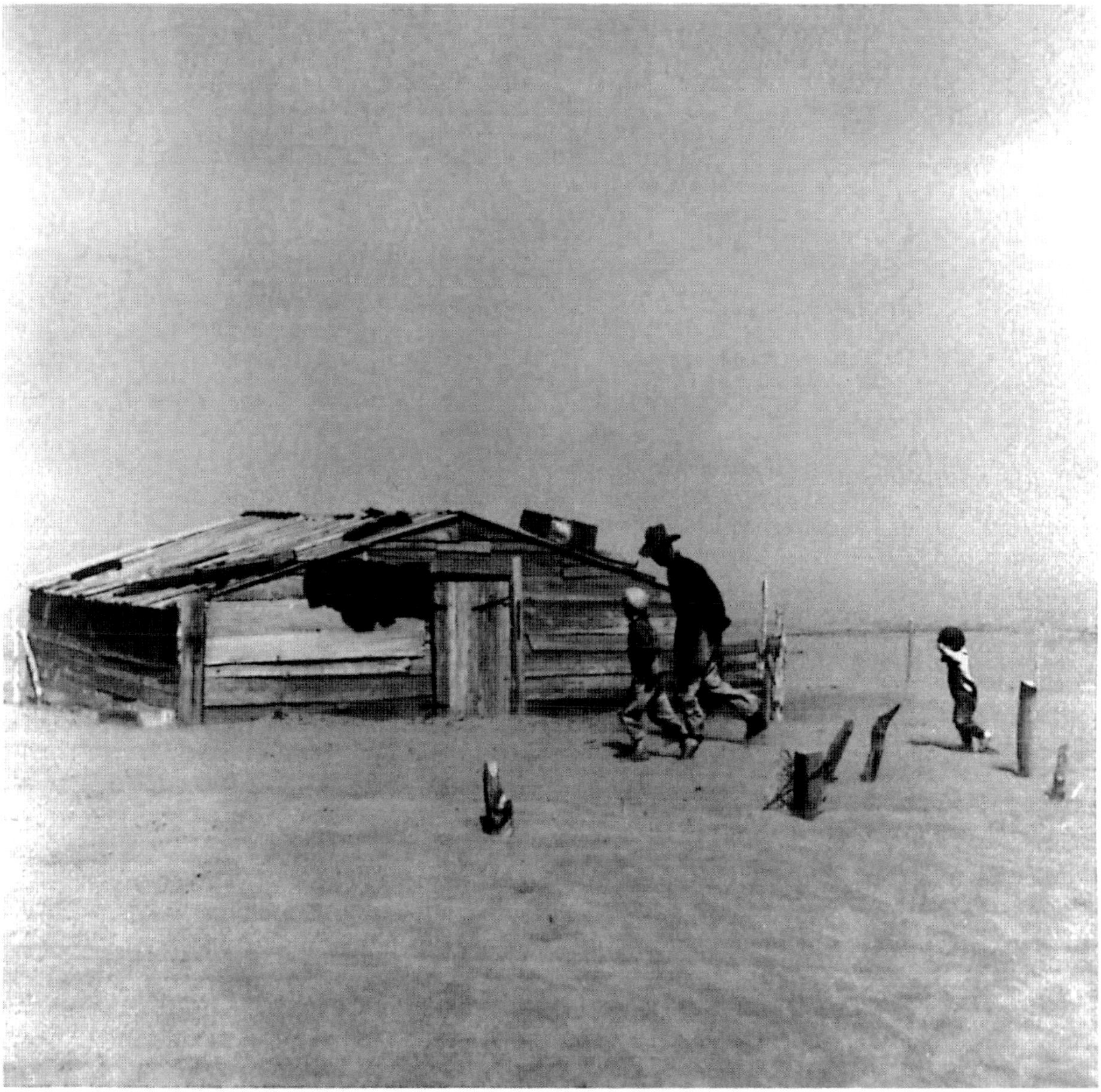

The best-known Dust Bowl photograph of the 1930s was taken by Farm Security Administration photographer Arthur Rothstein. Rothstein also visited Southern Illinois on several occasions—in 1939 and 1940—and most of the photographs in this book are his.

(1915–85), he had won more than fifty photography awards and completed nine books. He is responsible for two-thirds of the pictures in this book.

Stryker also hired the Ottawa, Illinois, engineer-artist-photographer Russell Lee, who did much of his best work in the Midwest and who took many of the remaining pictures in this volume. Lee worked for the FSA from 1936 to 1943 and left behind some of the most dramatic photos of the Great (Ohio River) Flood of 1937. He spent much of his post-FSA life as a free-lance photographer and college teacher and died in 1986 at the age of eighty-three.

John Vachon was another photographer who passed through the region and left his mark. Vachon's photos are frequently a blend of silence and sensitivity—comprehension without comment—and several of the best agricultural photos in this book are his. Following his FSA experience (1935–42), he spent much of the rest of his professional career with *Look* magazine (1947–71). He died in 1975 at the age of sixty-one.

The work of two other FSA staff photographers is also featured. Carl Mydans (born in 1907) worked only a year for the FSA (1935–36) before joining the initial staff of *Life*. While on assignment in the Philippines, he was taken prisoner by the Japanese and survived World War II prison camps in the islands and in China before being released in time to take one of the best-known pictures of the war—that of General Douglas MacArthur wading ashore in his famous 1945 "return" to the Philippines. Mydans took the earliest-dated FSA photo in this collection, May 1936. Arthur Siegel (1913–78) free-lanced as a photographer with a wide variety of magazines and with the Associated Press following his term with the FSA (1942–43). Siegel took the last-dated photo in this collection, June 1943.

Others who enhanced their photography credentials while with the Farm Security Administration included Walker Evans, the moody and temperamental artist whose photos of the Deep South in *Let Us Now Praise Famous Men* (1941) form an indelible record of the depression's effects on that region; the New York artist-photographer Ben Shahn, who translated his visual images to WPA murals; and Marion Post Wolcott, who relied on her personality traits of sensitivity and grit to help produce fine FSA records of several regions.

These were among the best-known of the full-time photographers, but there were also others who worked intermittently, or on a part-time basis, or whose work was acquired by the FSA, including C. William Horrell, the Southern Illinois University professor-photographer from Anna, whose work is also represented in this book.

Life on the road for an FSA photographer in the mid-1930s was anything but glamorous: equipped with three government-issue cameras as well as their own equipment, including flashbulbs, tripods, and film-processing chemicals, the photographers were paid about thirty-five dollars a week along with five to six dollars per day for food and lodging, and three to five cents a mile for travel. They were supposed to help "explain America to Americans" (as Tugwell put it) by seeking out and photographing that one-third of the nation described by FDR as "ill-housed, ill-clad, and ill-nourished"—regardless of the fact that the most promising subjects often lived at the end of the worst roads, not all of which had bridges, ditches, or gravel (or anything else to improve them).

Nearly all the pictures were taken with thirty-five-millimeter cameras in black and white (there are only sixteen hundred color prints in the entire FSA collection). The photographers carried their own film-processing chemicals in order to develop their film (in hotel bathrooms) before mailing the negatives back to Washington—along with information as to what town or hamlet with a post office they were headed to next.

In the return mails, they could expect ample directions from Stryker as to where to go and what, precisely, to photograph:

> "Get pictures of representative small farms," he wrote Arthur Rothstein.

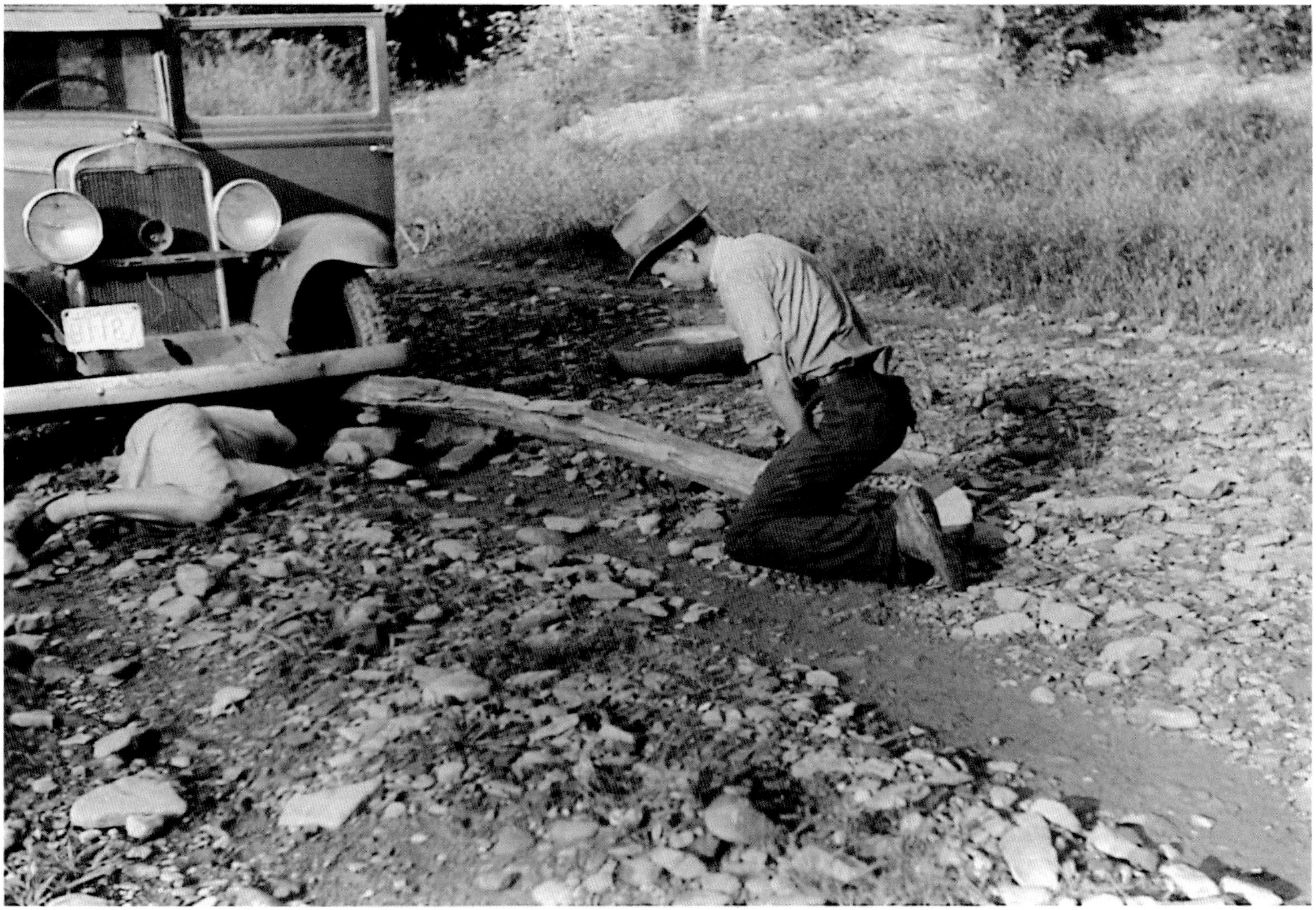

Life on the road had its hazards, especially when the roads were made for horses—a fact demonstrated by Farm Security Administration photographer Marion Post Wolcott, here seen (under the car) changing a tire with the help of a friend on a fence post.

> "Search for ideas to give the sense of loneliness experienced by the women folks who helped settle this country," he wrote Marion Post Wolcott as she headed off to the West. "This idea might be developed around an abandoned dwelling on a plains homestead. Look for interiors where the wallpaper still hangs to wall or ceiling."

> "Watch out, or you'll get caught in the flood raging in that part of the country," he wrote Russell Lee about the Ohio River's 1937 inundation of Southern Illinois. "Incidentally, if you get a chance to take any pictures . . . , be sure to get them."

Stryker might also advise his staff of a hundred other details, including the recent quality of their work, or send them on a new assignment.

A photographer assigned to Southern Illinois in 1939—the year many of these pictures were taken—would have found it relatively easy to get around. The Illinois Central Railroad running from Cairo northward stopped in virtually every small town, as did the Chicago and Eastern Illinois Railroad, with stops in Vienna, Marion, Johnston City, West Frankfort, and Benton. The highway system (minus interstate) was essentially the same as it would be a half-century later, and there were numerous bus routes connecting the towns.

The largest town in rural Southern Illinois was Centralia with a population of 16,000, the result of mining and railroad activity. Cairo, Mt. Vernon, West Frankfort, and Harrisburg followed in population in that order. No other towns in Southern Illinois had more than 10,000 inhabitants. Carbondale had 8,000; its university about 2,000.

Outside the towns, rural life was chancy following a decade in which drought, low prices, and overproduction had taken turns hammering farmers. Those most affected might qualify for one of the government's farm programs (the same act that created positions for the FSA's government photographers also provided relief for agriculture), and several of the pictures in this book depict farm "clients" undergoing "rehabilitation" — government language for the receipt of advice and loans or relocation to more productive land. Corn was the major farm crop, although the recently popularized soybean showed promise as a hardy new grain that could be adapted to the uncongenial soils of the region. Oats stood as a third important crop, an indicator of the great number of horses and mules in Southern Illinois in 1939.

Exploitation of mineral wealth was an uneven affair. Coal mining was both attractive and unattractive, depending on one's point of view: Franklin County coal was famous throughout the state as a high-energy fuel, but the men who mined it could never be sure of employment as a result of the increased reliance on mechanization. Some coal towns — such as Carterville, Cambria, and West Frankfort — resembled towns under siege, with piles of coal slag (or "slack") stacked high to the very edge of the municipal limits. Salem was prosperous because of its oil fields, one of the few such towns in the region, but it too had far too many men loitering on street corners at midday, or "on relief" — receiving either an outright dole or a make-work job through a federal agency such as the Works Progress Administration.

Life near the rivers was always risky. The Great Flood of 1937 washed away much of Old Shawneetown and every other Illinois town on the Ohio River except Cairo (its ancient levee withstood the flood by four inches). The Mississippi River routinely washed through river hamlets such as Grand Tower, and would continue to do so until the Mississippi levee system was completed after World War II. What was true of the major rivers was also true of the lesser ones, the Big Muddy, the Saline, and, in particular, the Little Wabash, which seemed to spend more time out of its banks than in.

A glimpse at either the Ohio or the Mississippi rivers in 1939 might have convinced a photographer he had returned to Mark Twain's day: many of the riverboats still ran on steam (fired by coal); paddle wheels provided the locomotion. There were also human vestiges of the past: Civil War veterans lived in some Southern Illinois towns (the last of the region's "boys in blue" would die in Karnak, near Cairo, in 1945).

Prices were also rooted in the past. A Hoover vacuum cleaner cost twenty dollars in 1939, a Philco radio half that, and the penny was still important: a large bar of Ivory soap and a man's tie both cost nine cents, the same as a pound of "dry salt jowl meat." Advertising of such goods might be placed in any of the numerous small town newspapers that survived the depression, or displayed more prominently in a store window, or more permanently on a barn: "Best in Egypt"—or some approximation thereof was popular. There was a strong sense of regional identity.

Lighted signs were common in towns, but there were few to none in the country for the reason that there was little or no electricity in the country. The home "light plant"—a combination of gasoline engine and batteries—could generate and store enough energy to power a light bulb over the kitchen table, an iron, and the family washing machine, but home light plants were rare.

This is not to say that the evenings of 1939 were without amusements: there was always the Southern Illinois mania for basketball (admission twenty cents), as well as the area's first and only radio station to listen to (WEBQ in Harrisburg), and the family Victrola, or possibly a Southern Illinois album that needed looking at. Or one could while away the dark Egyptian nights at the movies. There was a new movie every night or two at most Southern Illinois theaters. The affluent could buy a new Buick for under nine hundred dollars, fill the tank (at sixteen cents a gallon), and drive out to see the new "frog pond," which was to become Crab Orchard Lake, completed in 1939.

There was a hint of war throughout 1939—on page one of the newspapers, and in certain of the movies, and finally in the mock air attack on Carbondale staged by Army recruiters on the night of November 7.

Pearl Harbor signaled the end of the FSA and its photography unit. After December 7, 1941, pictures showing Americans as weak victims of circumstance drifted out of favor as the country rearmed and sought a more positive national image. By late 1942, the FSA had lost both its political and financial support and was abolished. The Historical Section of the FSA—with its photographers—was transferred to the Publication Bureau of the Office of War Information (OWI), where its chief product was wartime propaganda; in the new photos, soldiers trained while civilians produced munitions, rationed gas, and generally worked for the common good. By 1943, the pictorial unit was also abolished. The FSA and OWI prints and negatives were subsequently transferred to the Library of Congress in 1945, and by 1946 the FSA/OWI collection was complete. The two collections are now filed together.

The achievements of the FSA photographers are simply summarized: collectively, they helped invent and popularize the "documentary" style of photography in which pictures and their arrangement carry much of the information in a story. This accomplishment alone tends to offset the shortcomings of the collection, two of which are visible in this volume: there is a sameness about some of the pictures that justifies one FSA photographer's colloquial reference to them as "cookie cutters" (for some of the images are repeated again and again); also, because photographic emphasis was on generic themes rather than regional balance, certain gaps appear when the collection is approached in a strictly regional way. For this book, for example, there were scores of coal-mining pictures to choose from but only a handful of religious subjects, and numerous pictures of the Ohio River but none at all of the Mississippi.

When Roy Stryker received negatives from photographers in the field, he developed them and examined them in terms of their attributes and intent. His guiding criteria for selection or rejection was the quality of individual photos as these fitted into his plans to show certain themes of American life. Pictures that Stryker deemed acceptable were saved. Others—perhaps 100,000—he destroyed. Pictures that were distributed to the media, or saved but not distributed, were assigned a number and then filed in the Farm Security Administration archives in the Library of Congress, Washington, DC 20540. The captions—original with the photographers in the field—were filed with the photographs. The original captions are used in this book, although a handful of idiosyncratic instances of spelling, grammar, and nomenclature have been revised. File numbers of the photos are listed on pages 125–26.

FARMING AND FARM TOWNS

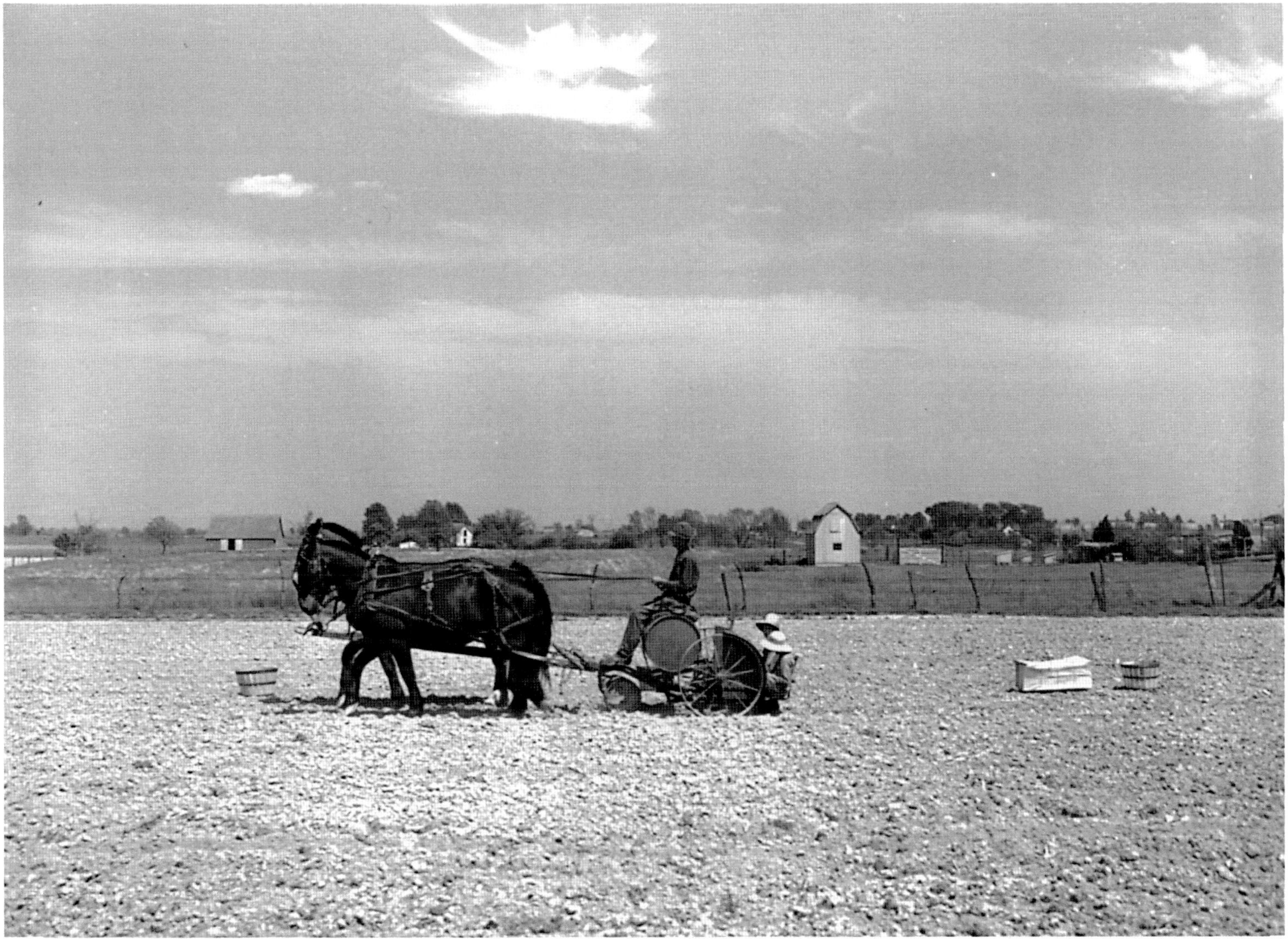

FSA rehabilitation borrower planting tomatoes with the help of his two little daughters.
Crawford County. May, 1940.
John Vachon

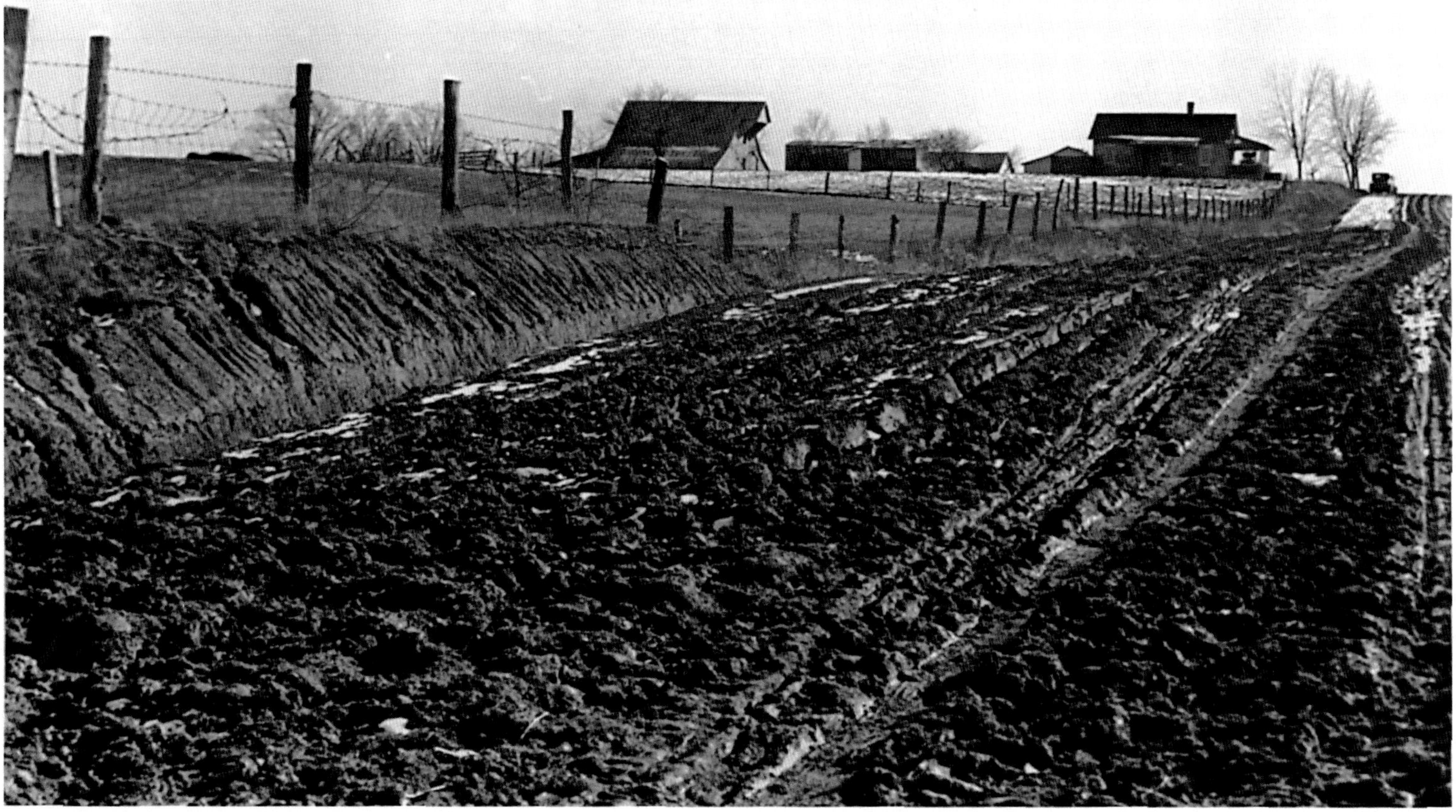

Rural land.
Saline County. January, 1939.
Arthur Rothstein

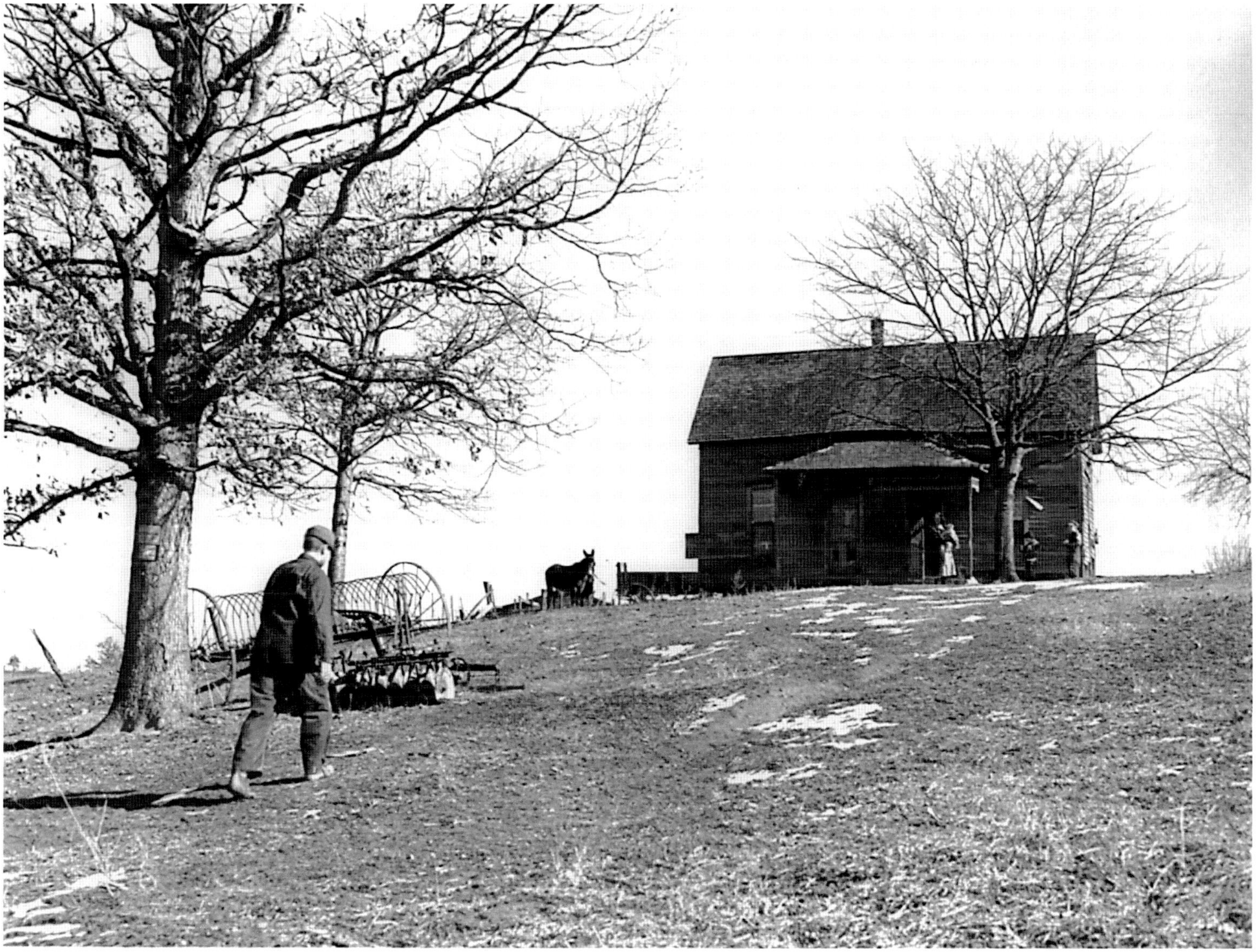

On the 80-acre tenant farm of an FSA rehabilitation client.
Home of Opal Shaw.
Gallatin County. January, 1939.
Arthur Rothstein

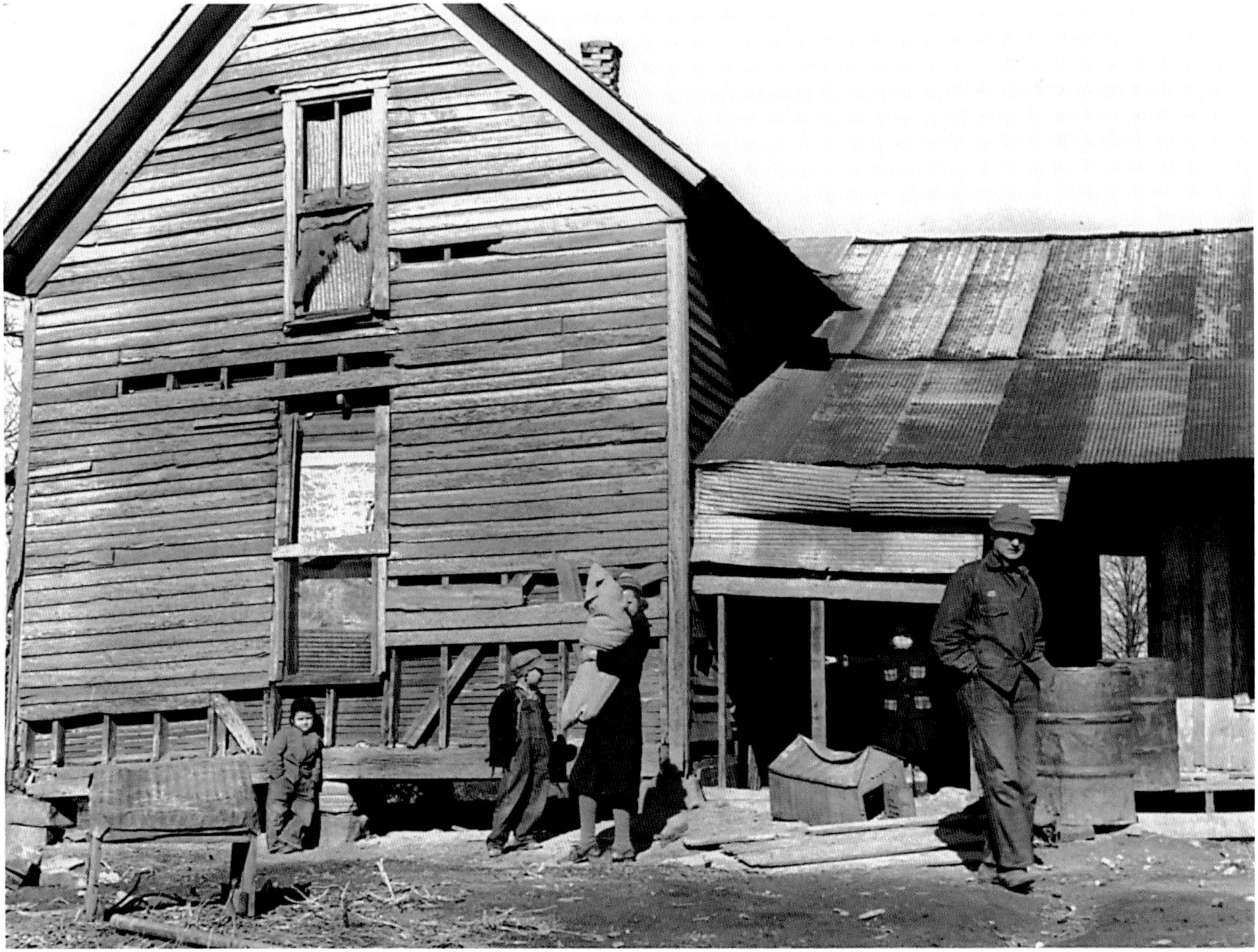

On the 80-acre tenant farm of an FSA rehabilitation client.
Home of Opal Shaw.
Gallatin County. January, 1939.
Arthur Rothstein

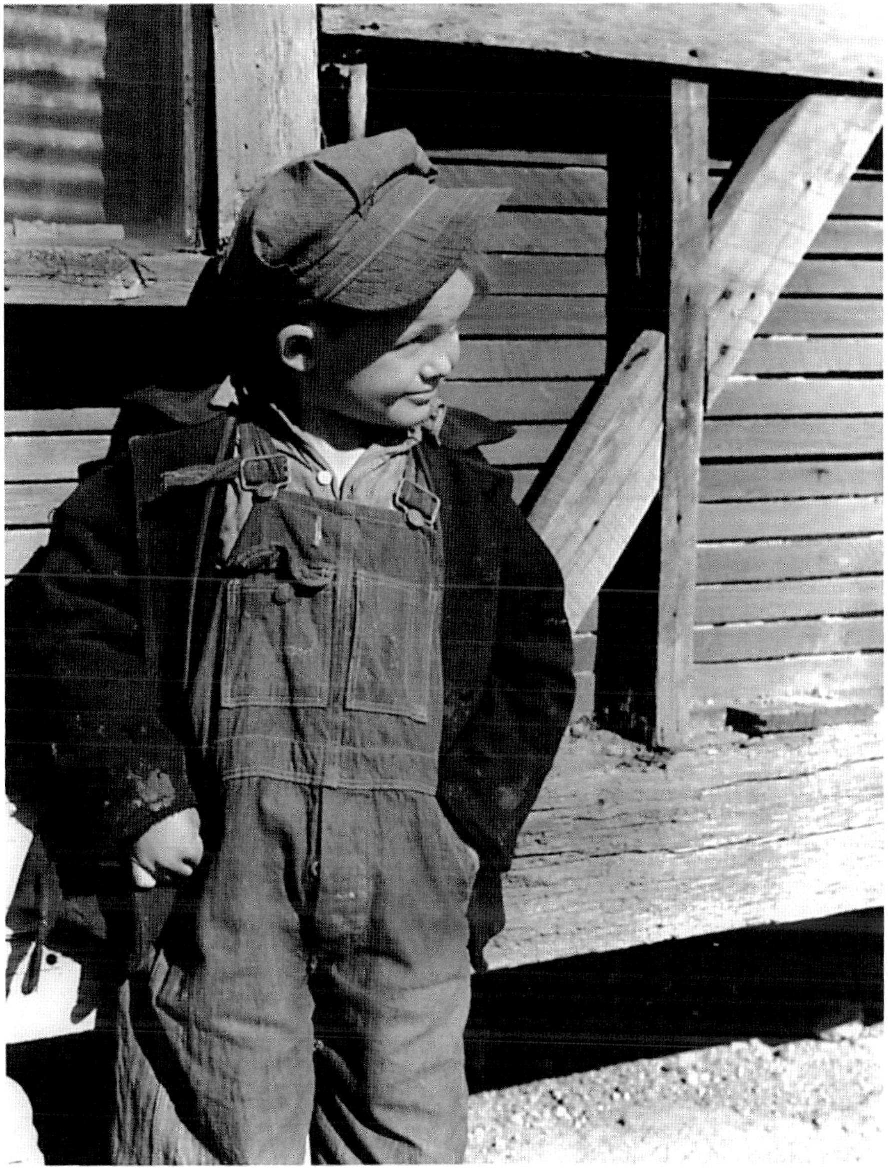

On the 80-acre tenant farm of an FSA rehabilitation client. The son of Opal Shaw.
Gallatin County. January, 1939.
Arthur Rothstein

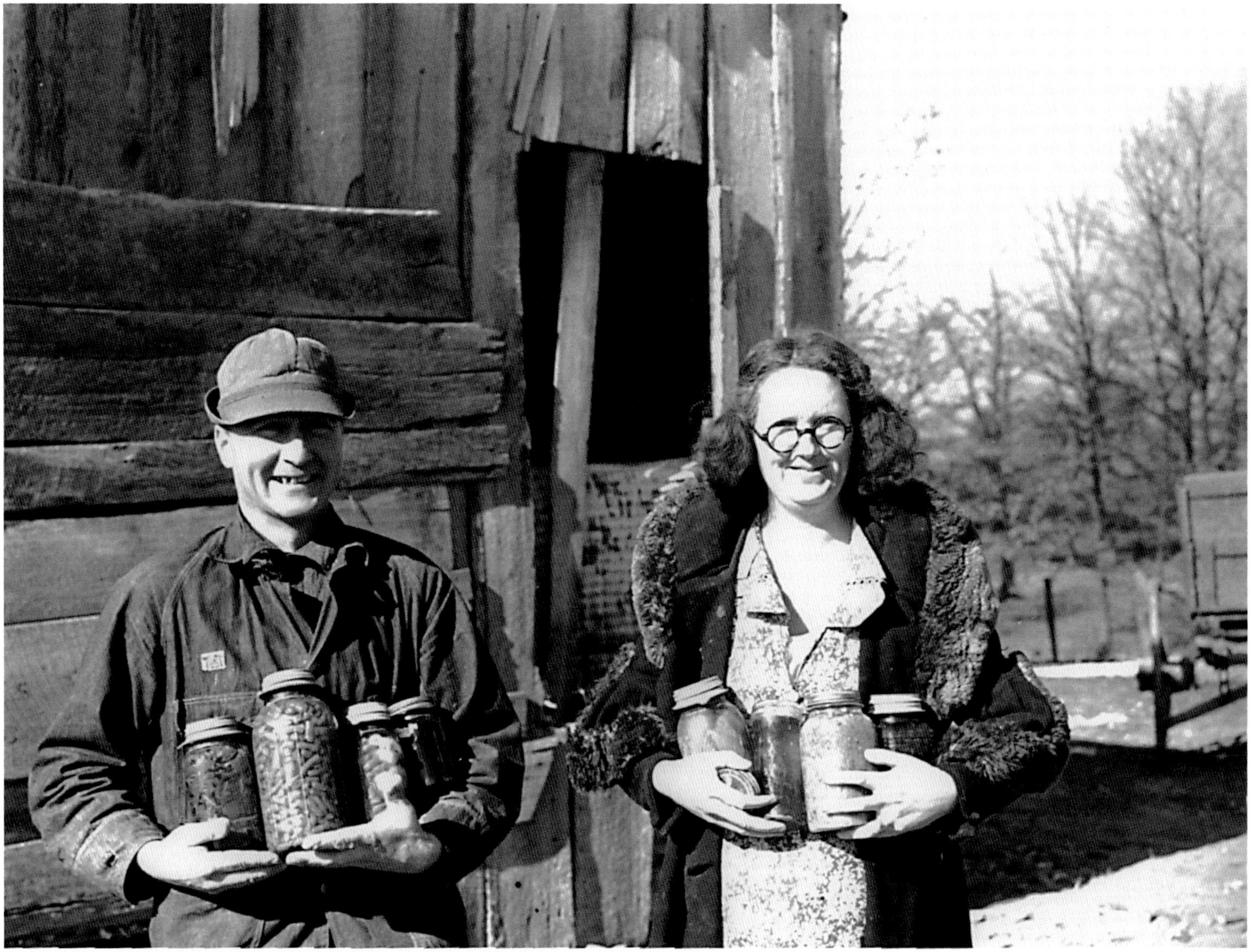

On the 80-acre tenant farm of an FSA rehabilitation client.
Opal Shaw and his wife, who holds canned produce she made.
Gallatin County. January, 1939.
Arthur Rothstein

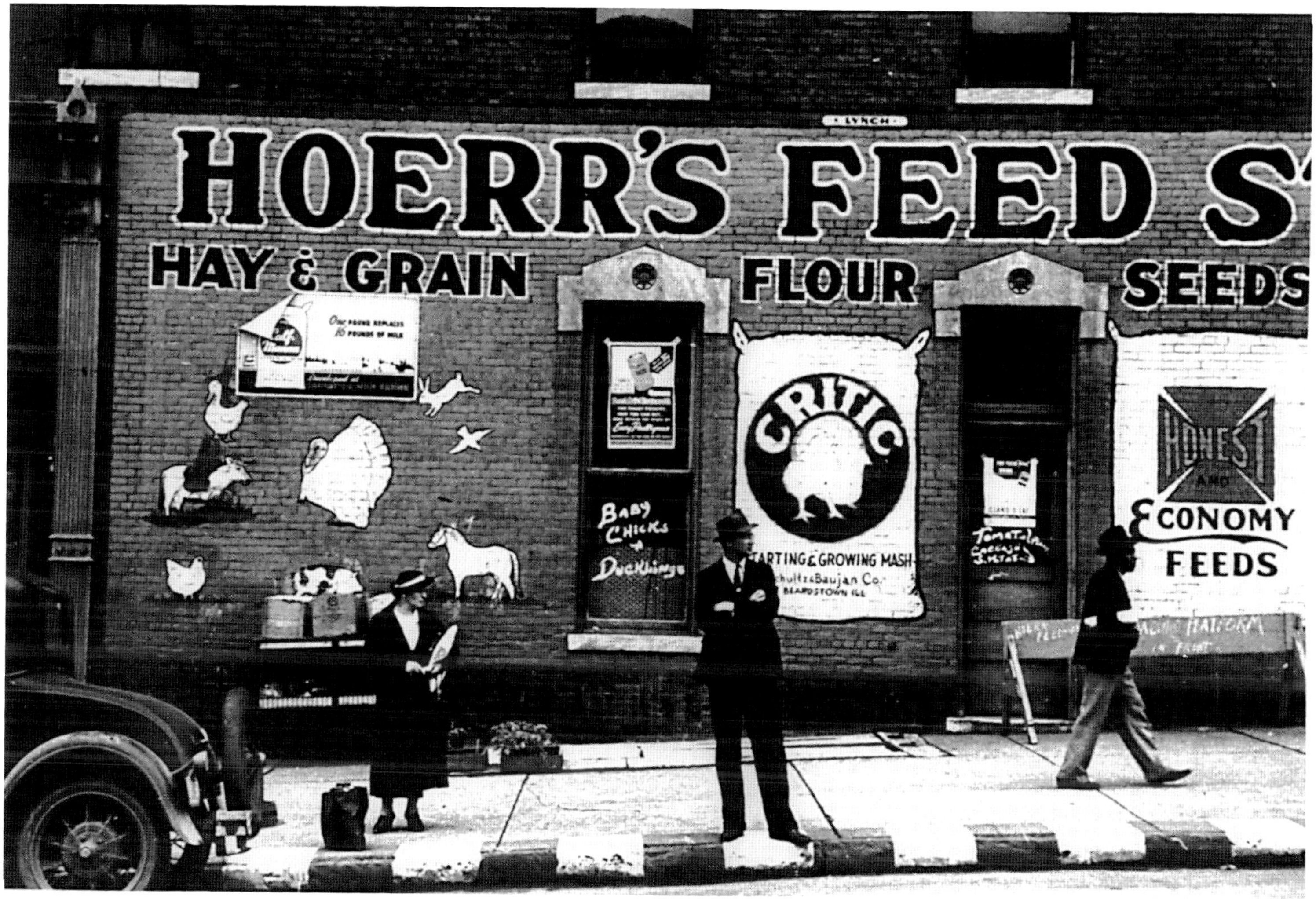

Grayville. May, 1940.
John Vachon

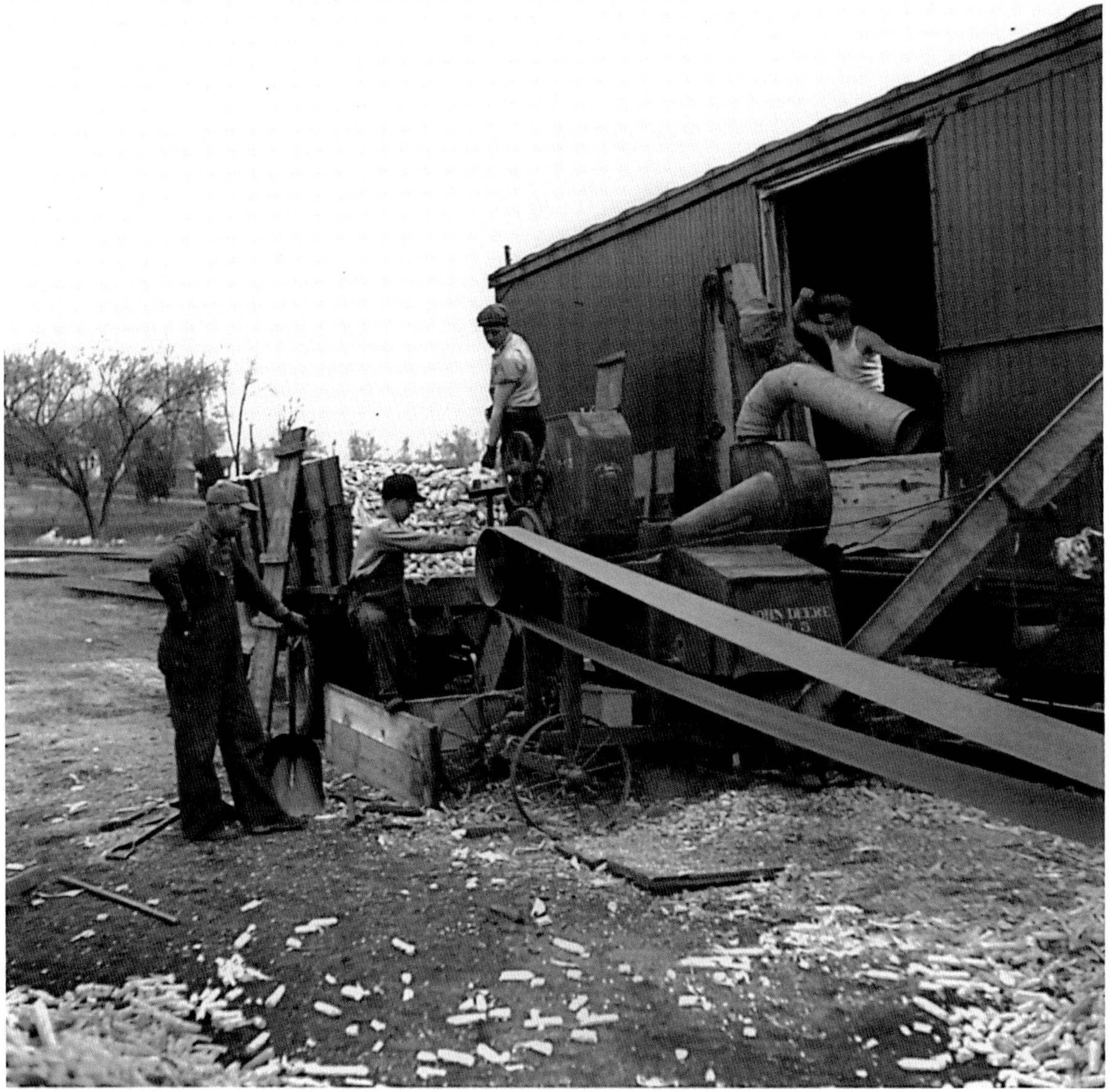

Shelling corn directly into a boxcar.
Newton. April, 1937.
Russell Lee

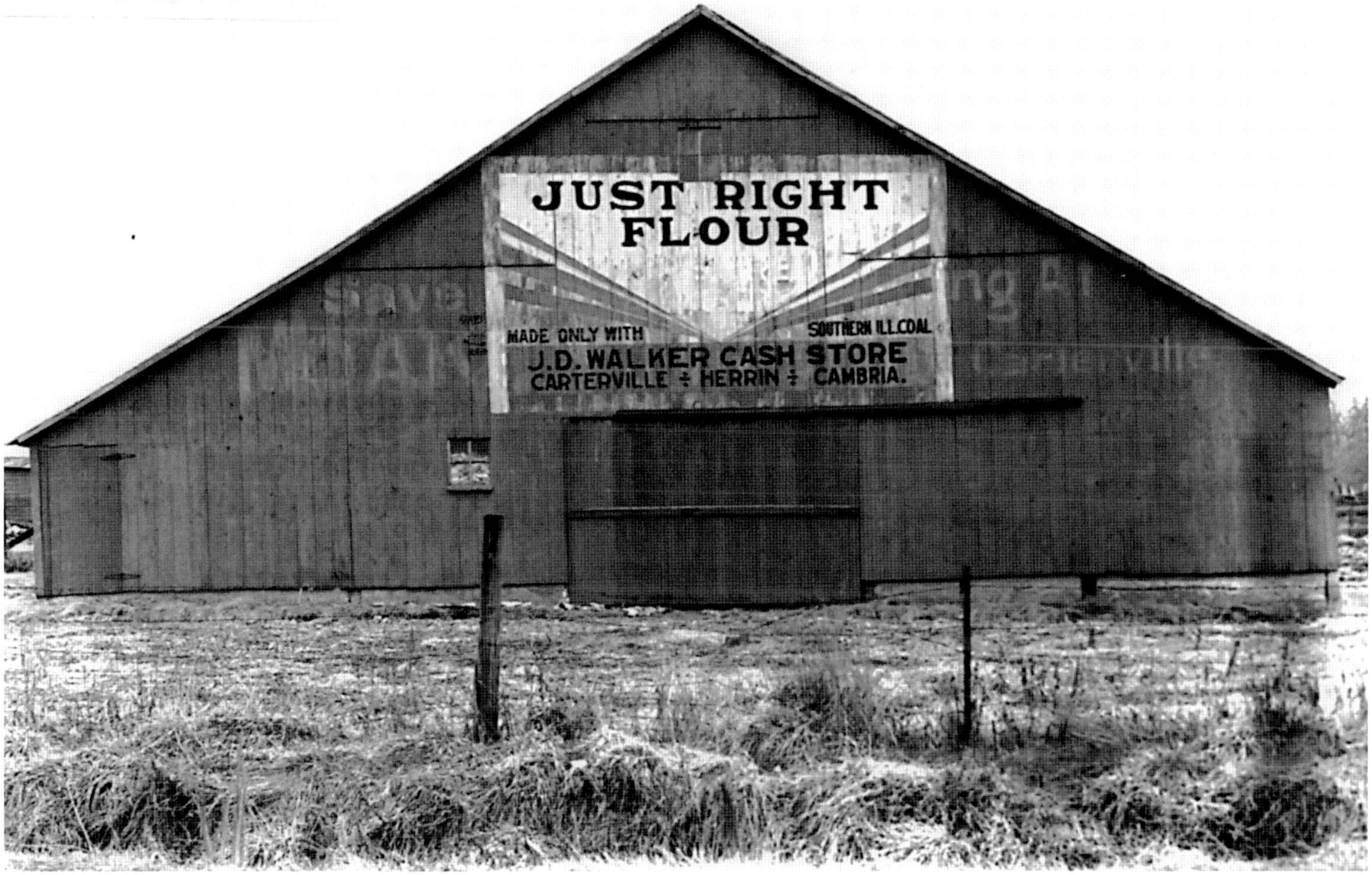

A barn.
Williamson County. January, 1939.
Arthur Rothstein

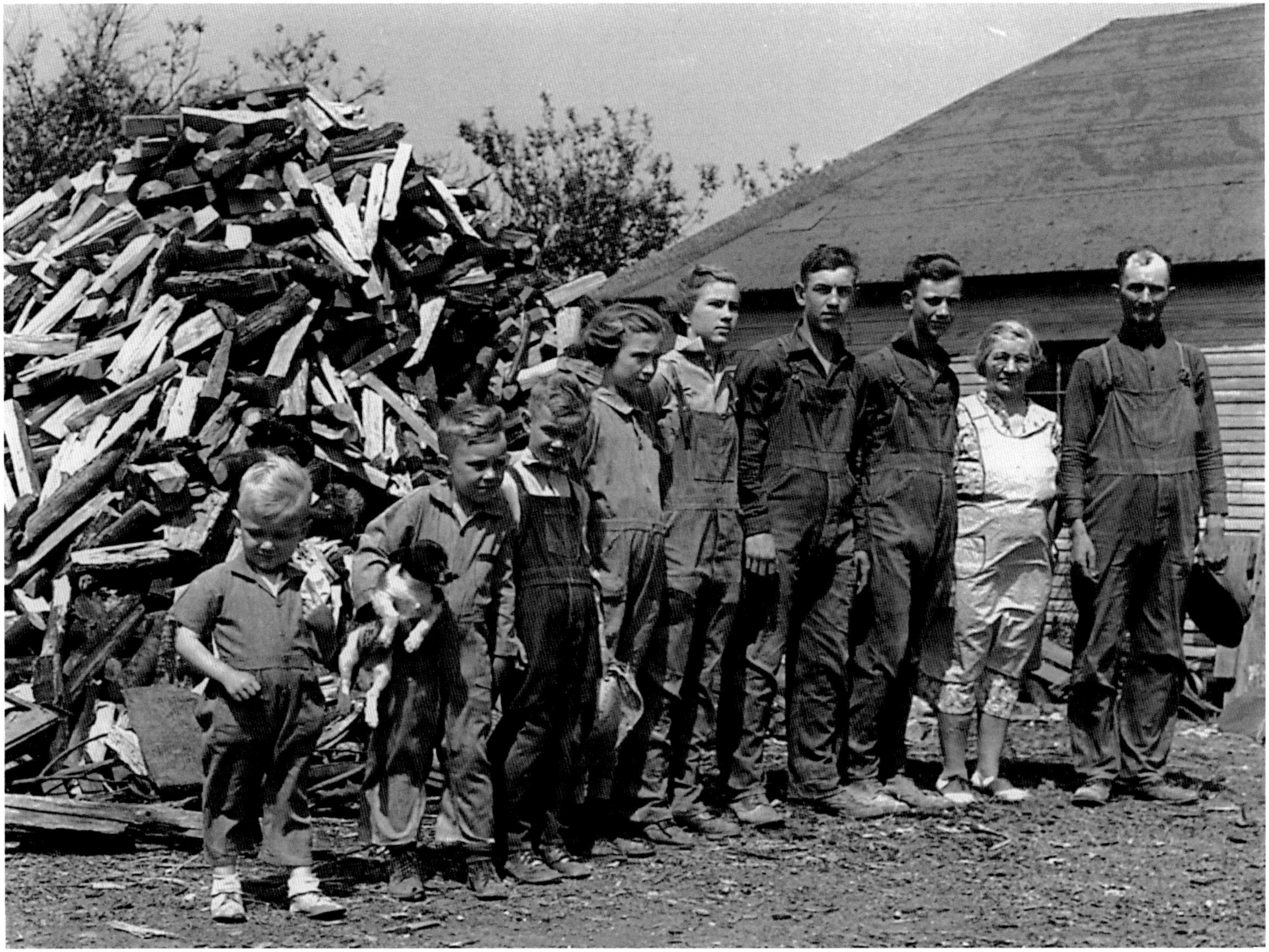

FSA rehabilitation borrower with his family.
Crawford County. May, 1940.
John Vachon

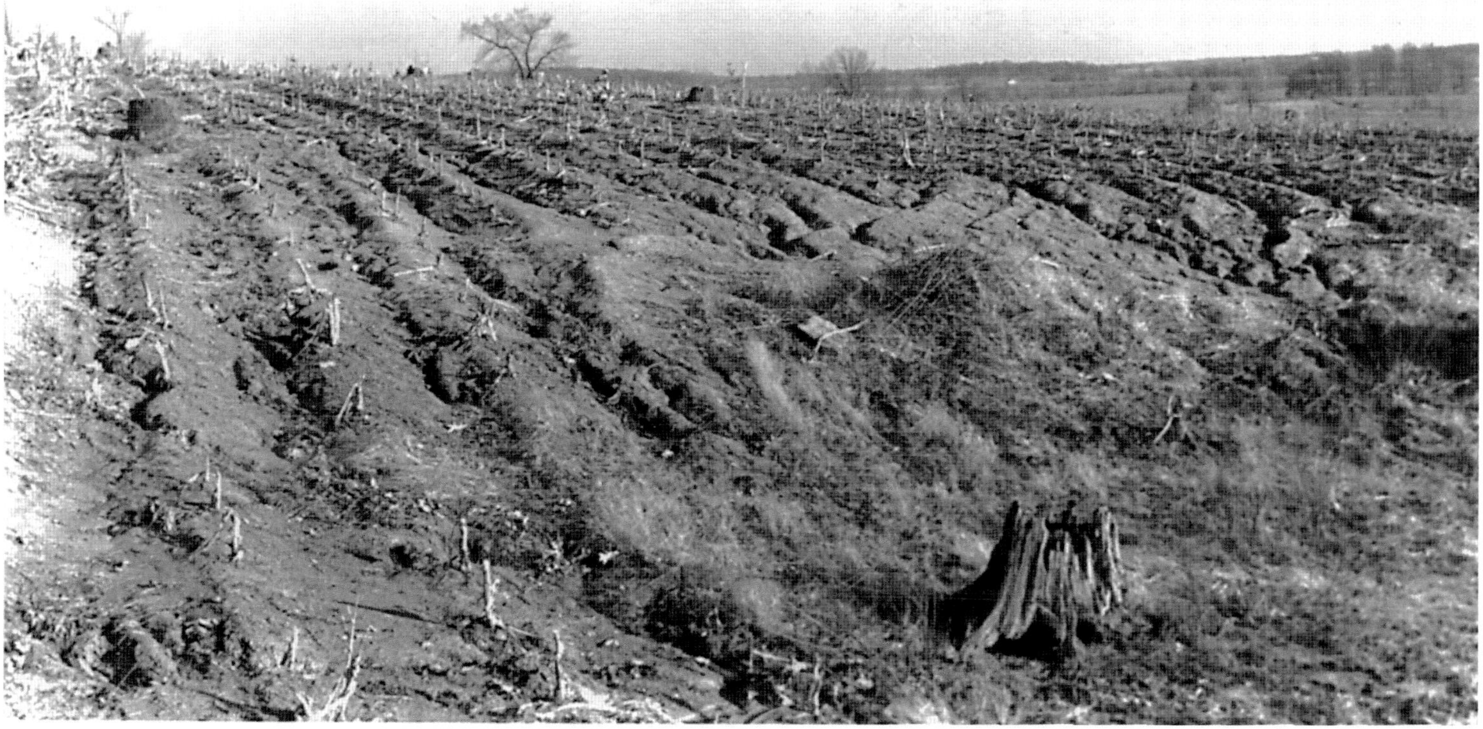

Soil erosion on land that has been cleared of timber and put into corn; note stumps of trees and beginning of erosion gullies. Hamilton County. February, 1937.
Russell Lee

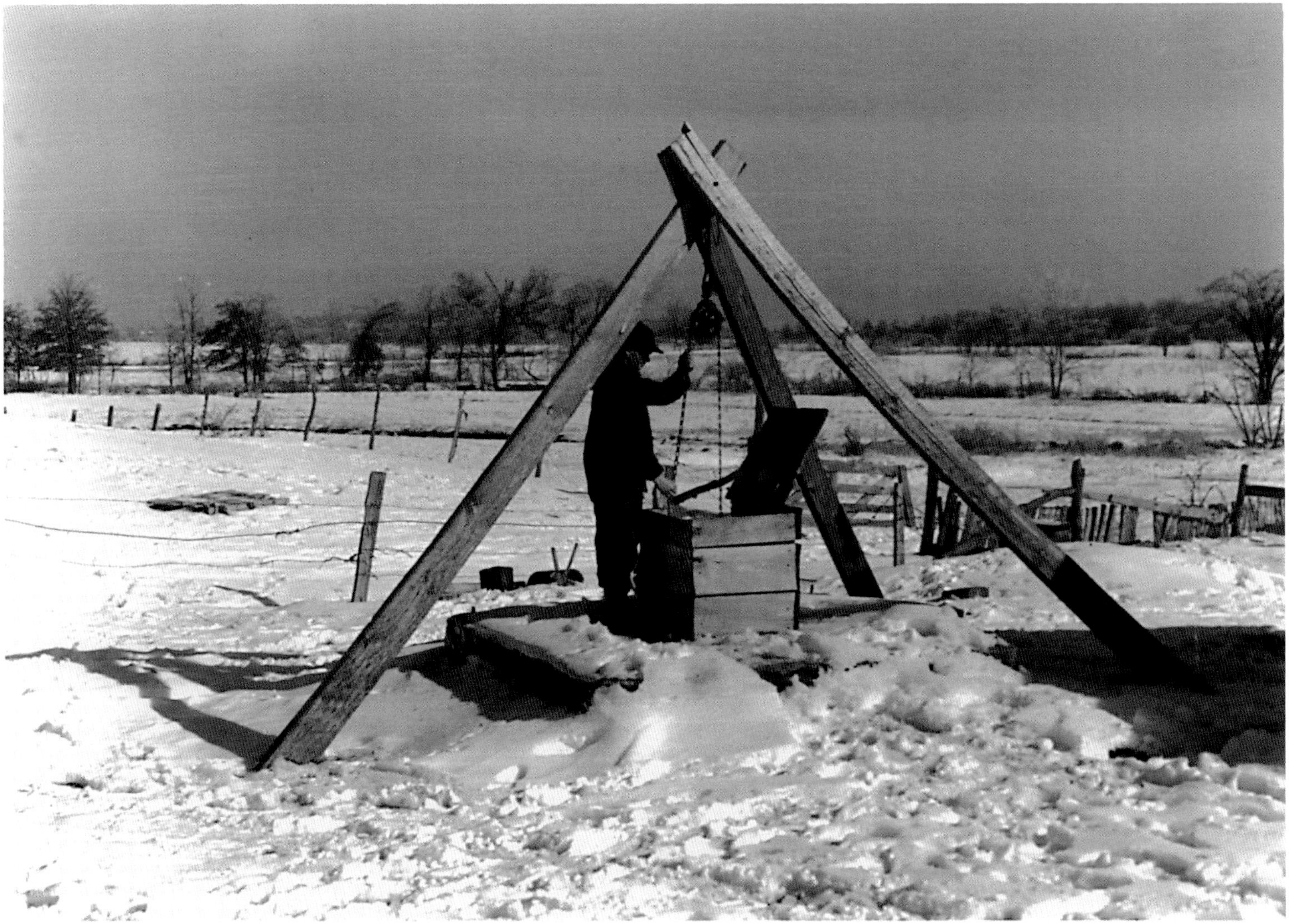

Oscar Gaither, a tenant farmer, hoisting water from his well.
McLeansboro (vicinity). February, 1937.
Russell Lee

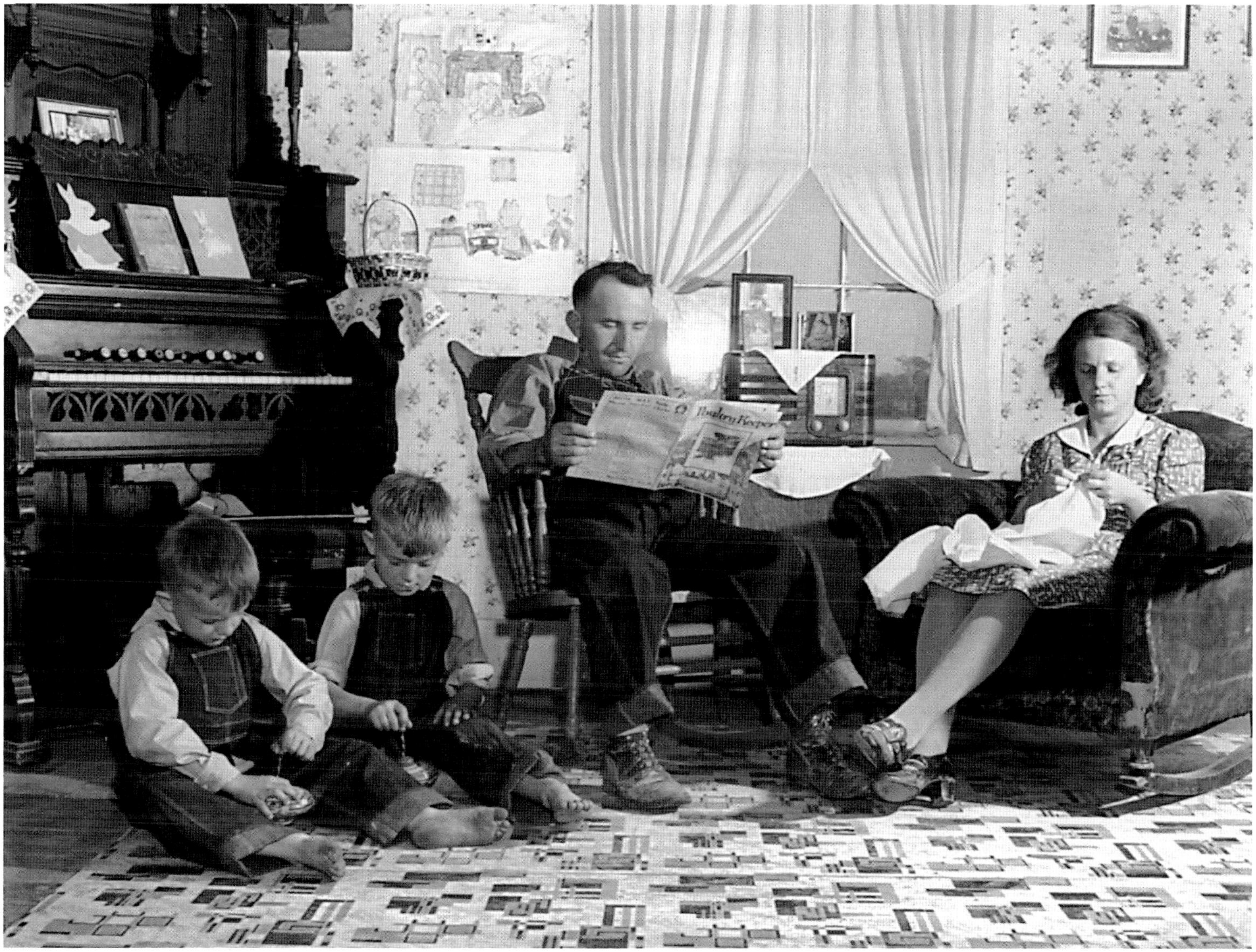

FSA tenant purchase borrower and his family.
Crawford County. May, 1940.
John Vachon

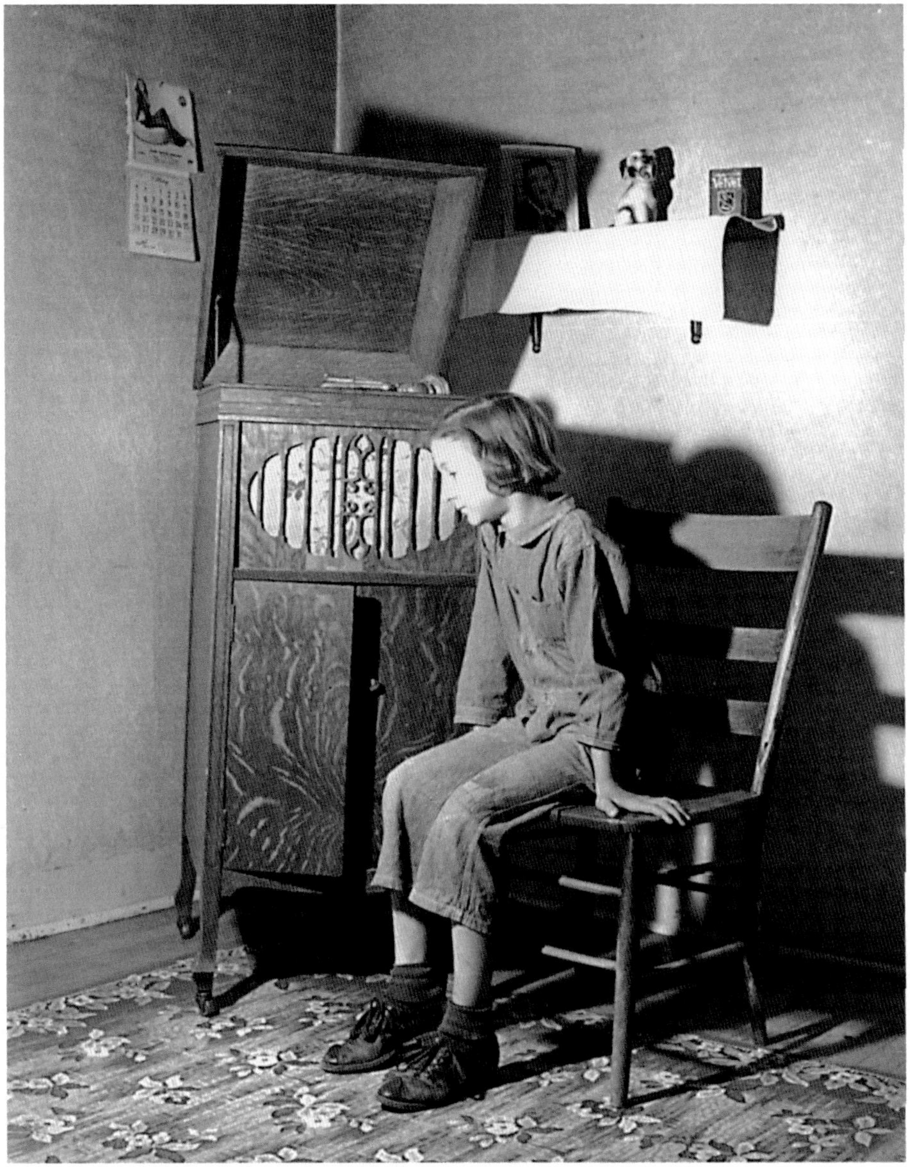

Daughter of an FSA rehabilitation borrower listening to a phonograph.
Crawford County. May, 1940.
John Vachon

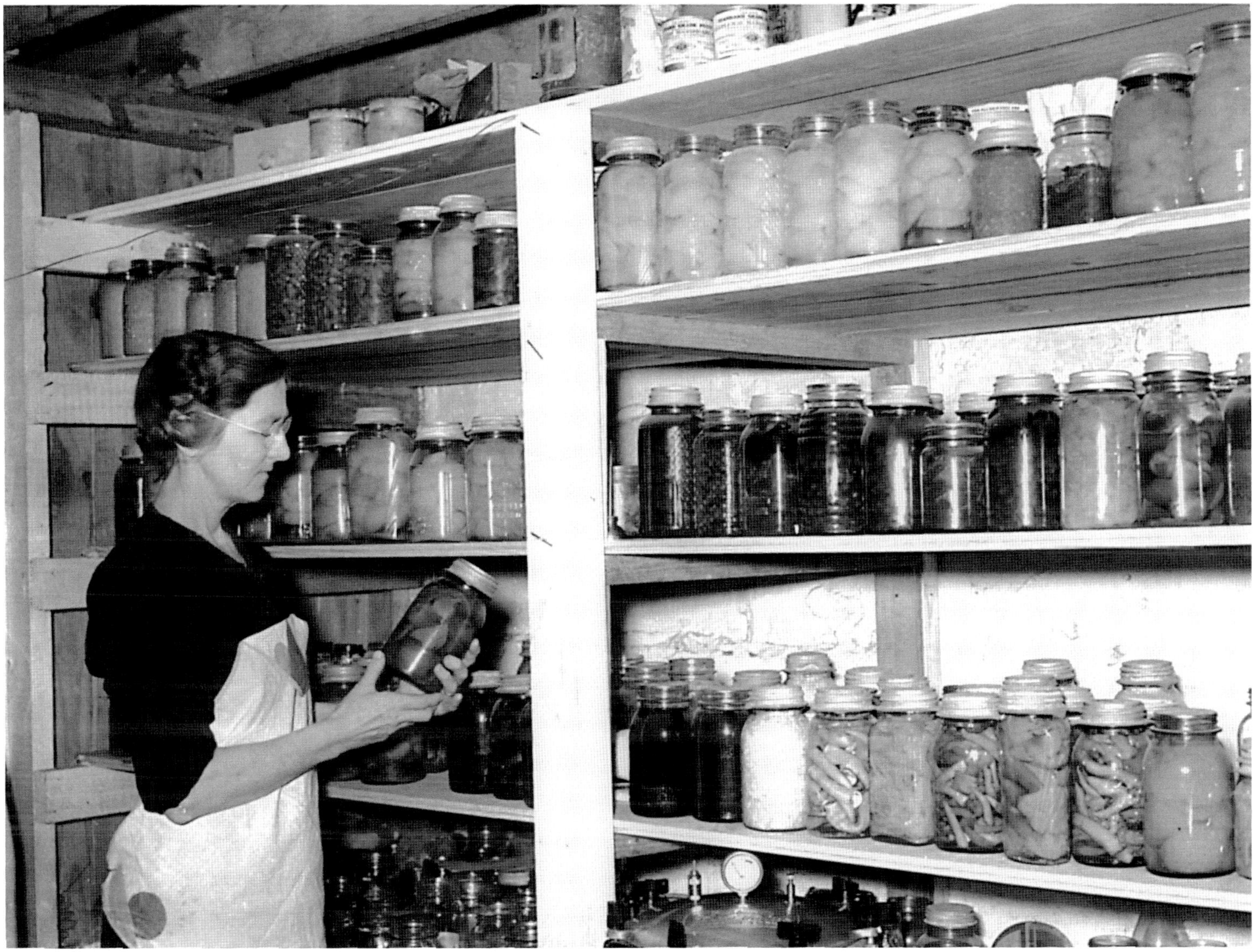

Loomis Hardesty, FSA tenant purchase client, acquired a 260-acre farm with livestock and equipment through the FSA. Mrs. Hardesty with her canned goods.
Saline County. January, 1939. Arthur Rothstein

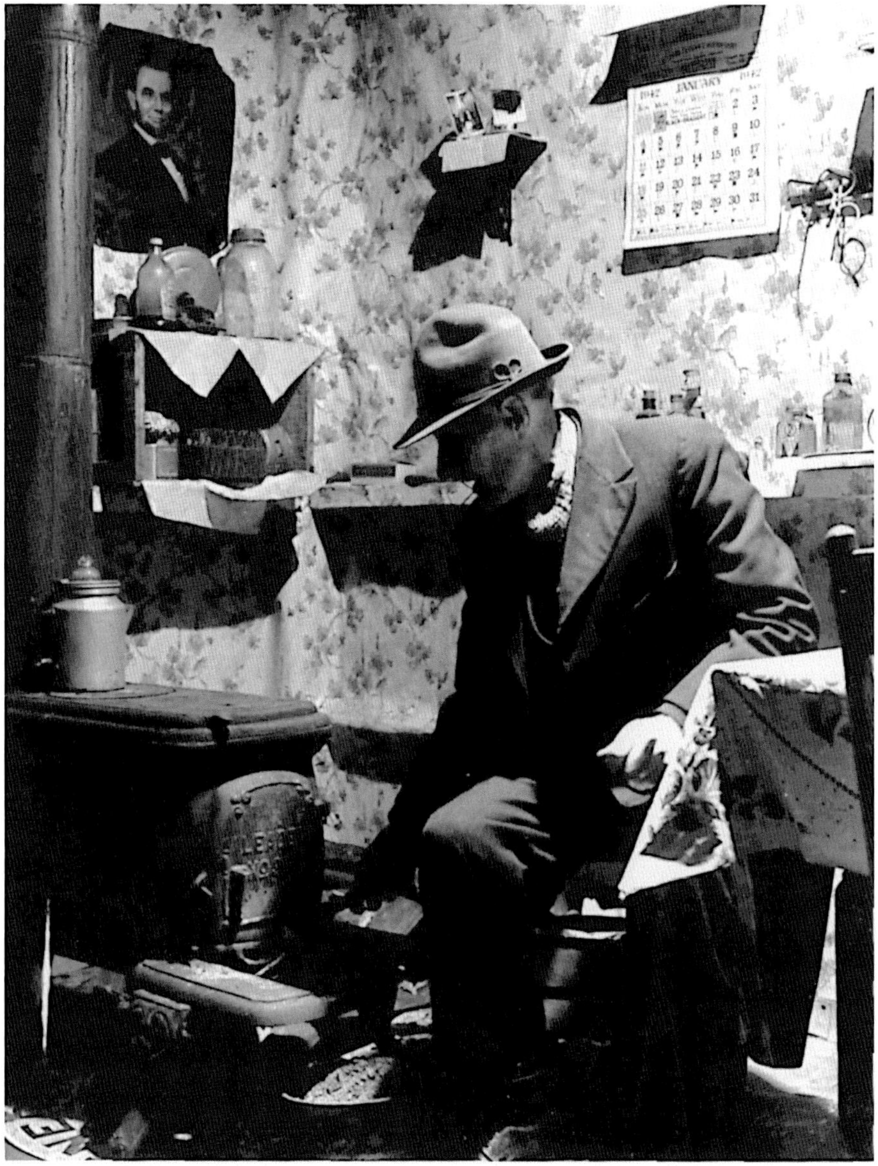

Billy Williams, 65-year-old squatter, living in a shack he built himself.
Washington County. February, 1942.
John Vachon

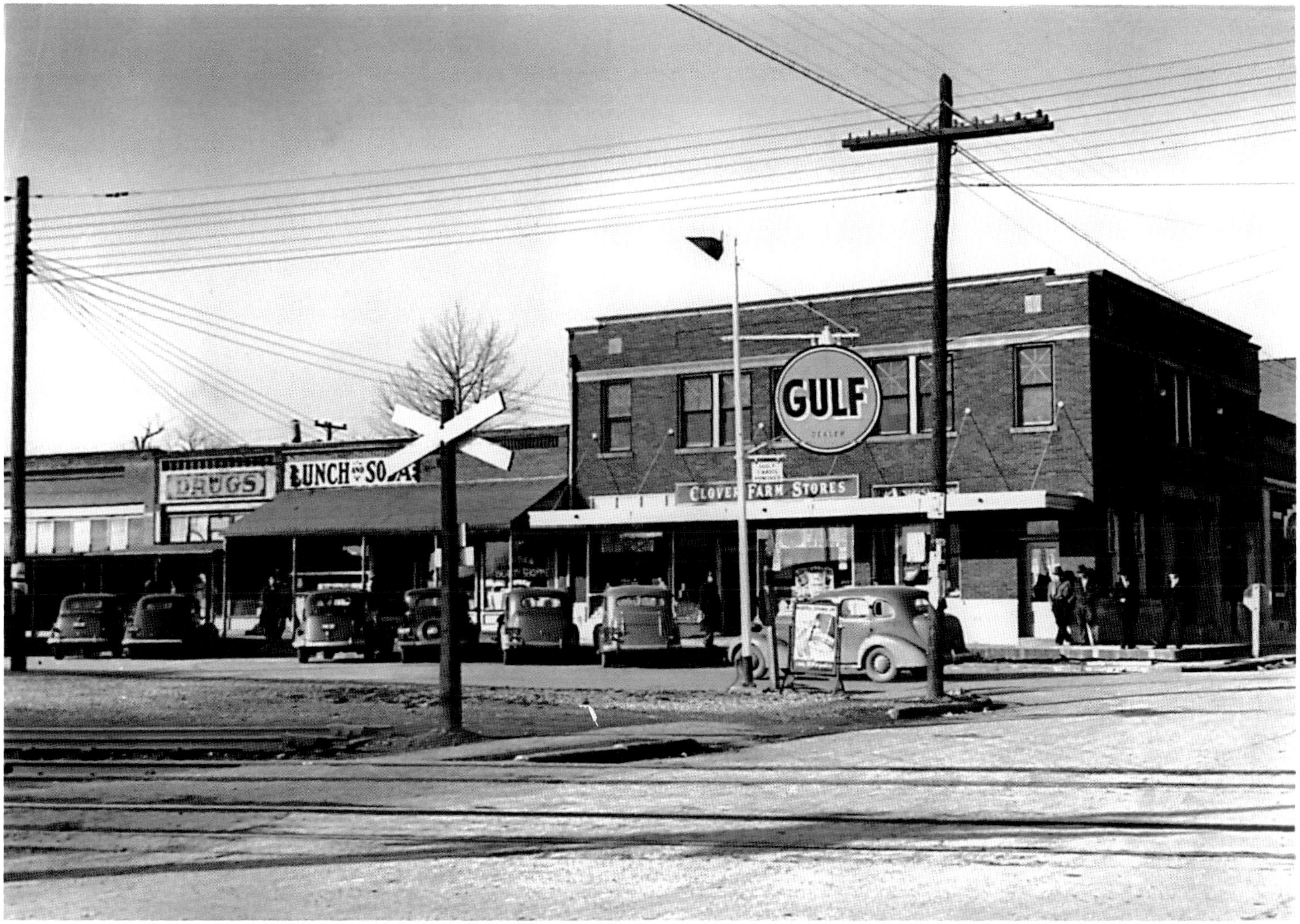

Street corner.
Carrier Mills. January, 1939.
Arthur Rothstein

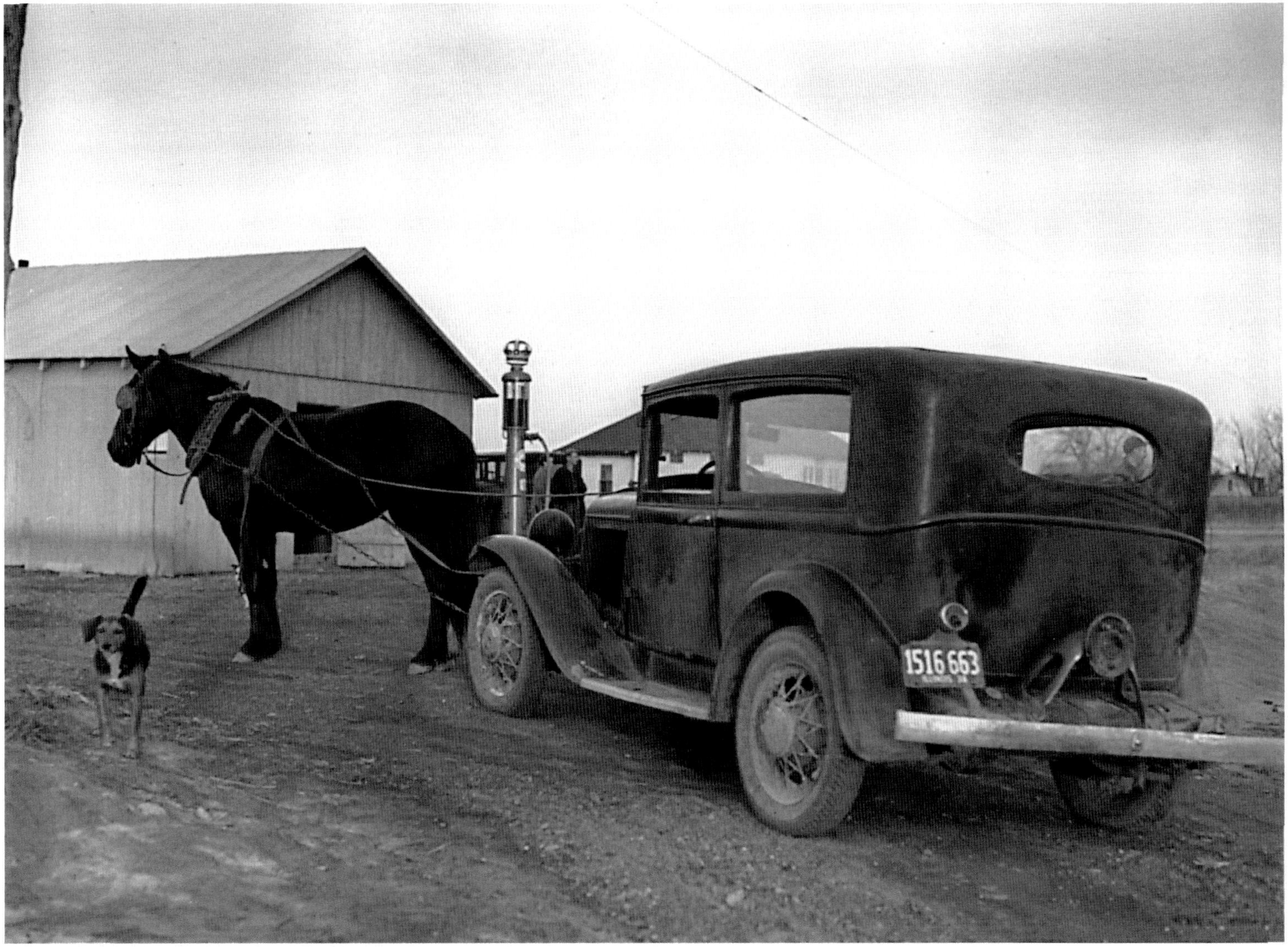

Emergency horse power.
Franklin County. January, 1939.
Arthur Rothstein

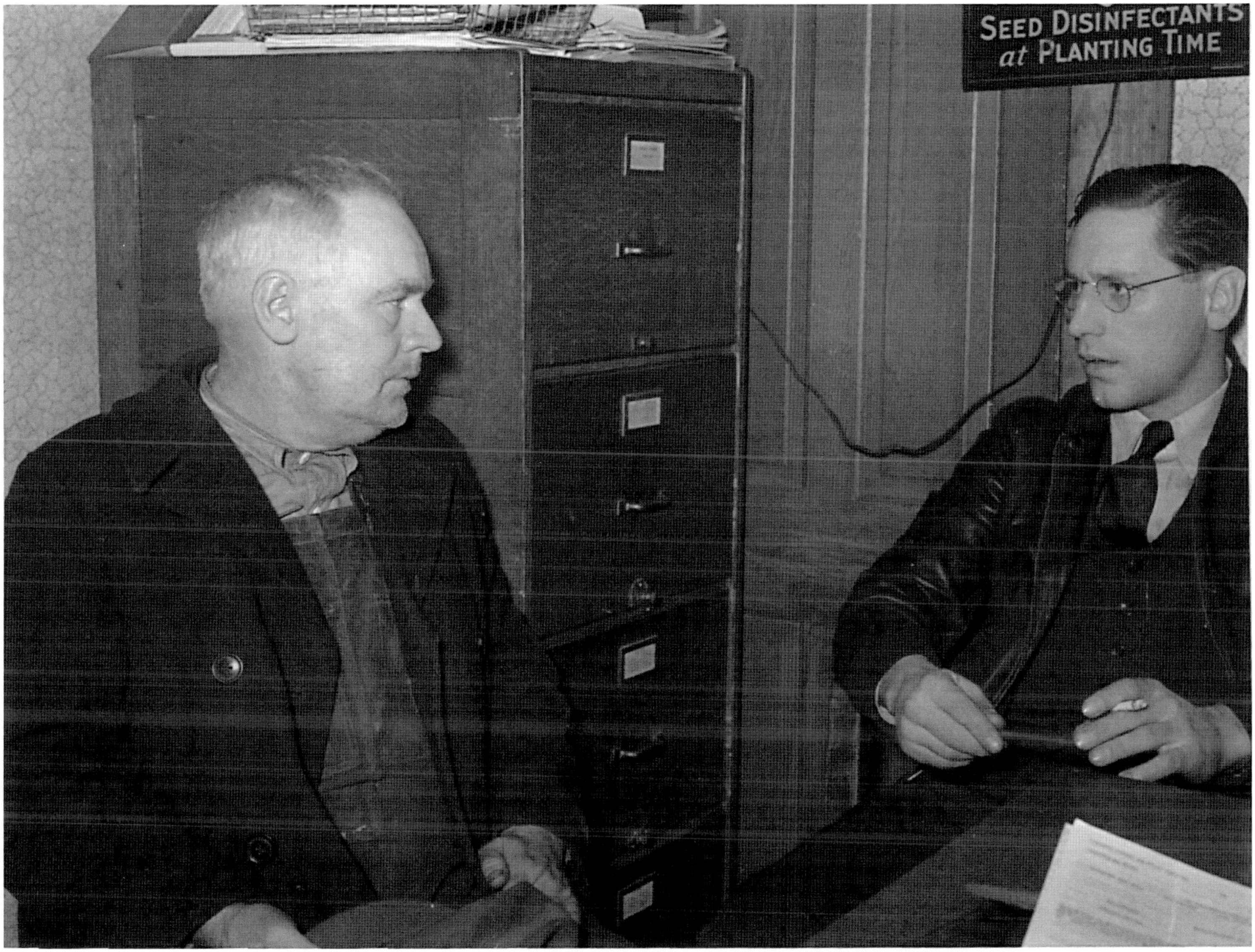

FSA rehabililution supervisor with a client.
Ridgway. January, 1939.
Arthur Rothstein

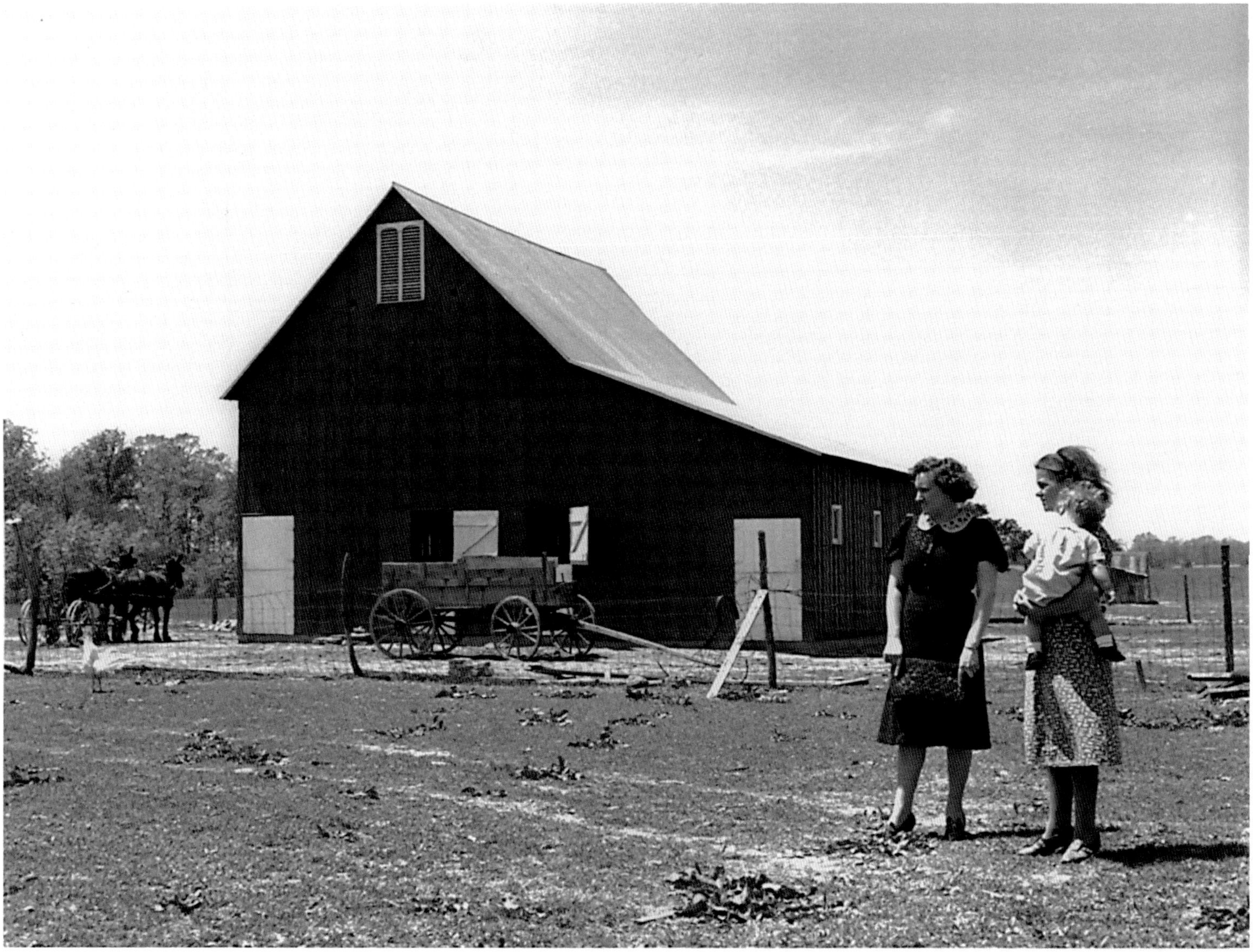

Wife of an FSA tenant purchase borrower talking with
a home supervisor.
Crawford County. May, 1940.
John Vachon

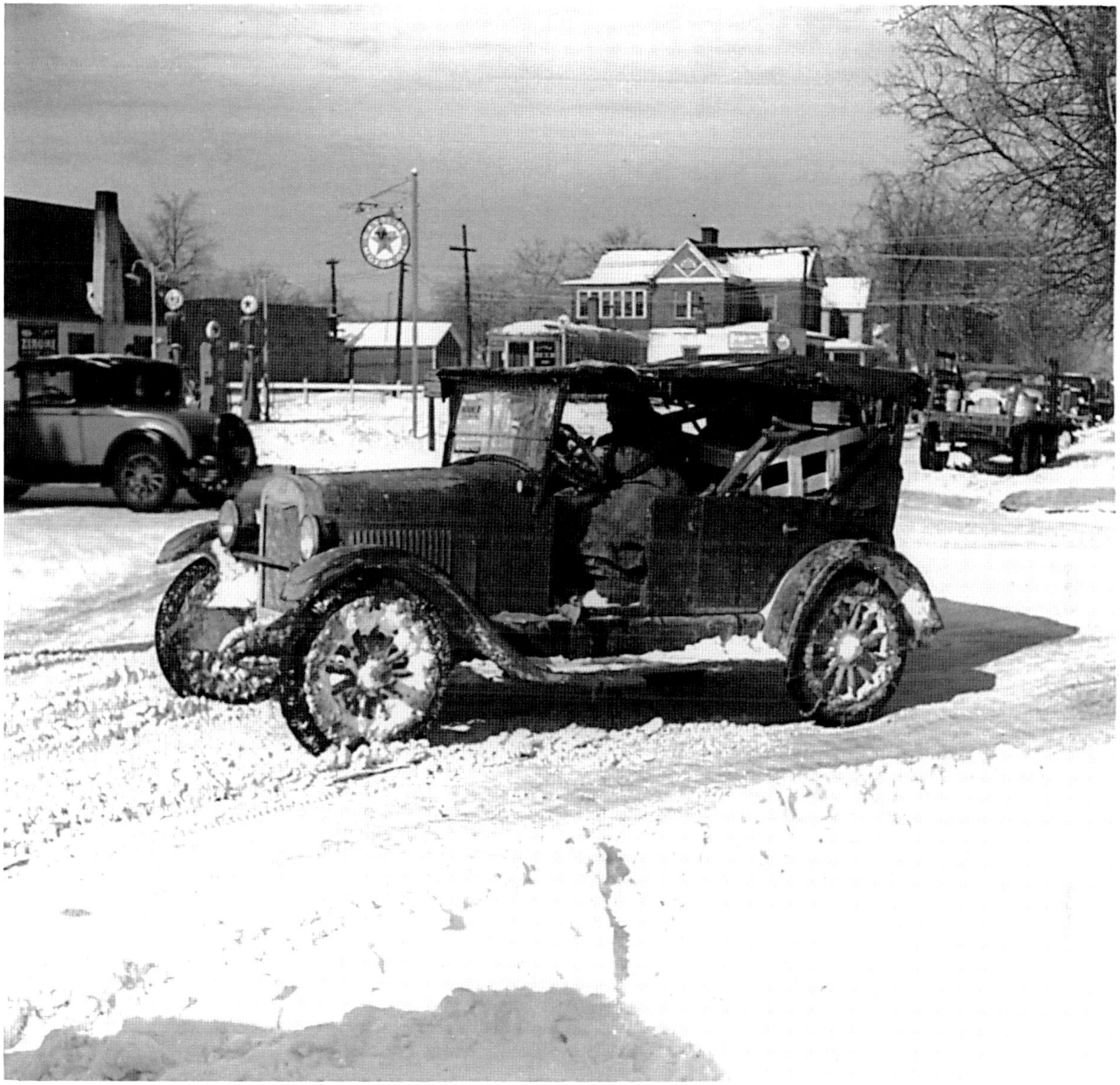

Typical transportation of Southern Illinois farmers. Several farmers often pool resources to buy a car and divide its use among themselves.
Hamilton County. February, 1937. Russell Lee

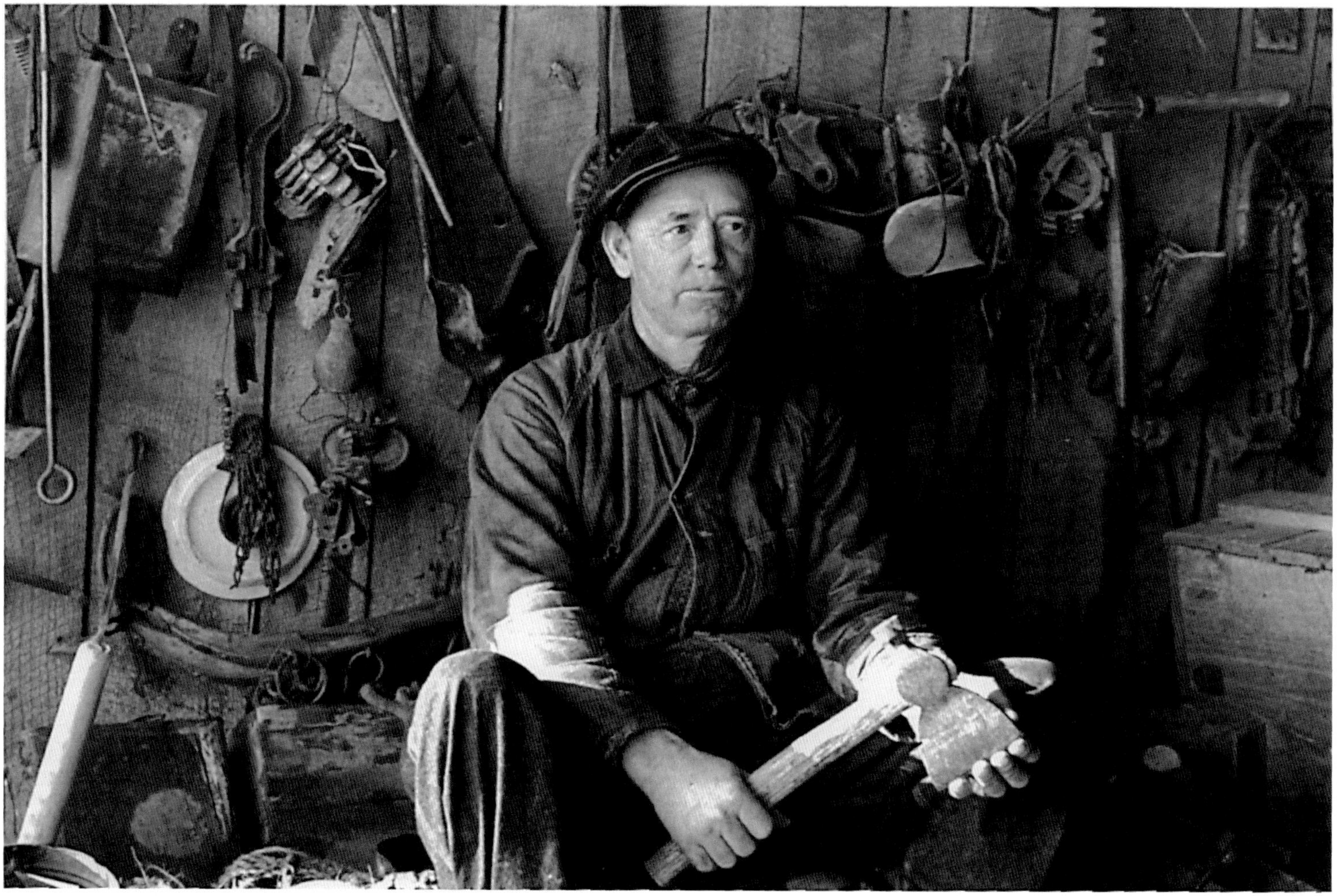

A farmer in his toolhouse.
McLeansboro (vicinity). January, 1937.
Russell Lee

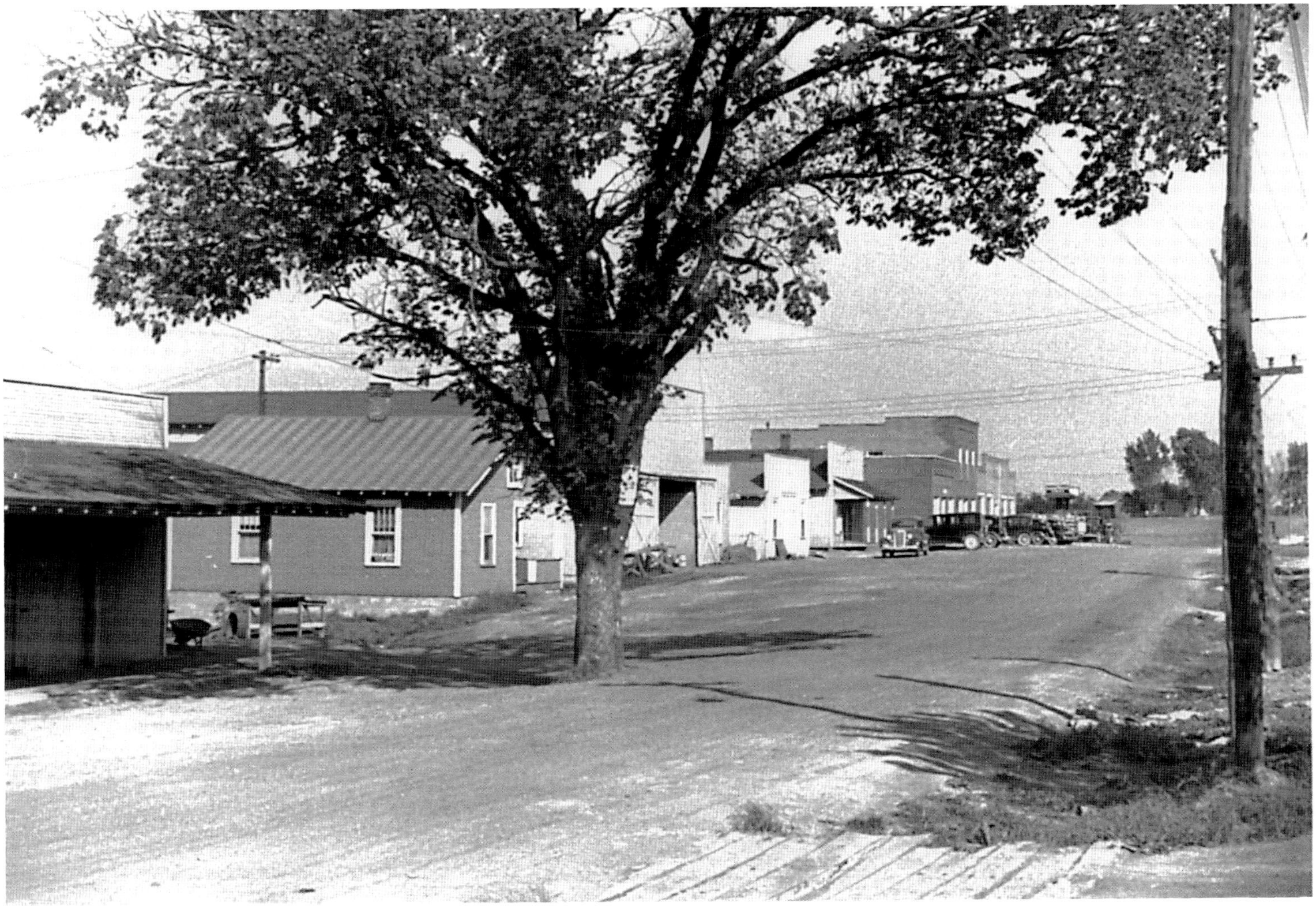

The one-man town near which the US Resettlement Administration has a project.
Robbs. May, 1936.
Carl Mydans

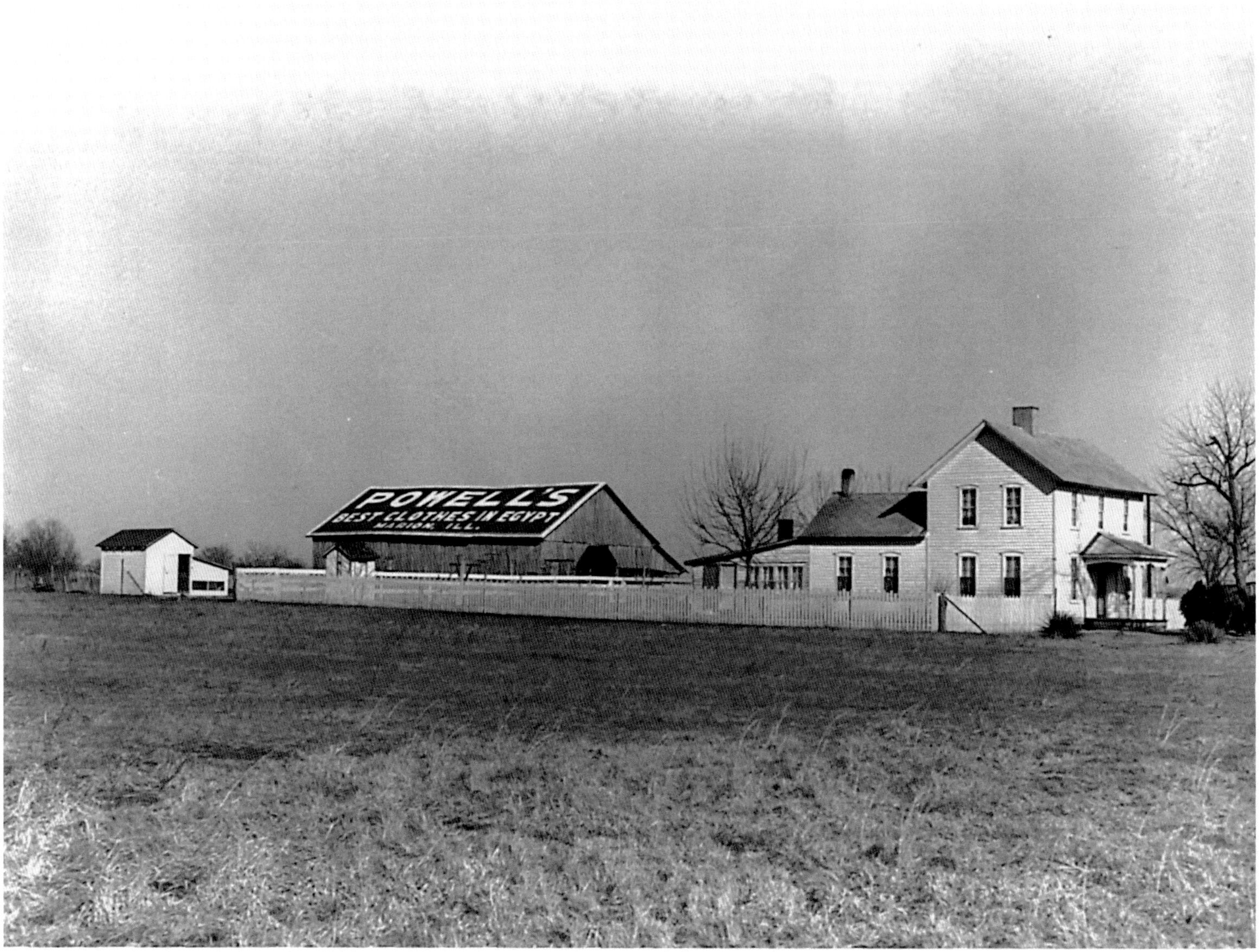

A farm.
Williamson County. January, 1939.
Arthur Rothstein

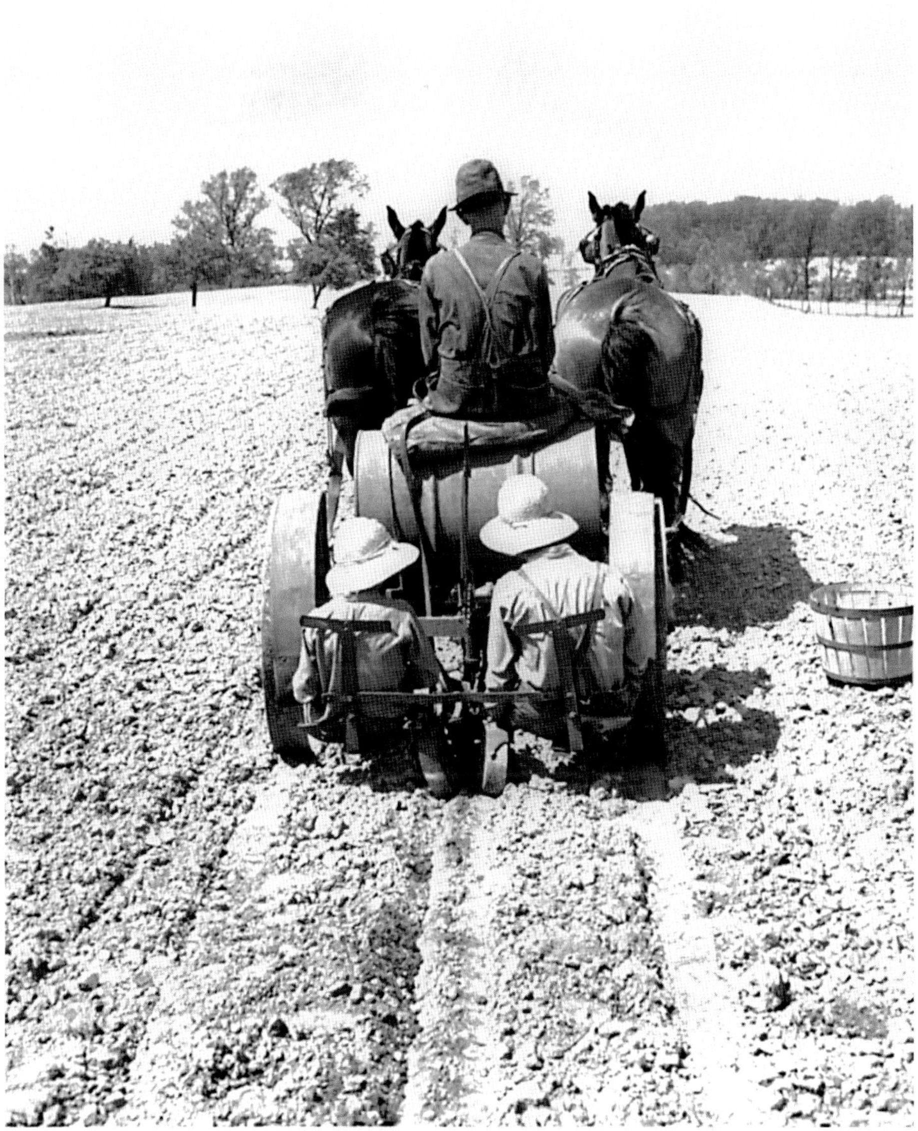

FSA rehabilitation borrower driving a tomato planter. His two little girls, sitting in the back, drop the plants into the ground and cover them up.
Crawford County. May, 1940. John Vachon

MINERS AND MINERAL WEALTH

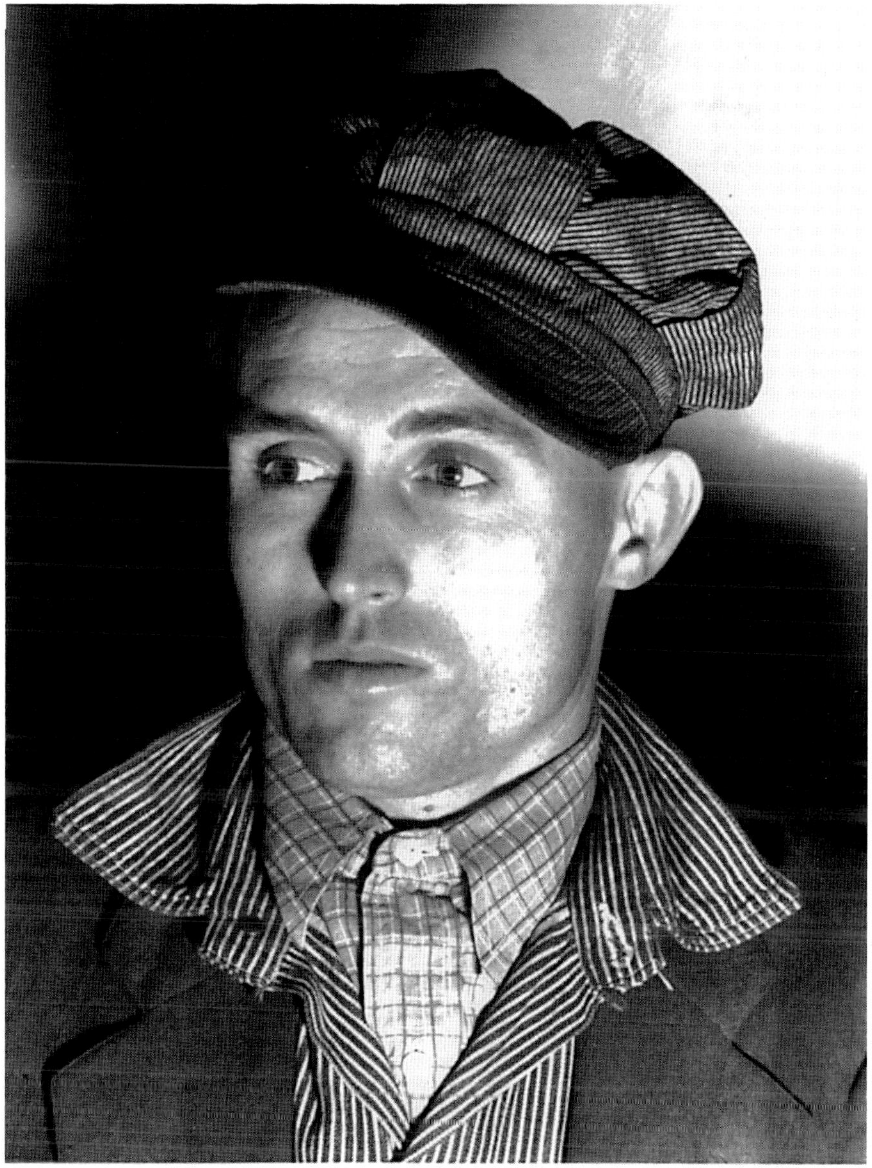

An unemployed miner.
Herrin. January, 1939.
Arthur Rothstein

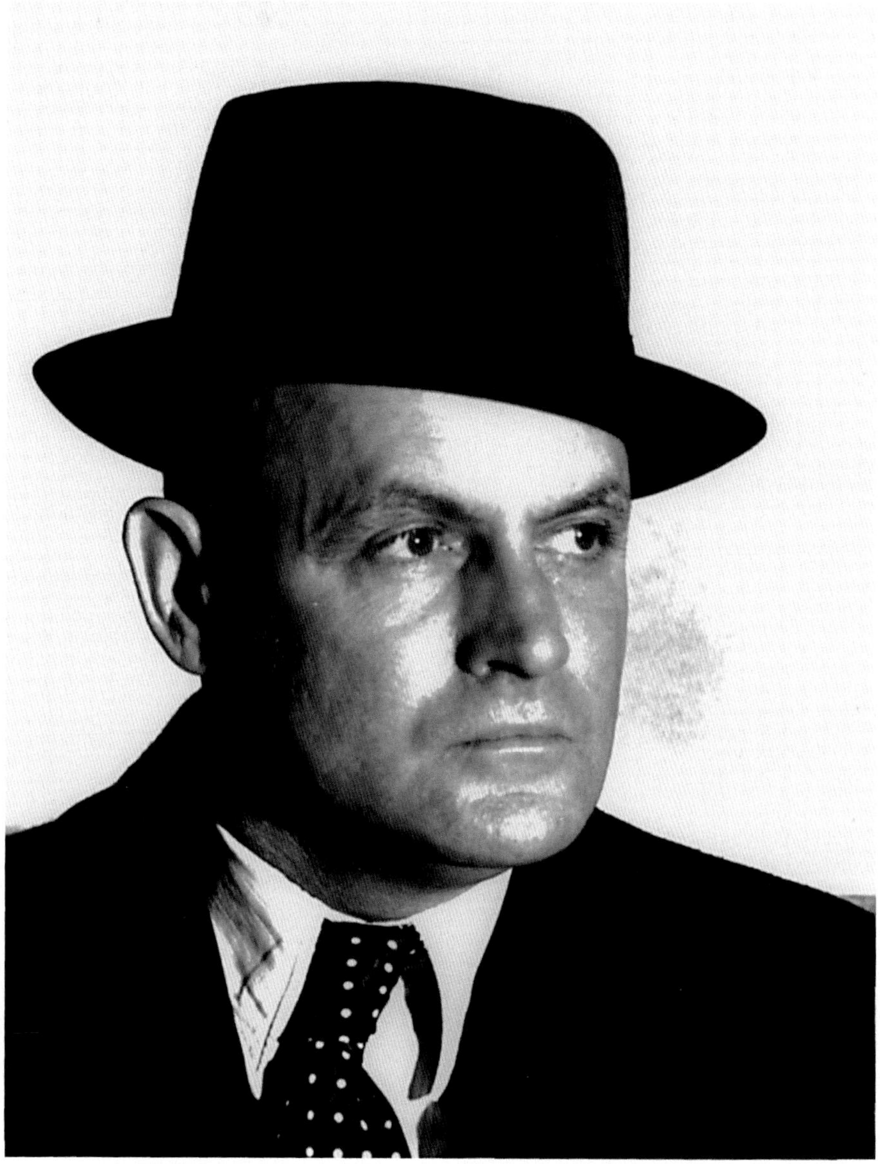

Officer of the United Mine Workers of America.
Herrin. January, 1939.
Arthur Rothstein

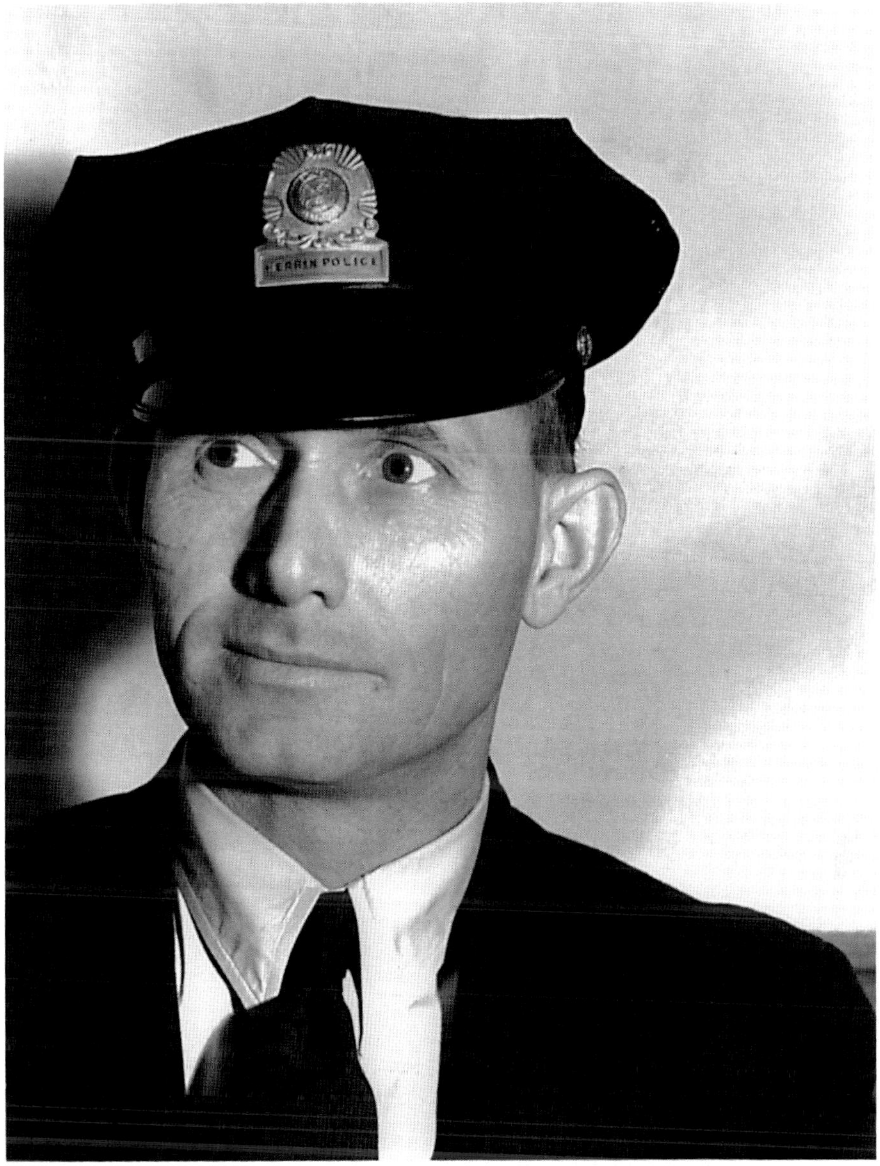

A policeman.
Herrin. January, 1939.
Arthur Rothstein

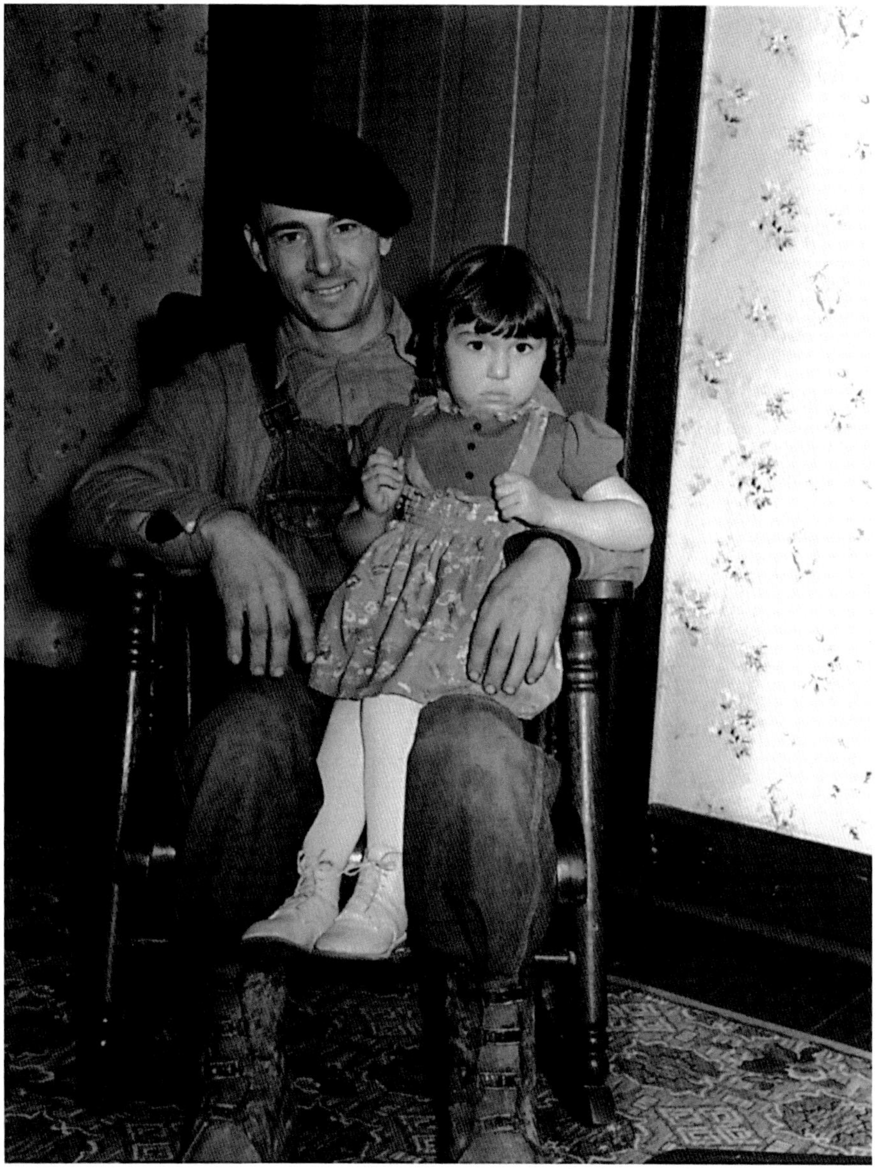

Coal miner and daughter.
Bush. January, 1939.
Arthur Rothstein

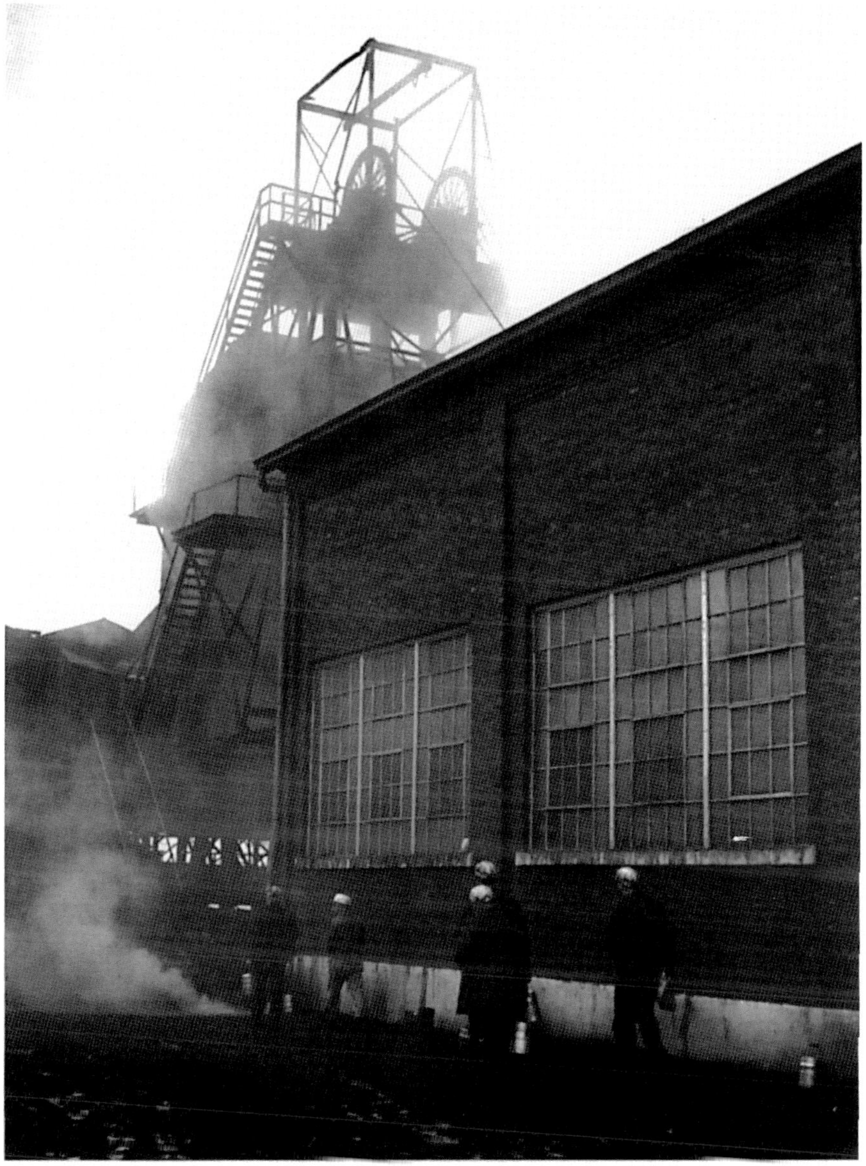

Old Ben Mine No. 8. Miners on their way underground at 7:00 A.M.
West Frankfort. January, 1939.
Arthur Rothstein

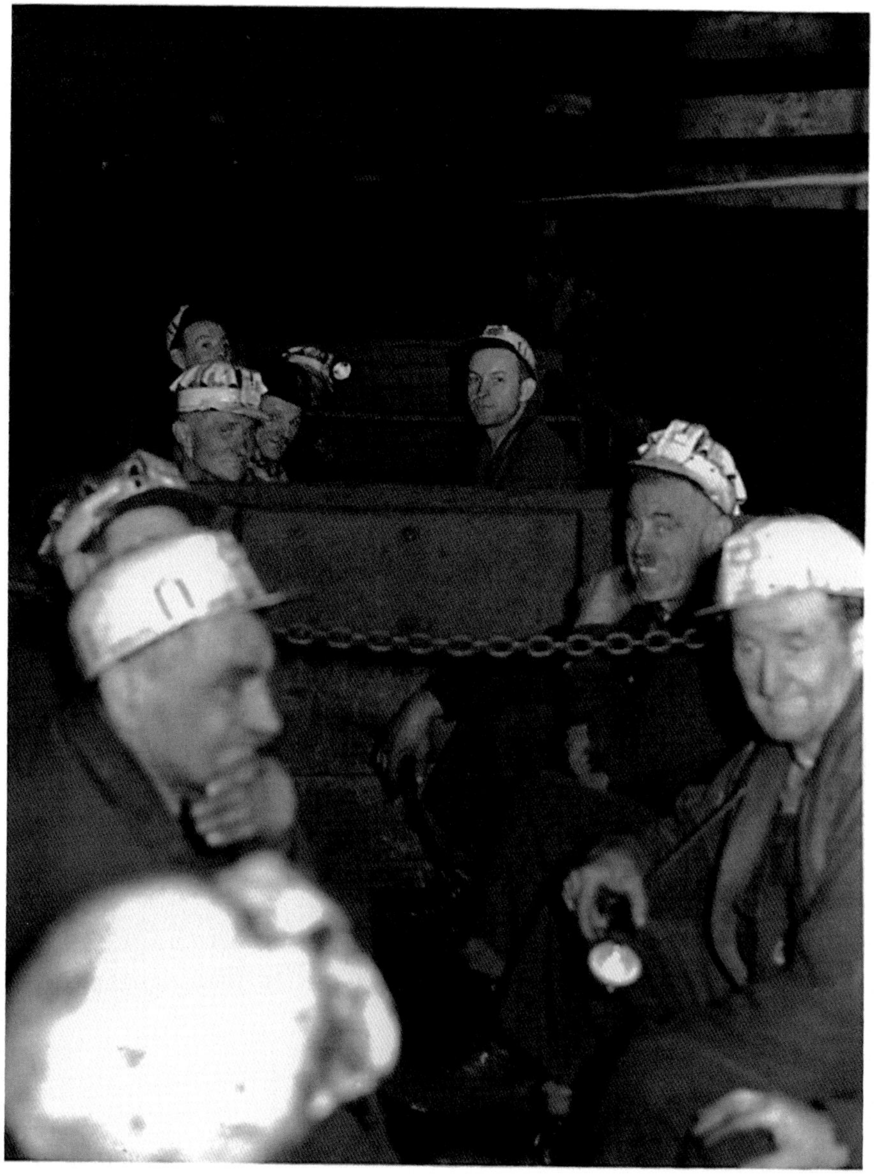

Old Ben Mine No. 8. These men are on a "man trip" that goes 3½ miles to the face of the coal.
West Frankfort. January, 1939.
Arthur Rothstein

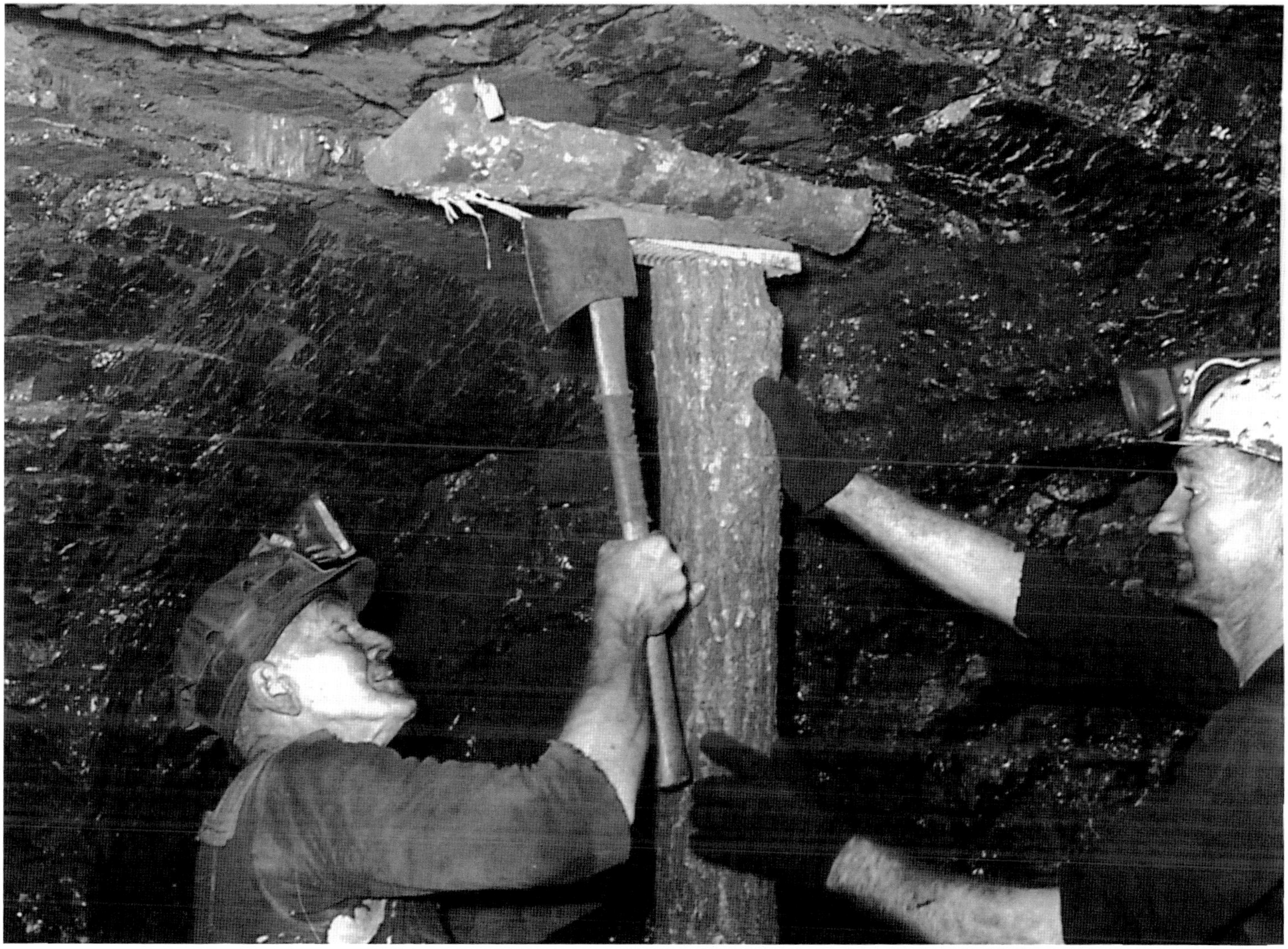

Old Ben Mine No. 8. Miners shoring up the roof of the mine.
West Frankfort, January, 1939.
Arthur Rothstein

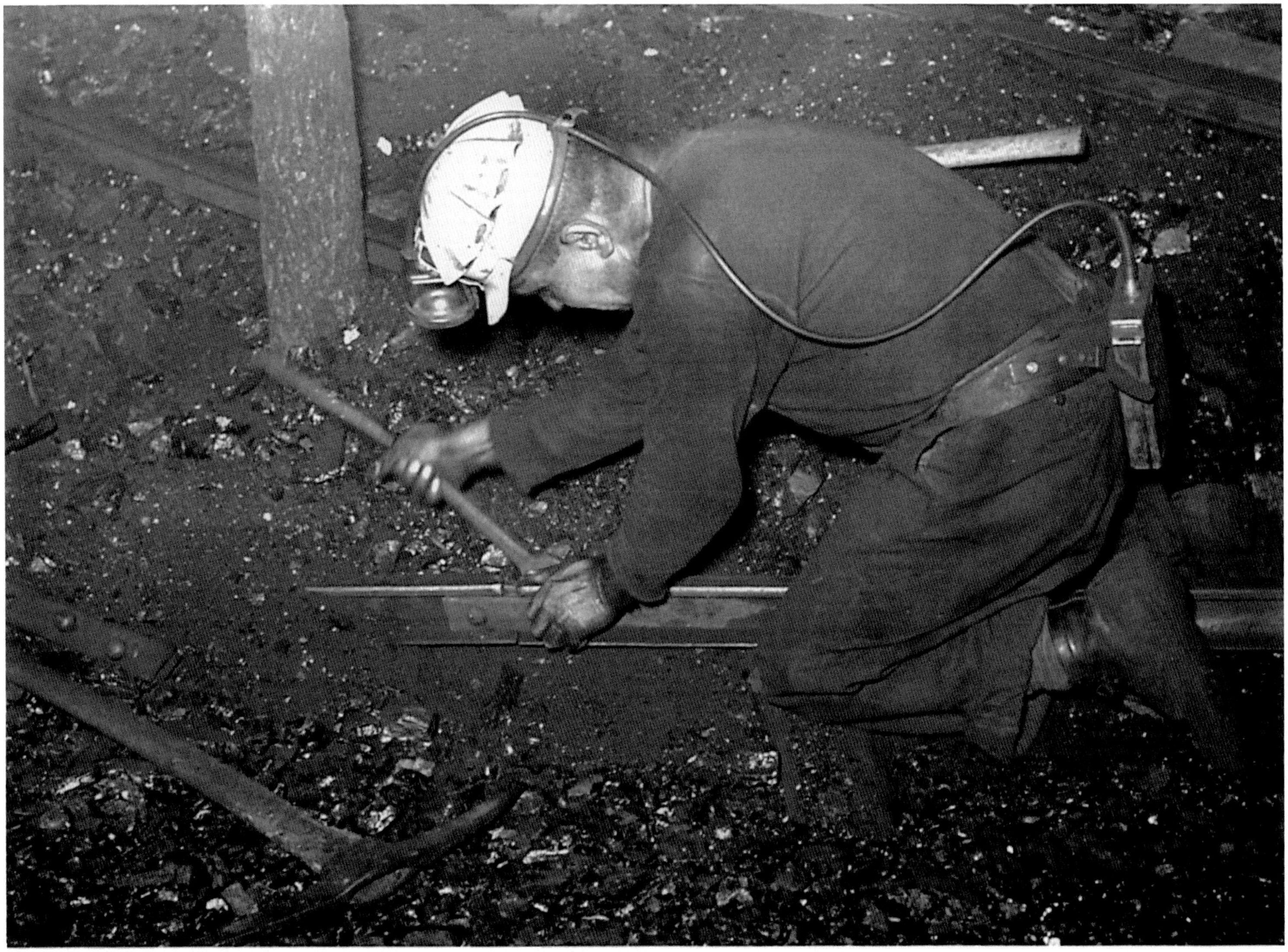

Old Ben Mine No. 8. Laying track underground.
West Frankfort. January, 1939.
Arthur Rothstein

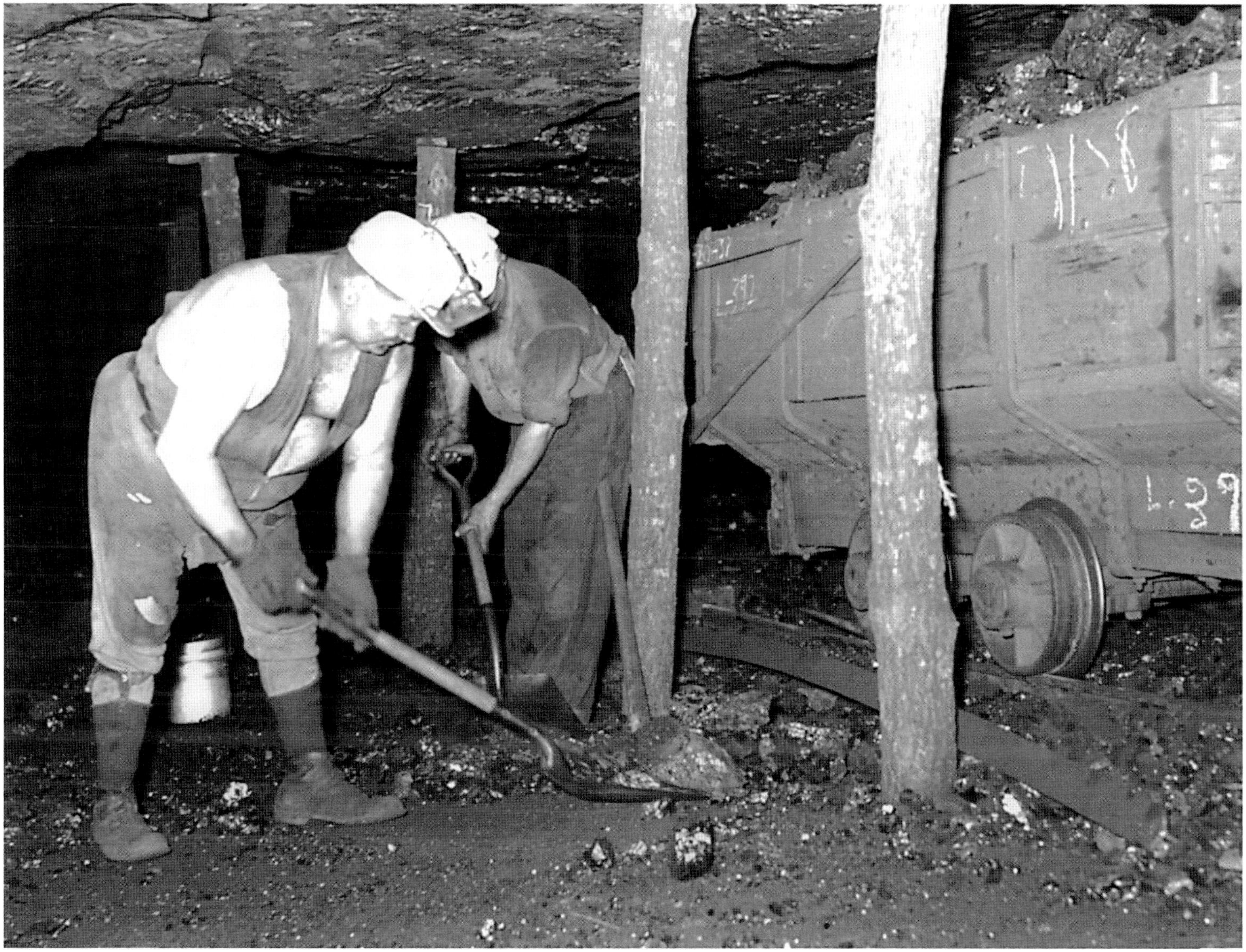

Old Ben Mine No. 8. Miners hand loading into a pit car.
West Frankfort. January, 1939.
Arthur Rothstein

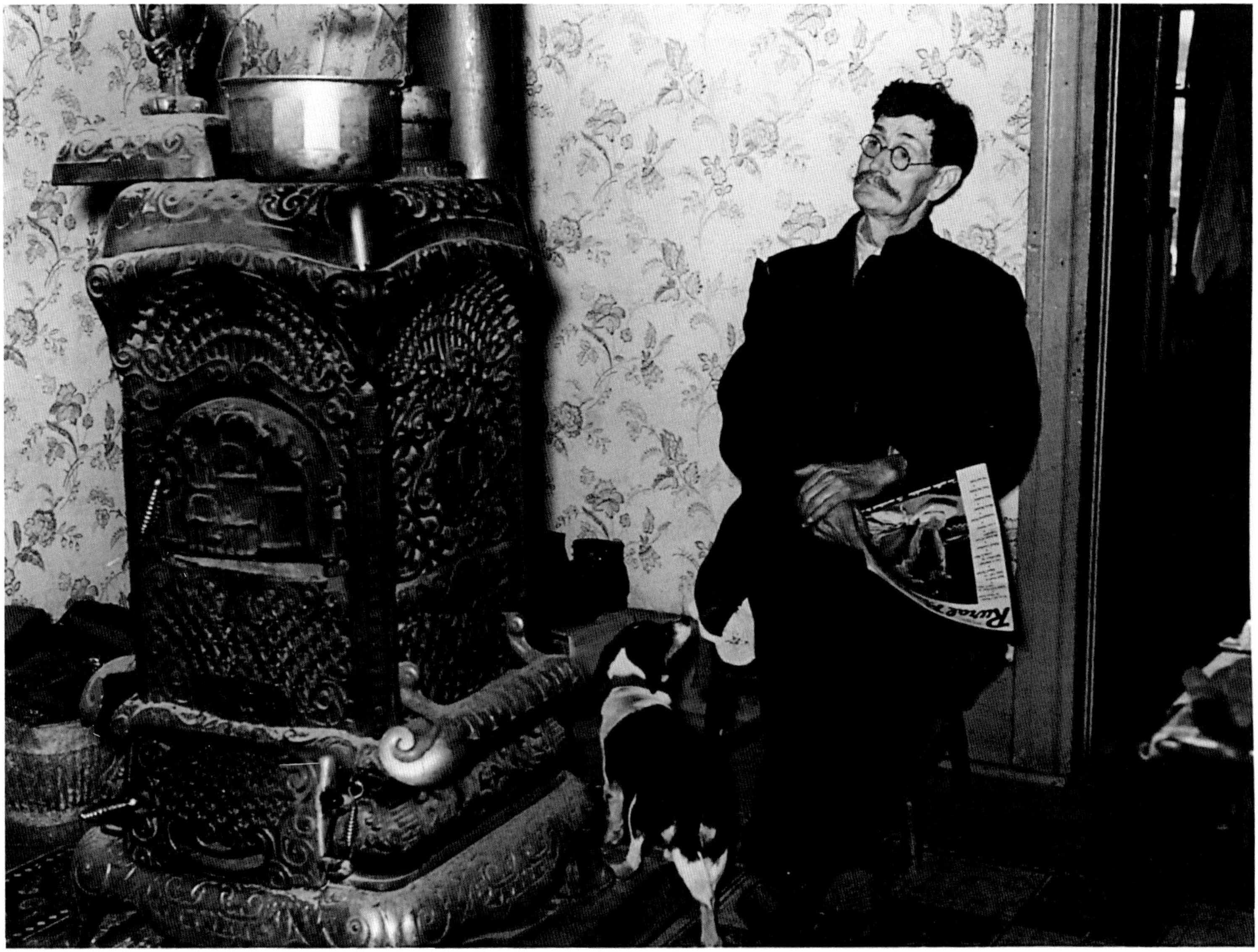

Unemployed mine worker.
Bush. January, 1939.
Arthur Rothstein

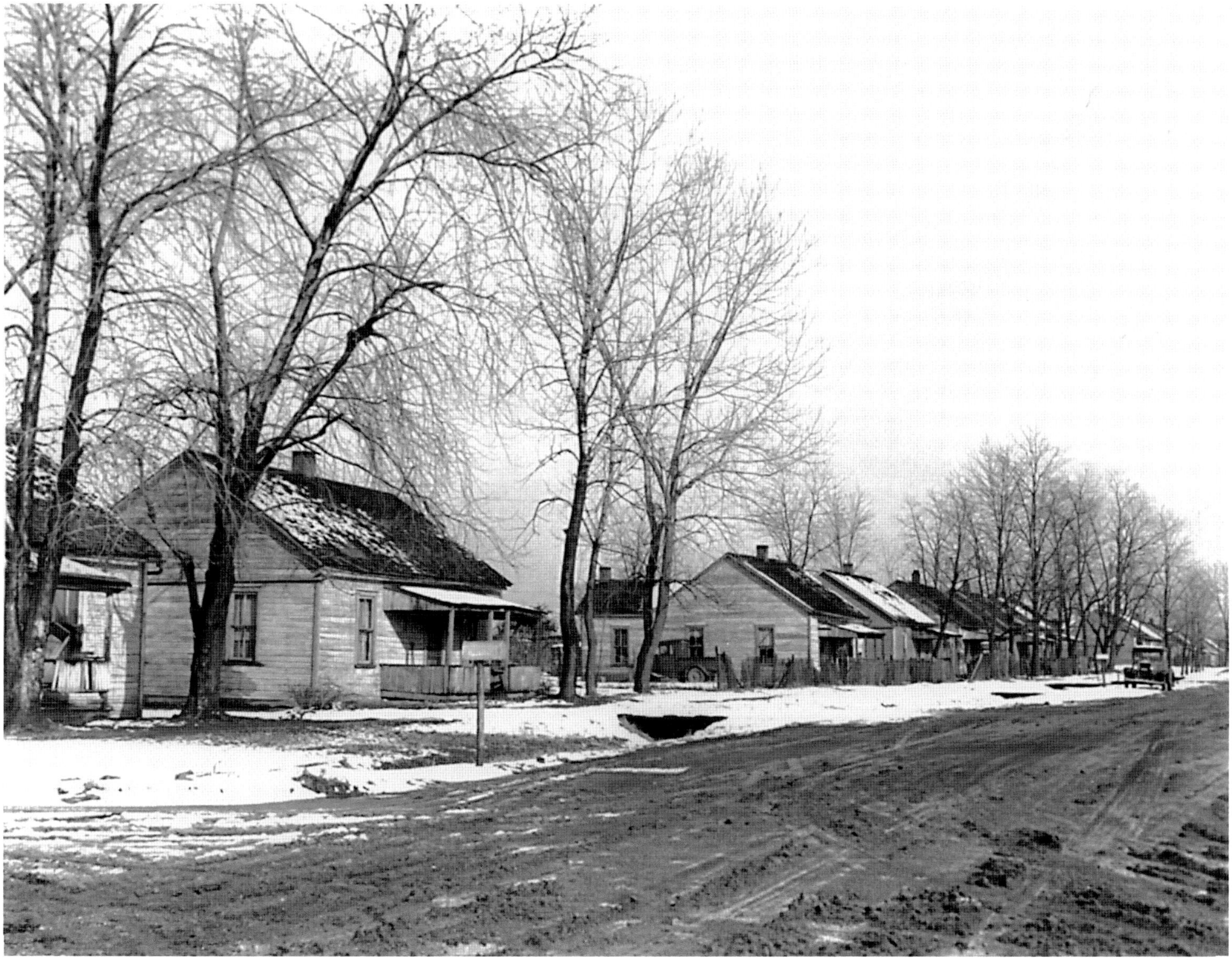

Miners' homes.
Bush. January, 1939.
Arthur Rothstein

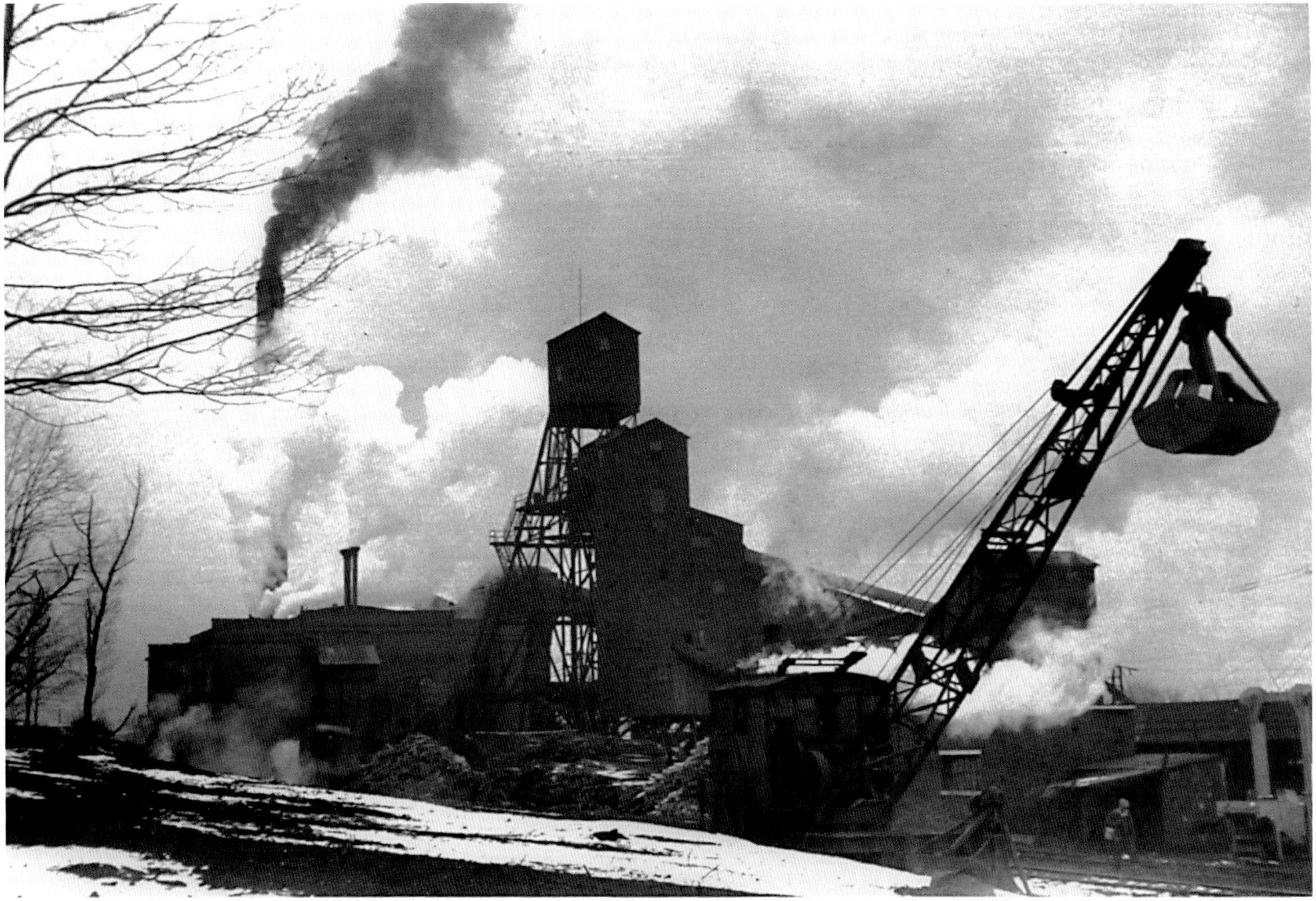

The Orient No. 1, one of the largest coal mines in the world.
Franklin County. January, 1939.
Arthur Rothstein

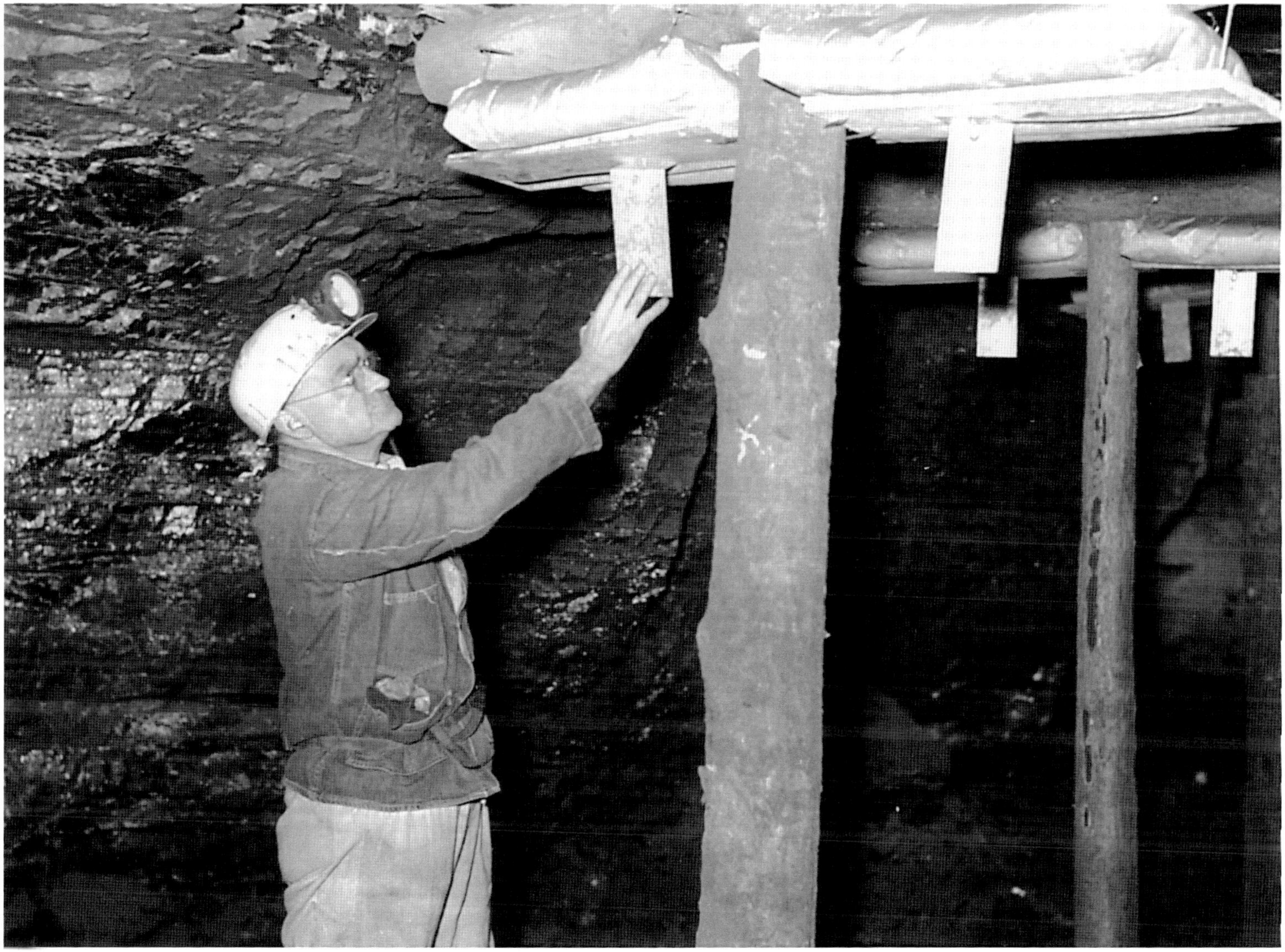

A safety engineer with rock dust traps to prevent the spreading of mine explosions.
West Frankfort. January, 1939.
Arthur Rothstein

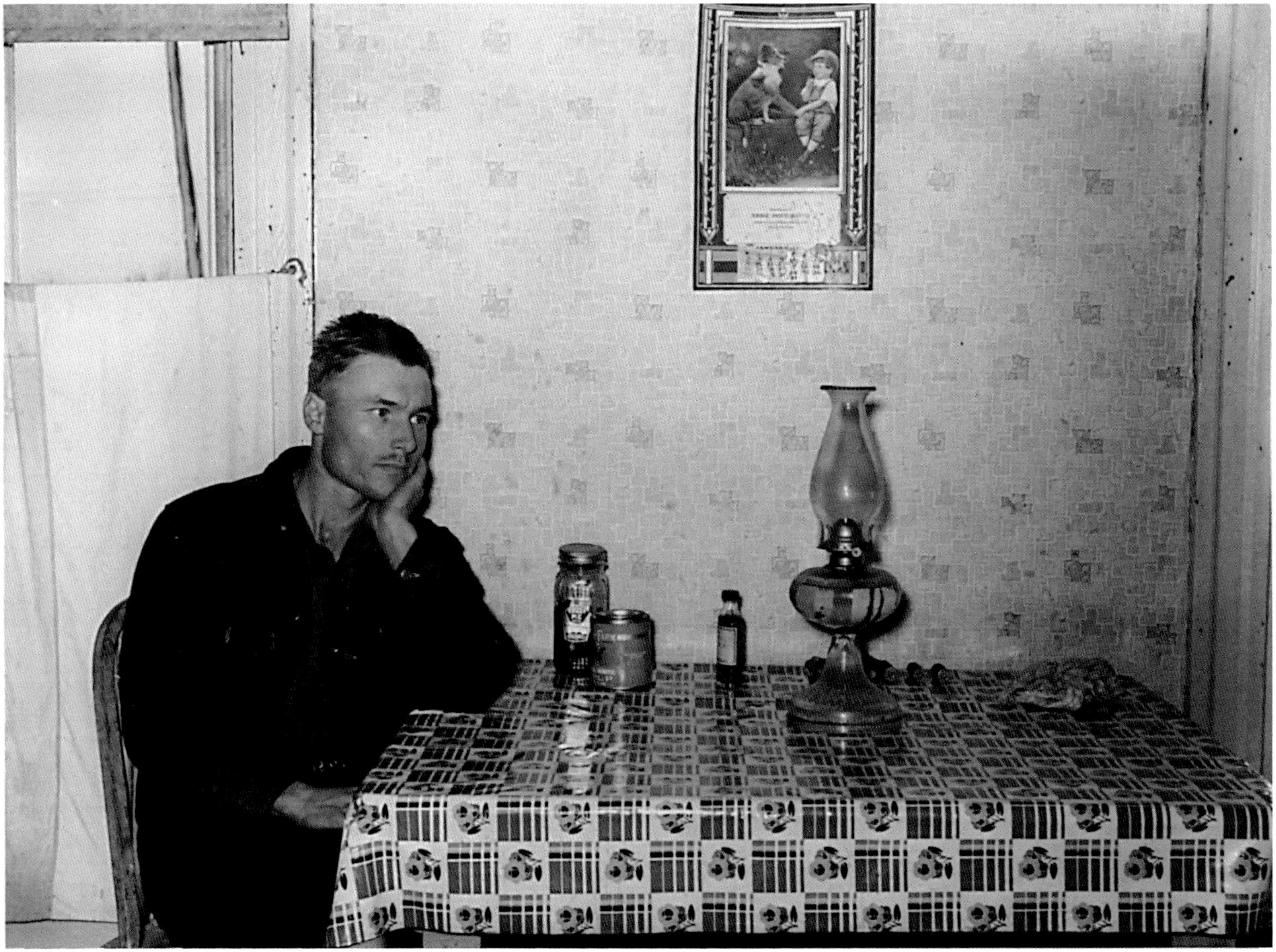

Unemployed coal miner.
Bush. January, 1939.
Arthur Rothstein

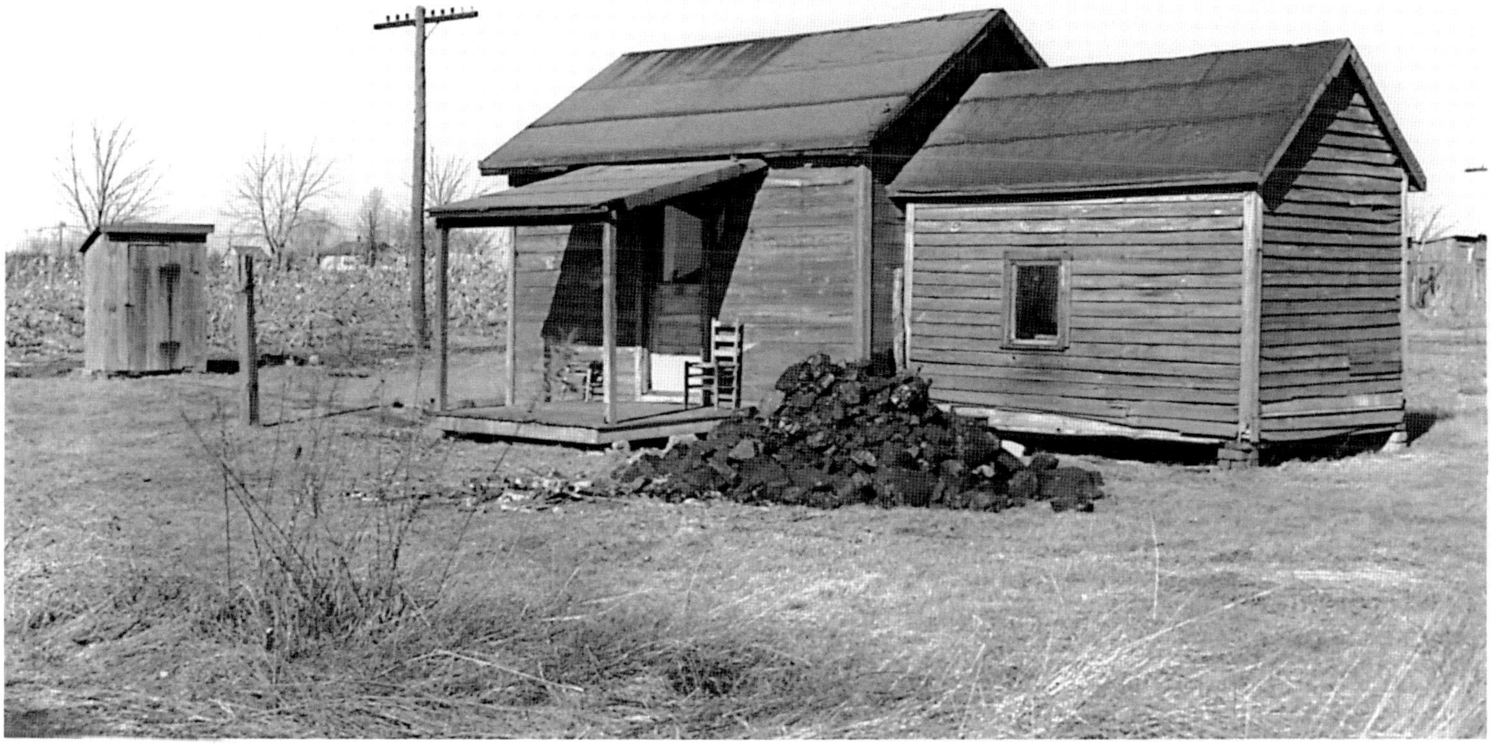

A miner's home.
Royalton. January, 1939.
Arthur Rothstein

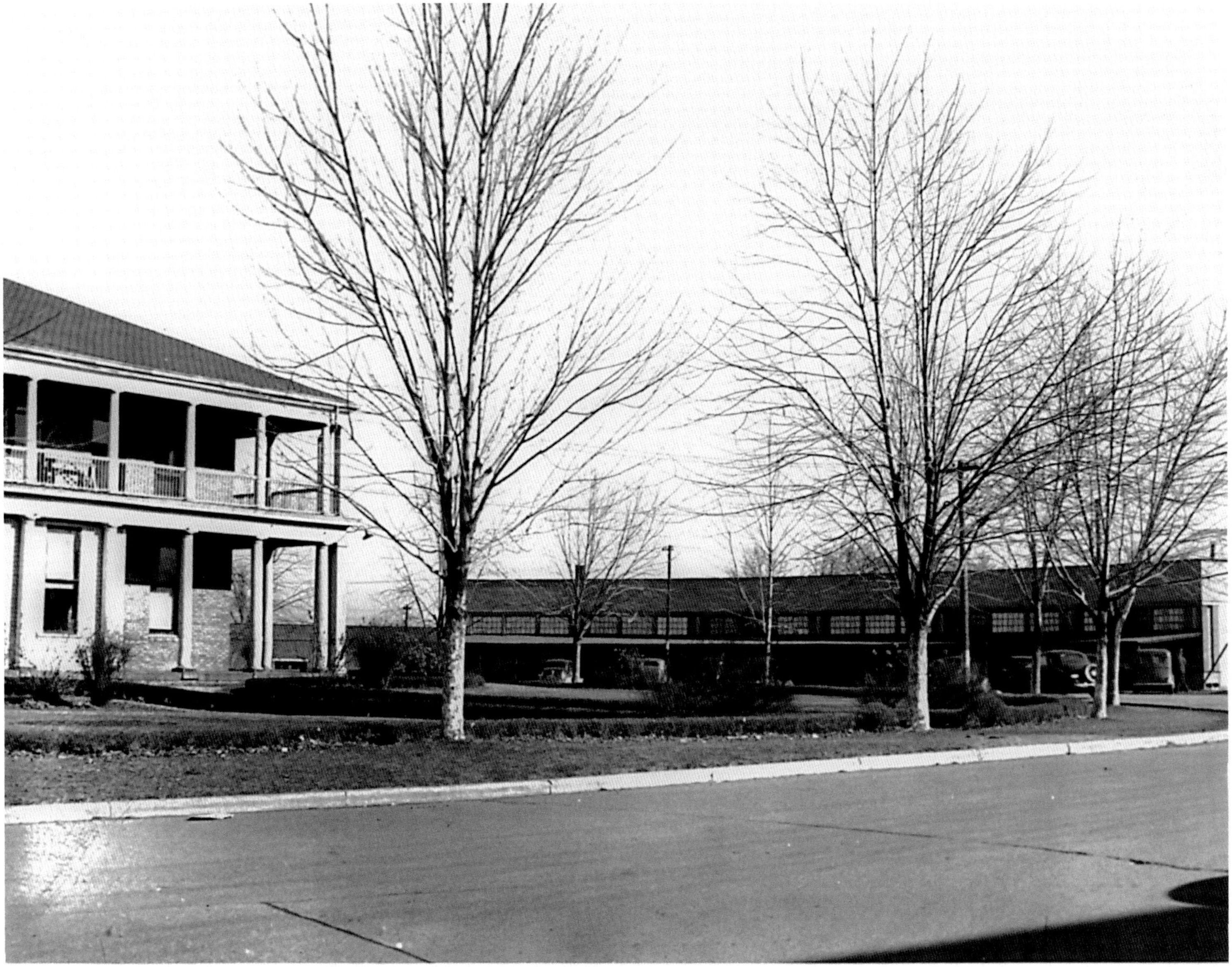

The mine office. The company store is on the right.
Zeigler. January, 1939.
Arthur Rothstein

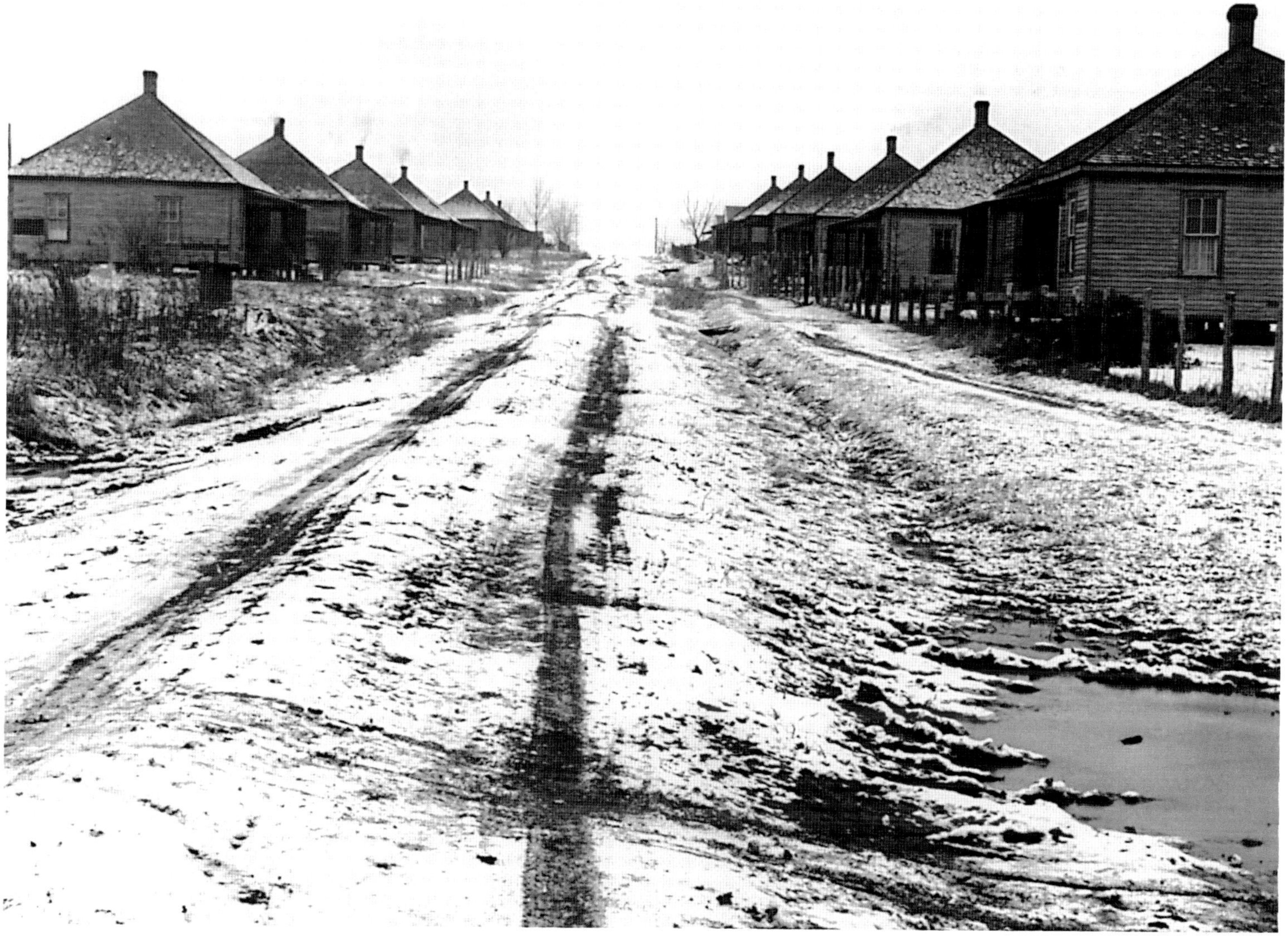

Miners' homes.
Freeman Spur. January, 1939.
Arthur Rothstein

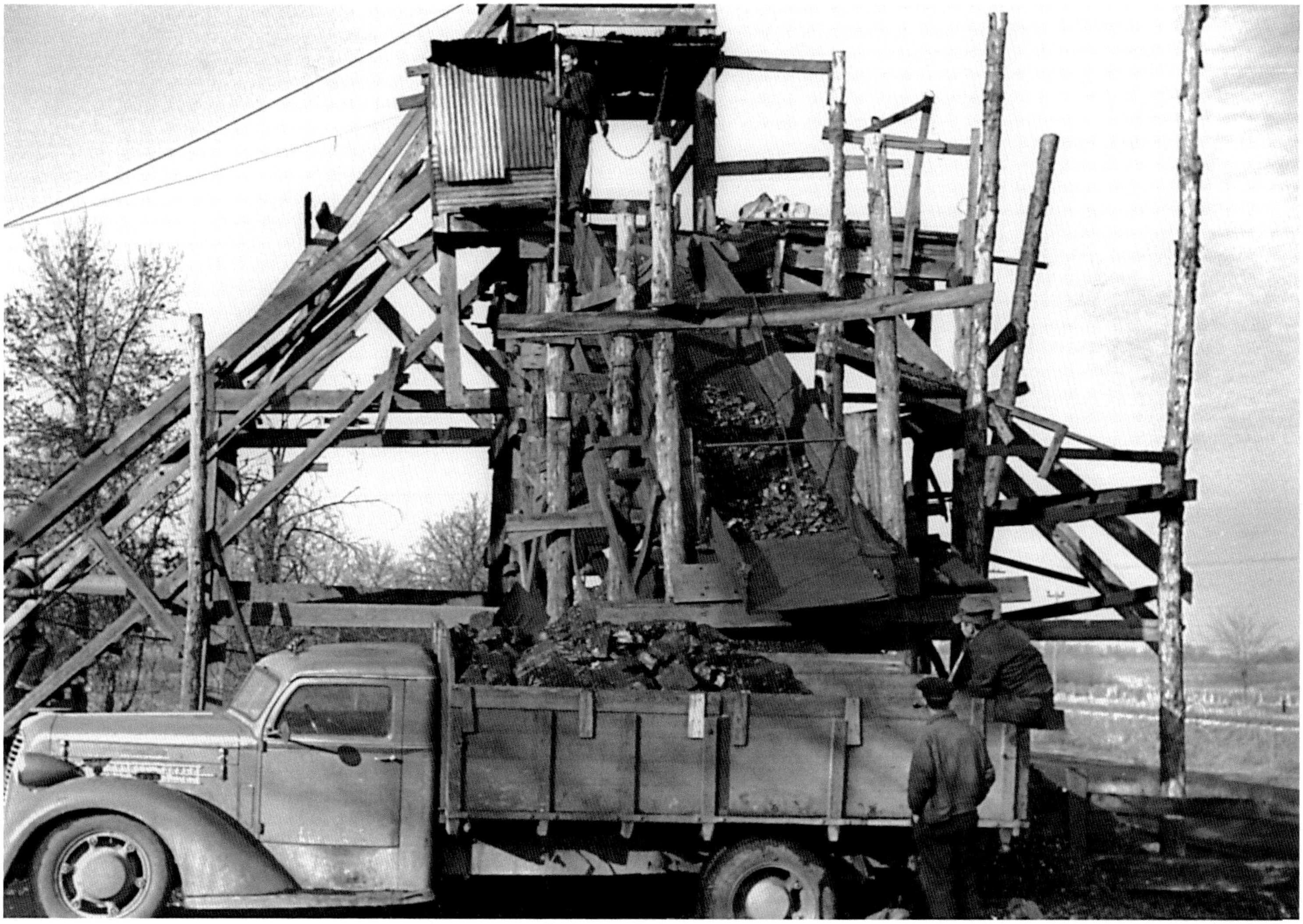

An abandoned mine, known as a gopher hole, in which the unemployed miners have opened primitive workings on the coal seam. Gopher hole showing a tipple and screen.
West Mine, West Frankfort. January, 1939. Arthur Rothstein

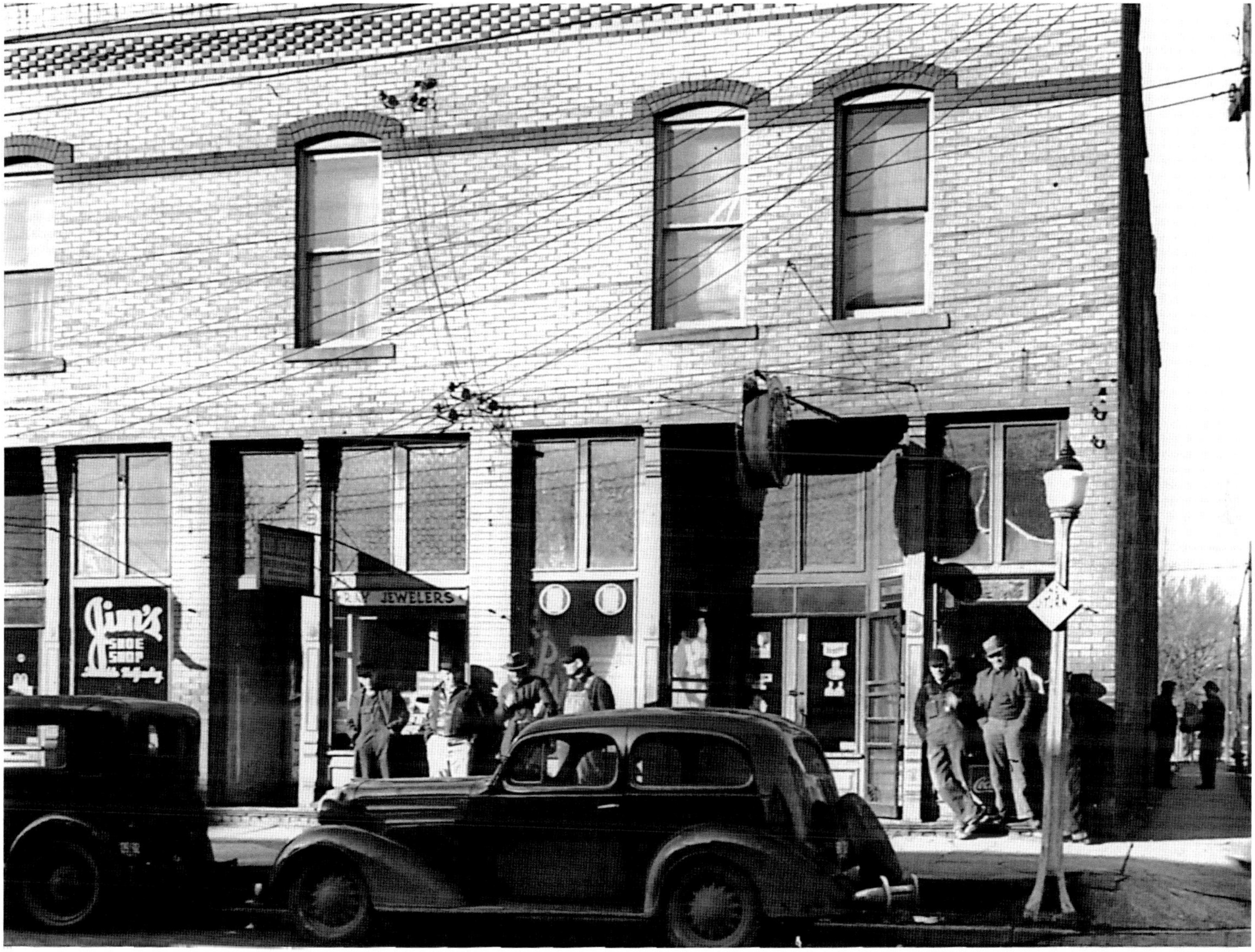

Unemployed miners on a street corner.
Johnston City. January, 1939.
Arthur Rothstein

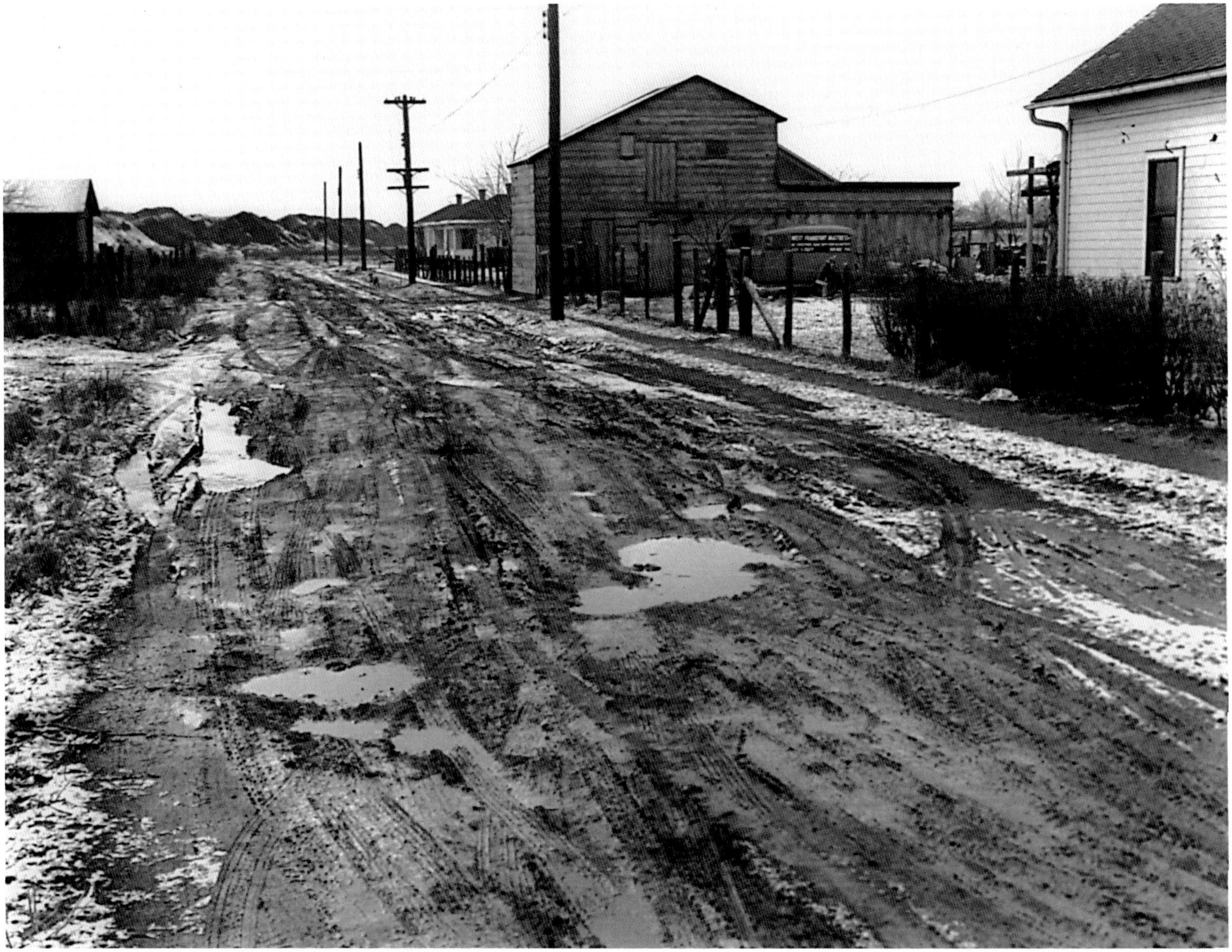

A side street.
West Frankfort. January, 1939.
Arthur Rothstein

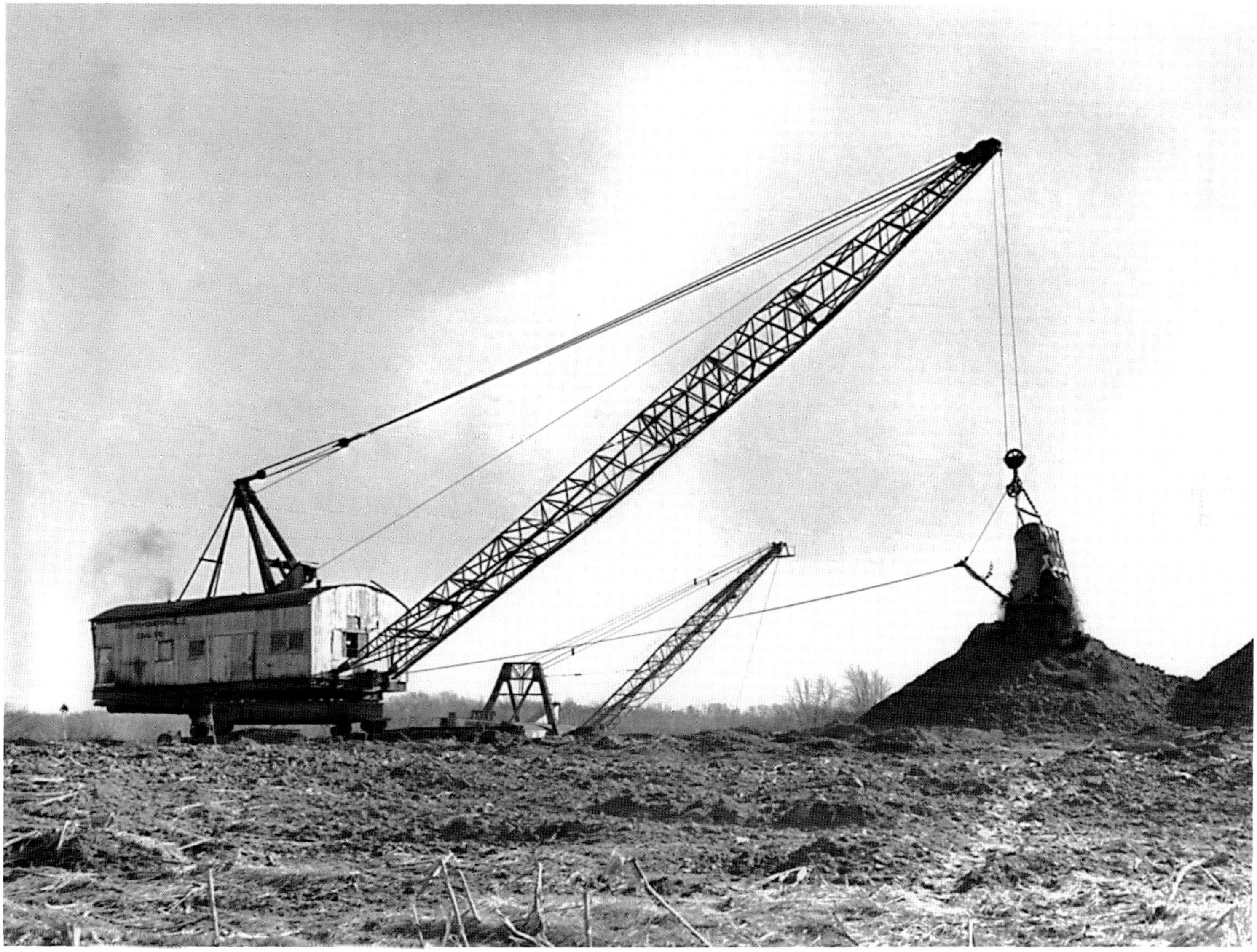

A strip coal mine.
Carterville (vicinity). January, 1939.
Arthur Rothstein

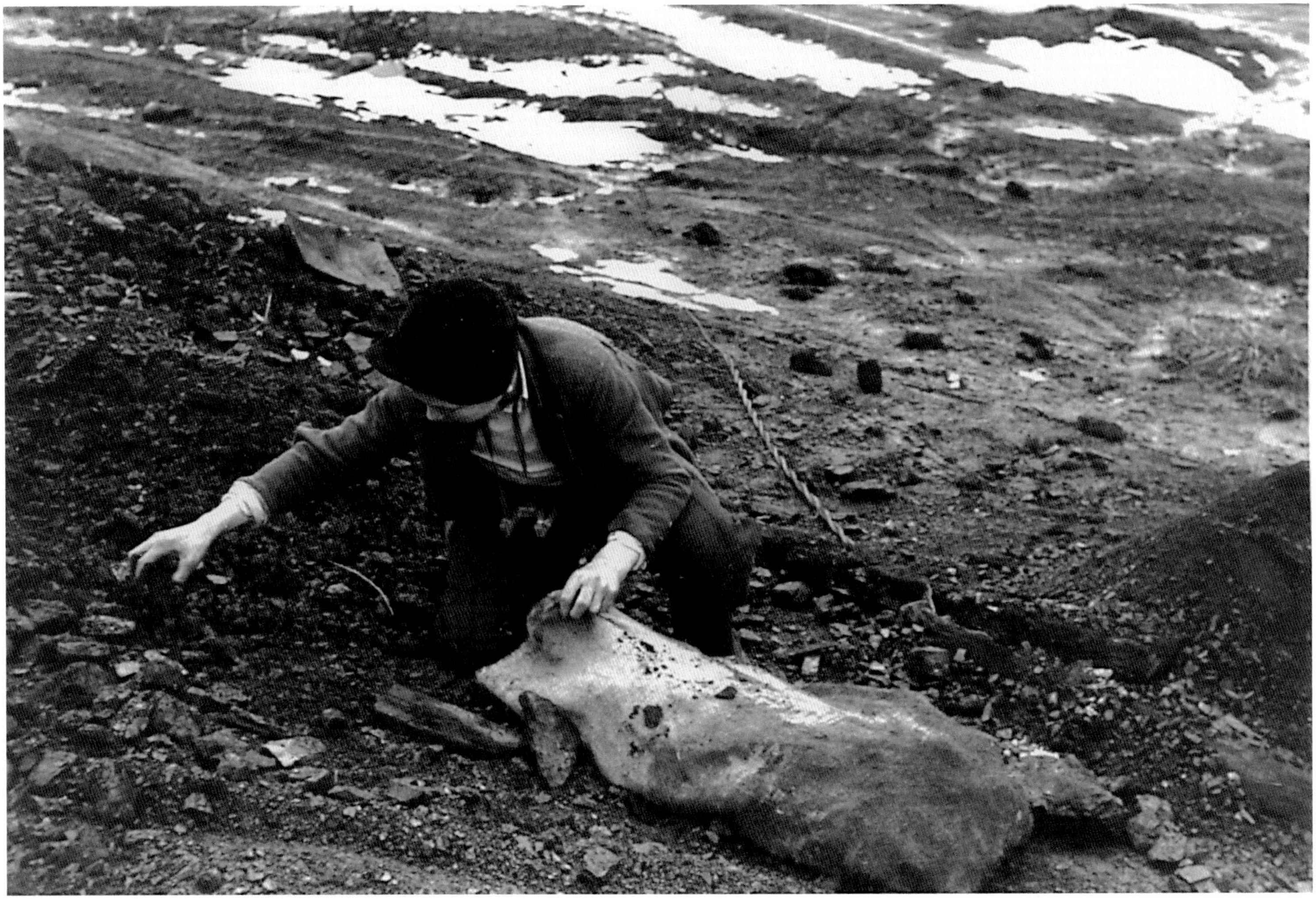

A boy hunting for coal on a slack pile.
Stiritz. January, 1939.
Arthur Rothstein

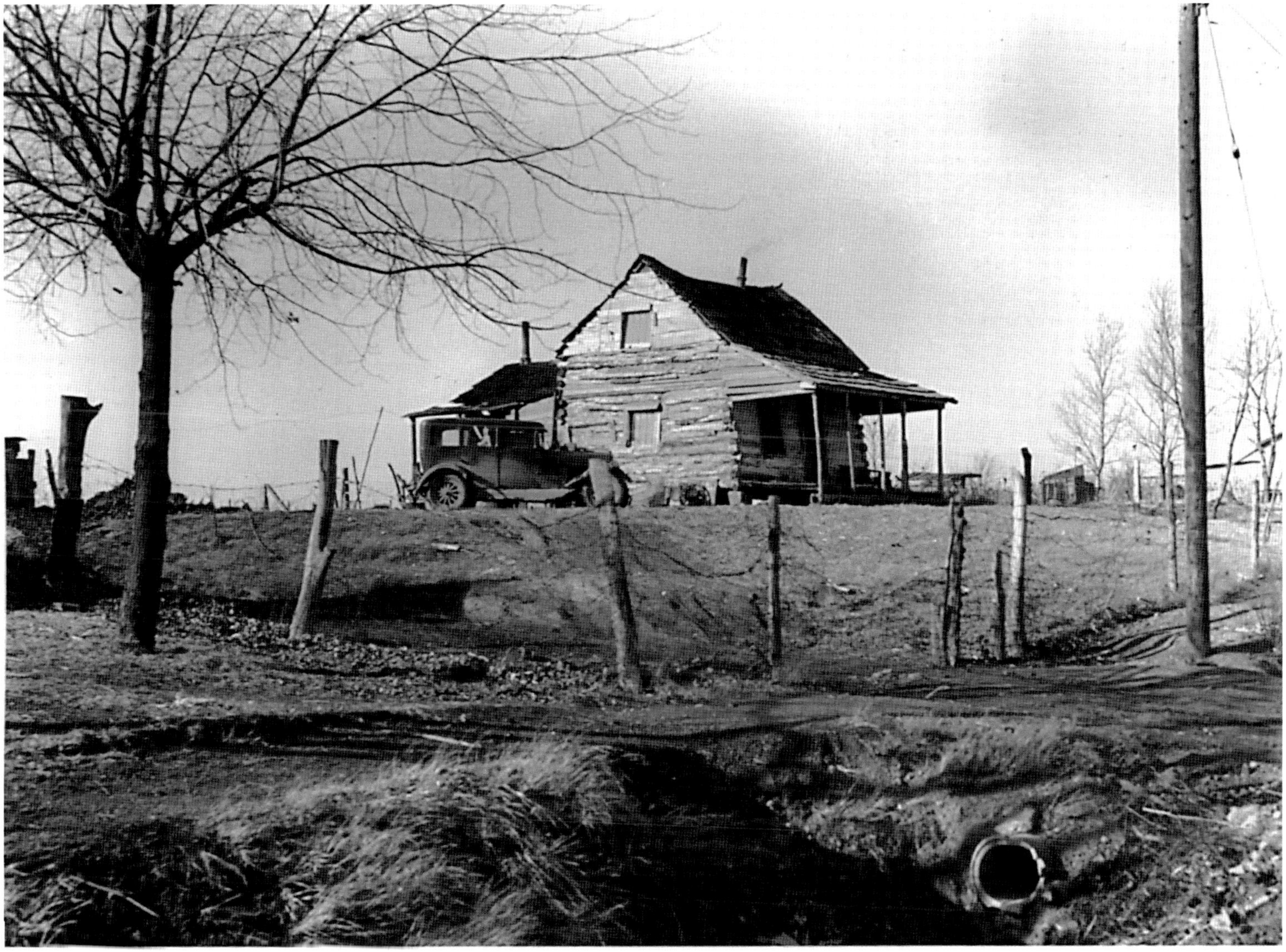

Miner's home.
Carrier Mills. January, 1939.
Arthur Rothstein

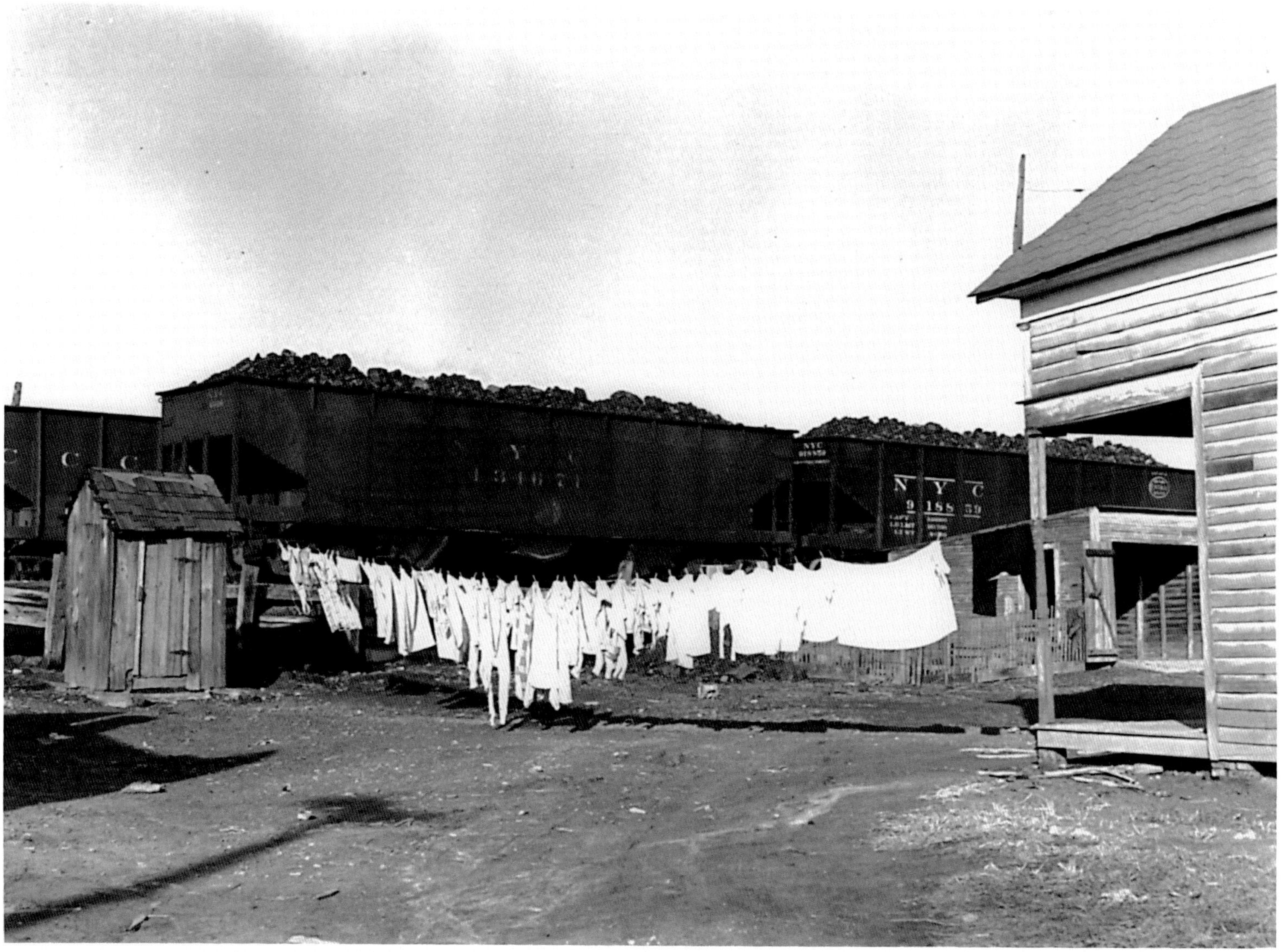

Clean clothes.
Carrier Mills. January, 1939.
Arthur Rothstein

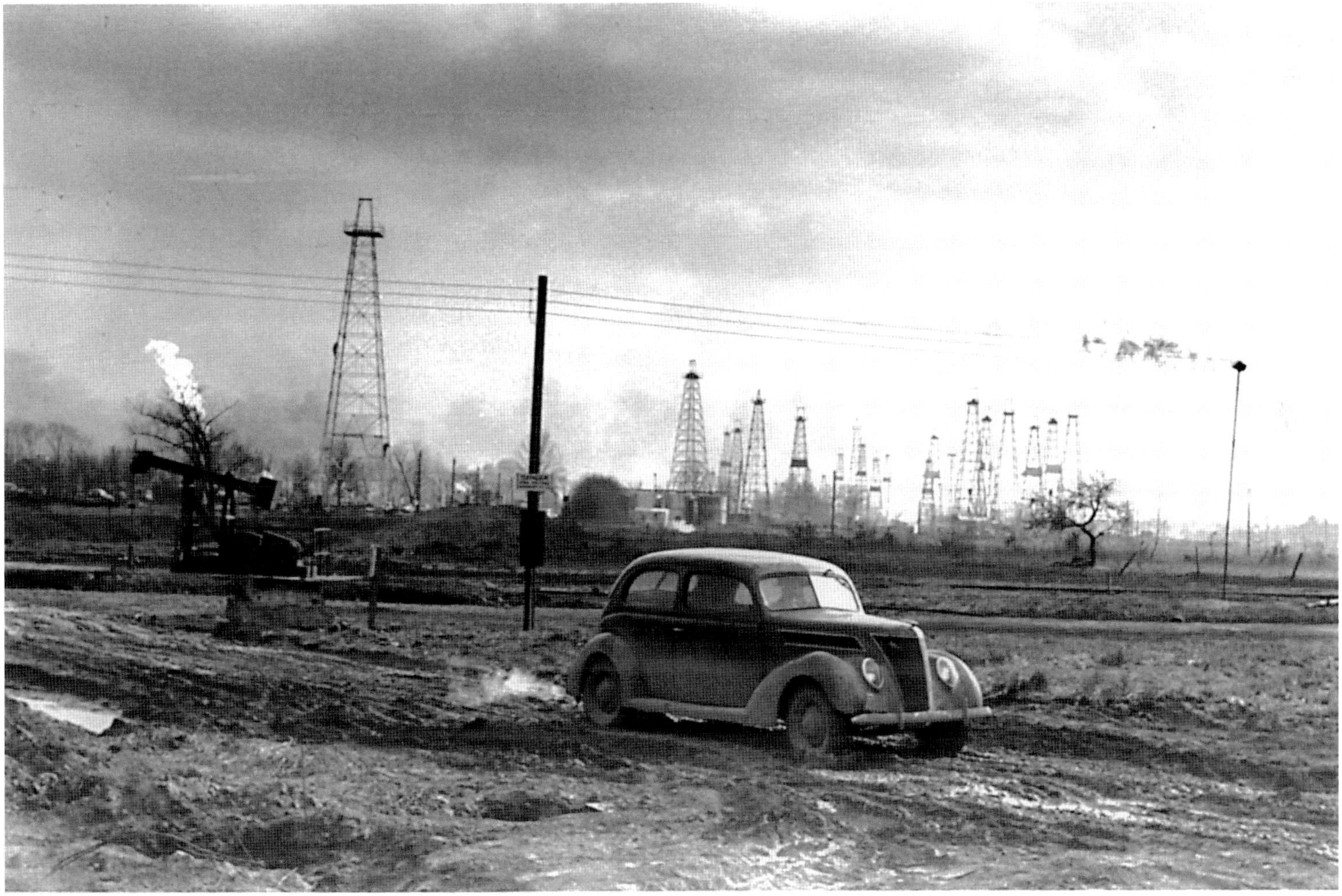

Oil field.
Marion County. February, 1940.
Arthur Rothstein

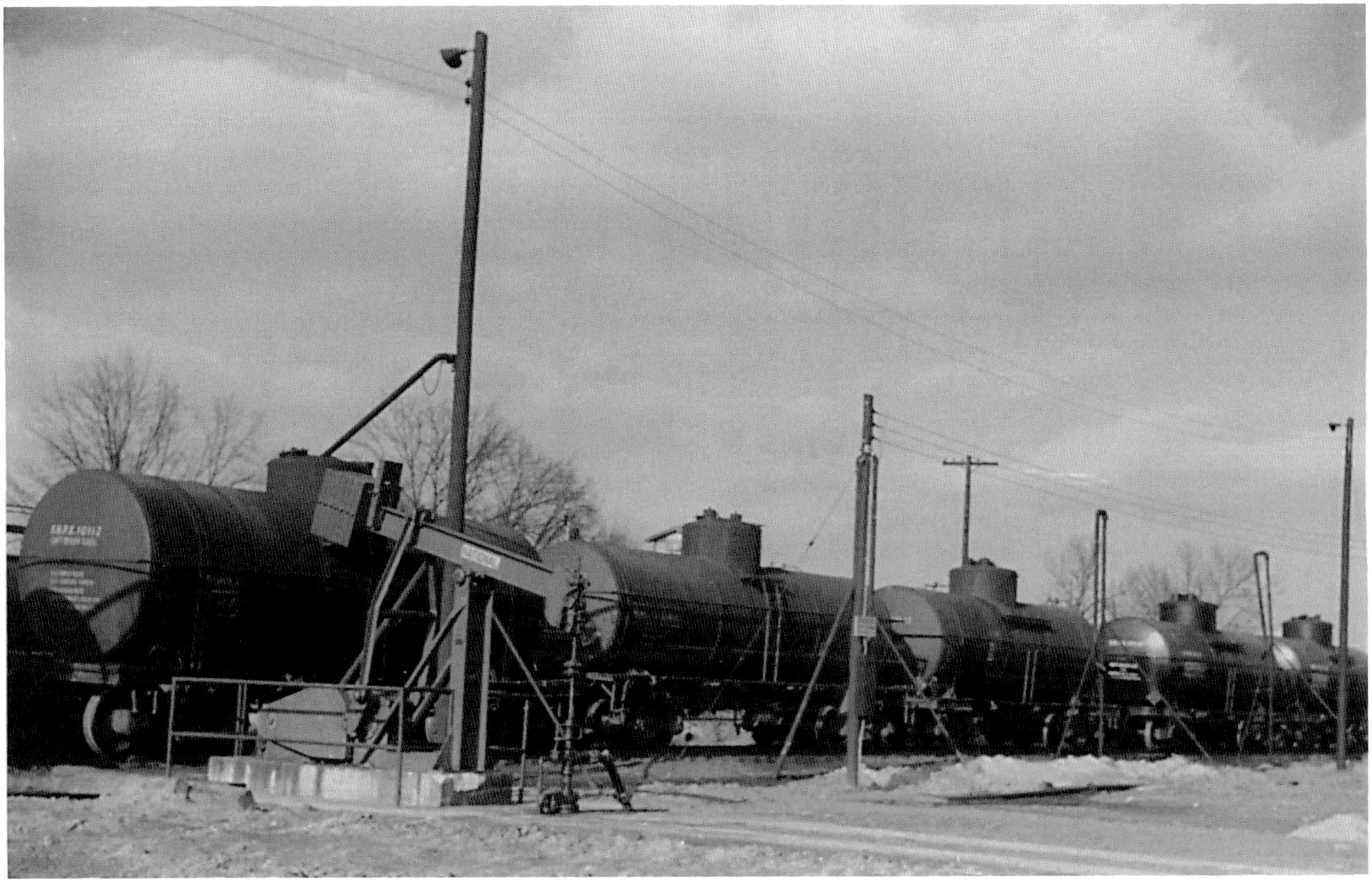

Tank cars at an oil field.
Marion County. February, 1940.
Arthur Rothstein

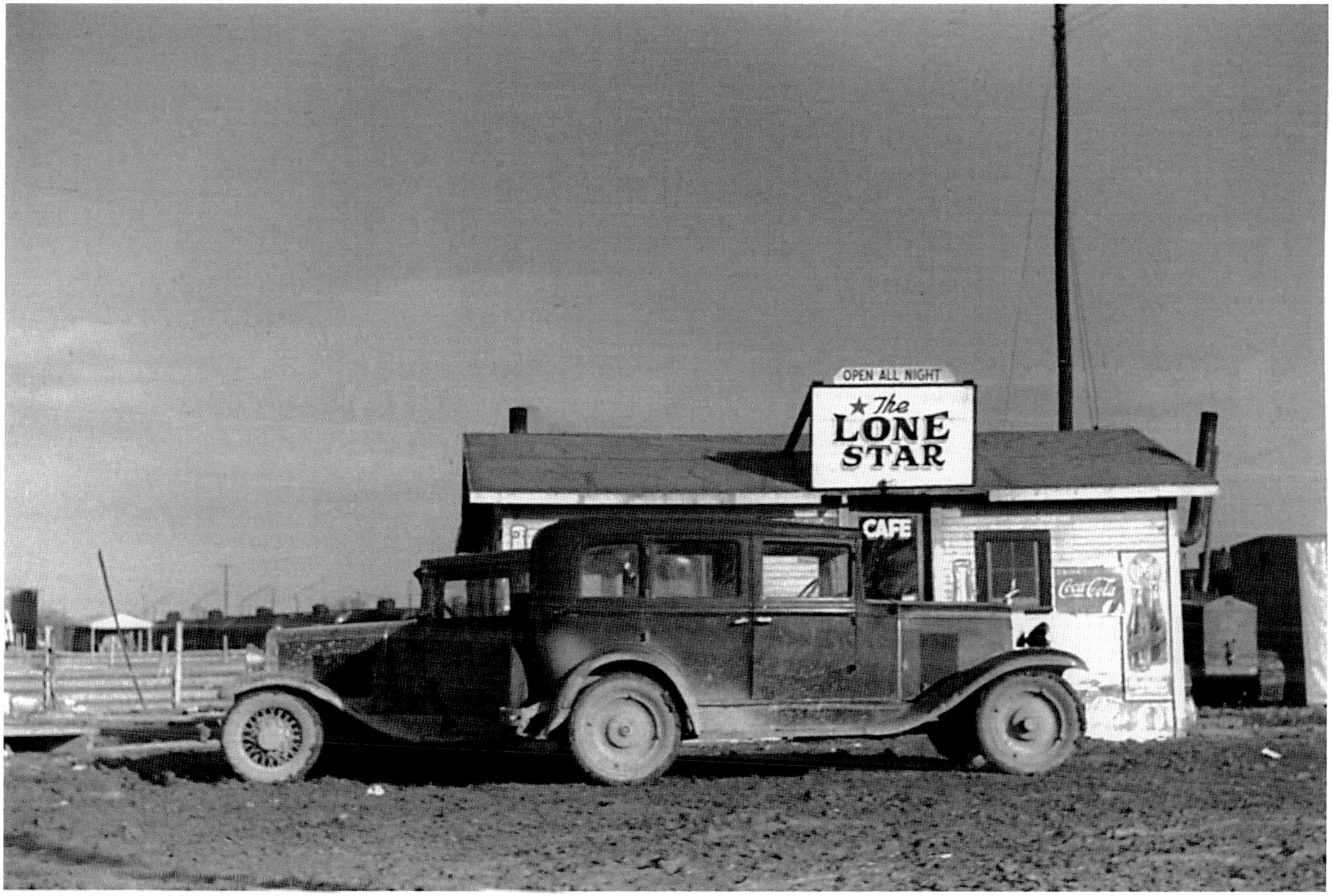

Cafe in an oil field.
Salem. February, 1940.
Arthur Rothstein

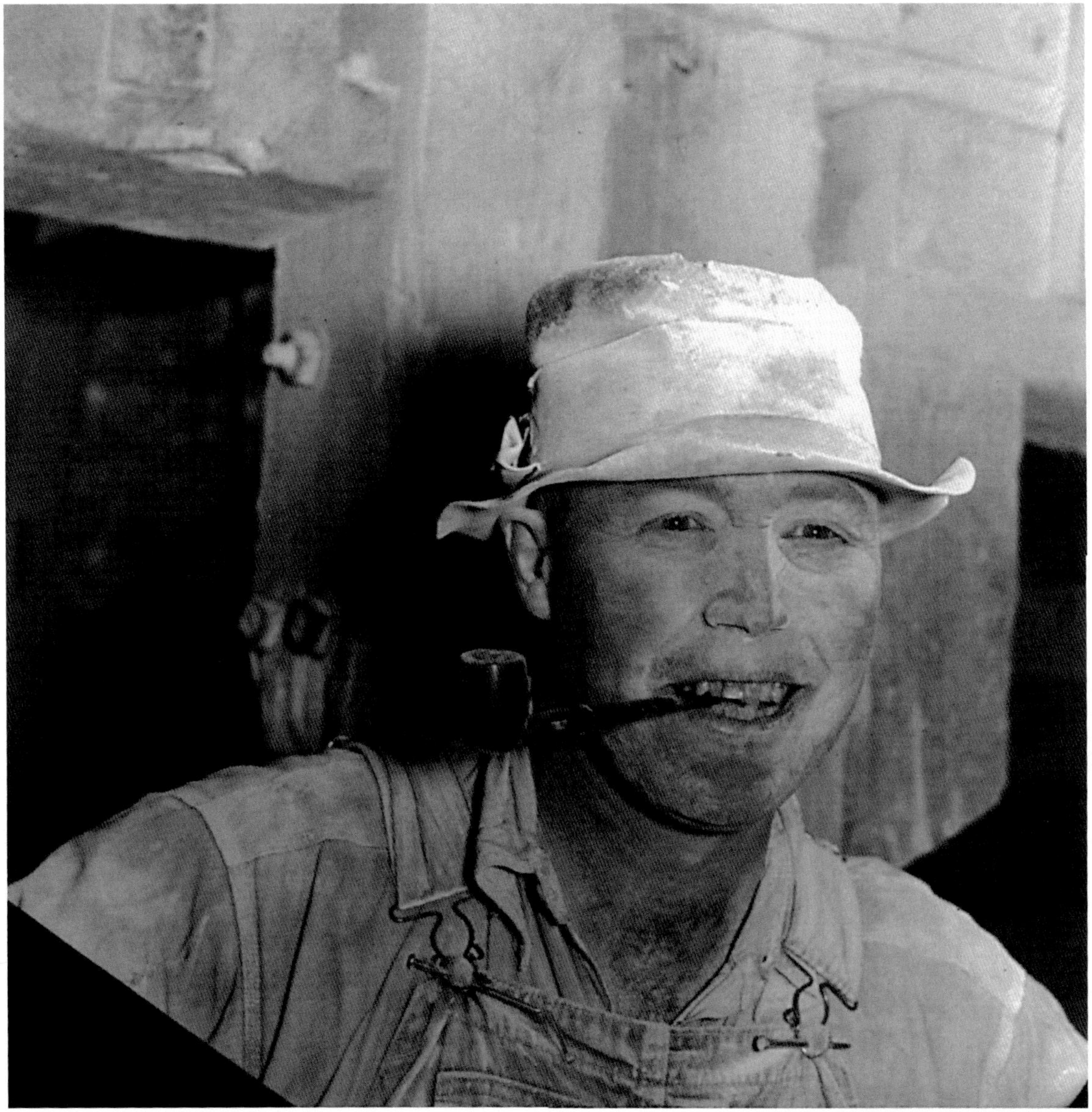

"Crusher man" at the Anna stone quarry.
Anna. June, 1940.
C. William Horrell

LIFE ON THE RIVER AND SHORE

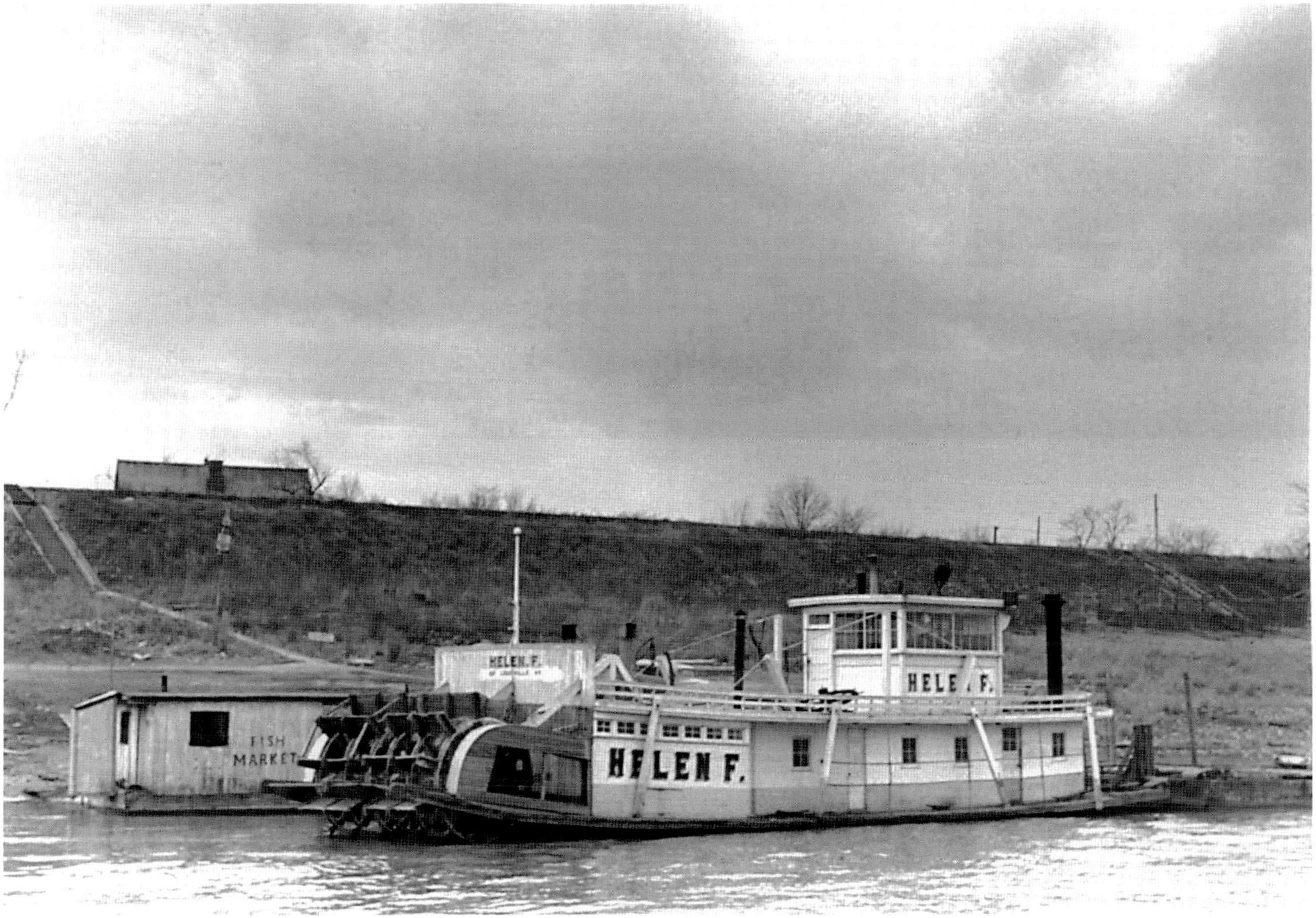

Ohio River steamboat.
Shawneetown. January, 1939.
Arthur Rothstein

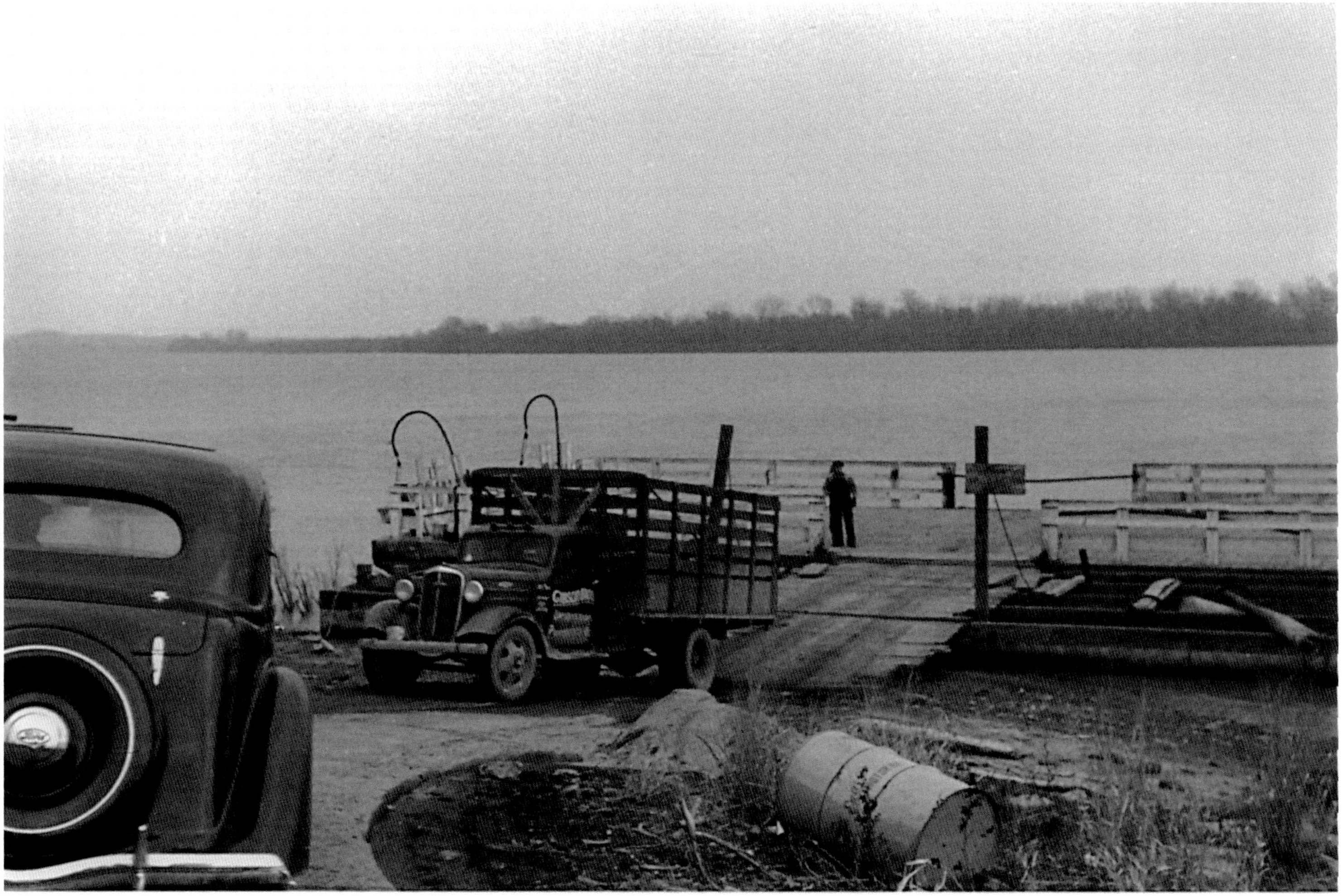

A ferry crossing on the Ohio River.
Shawneetown. January, 1939.
Arthur Rothstein

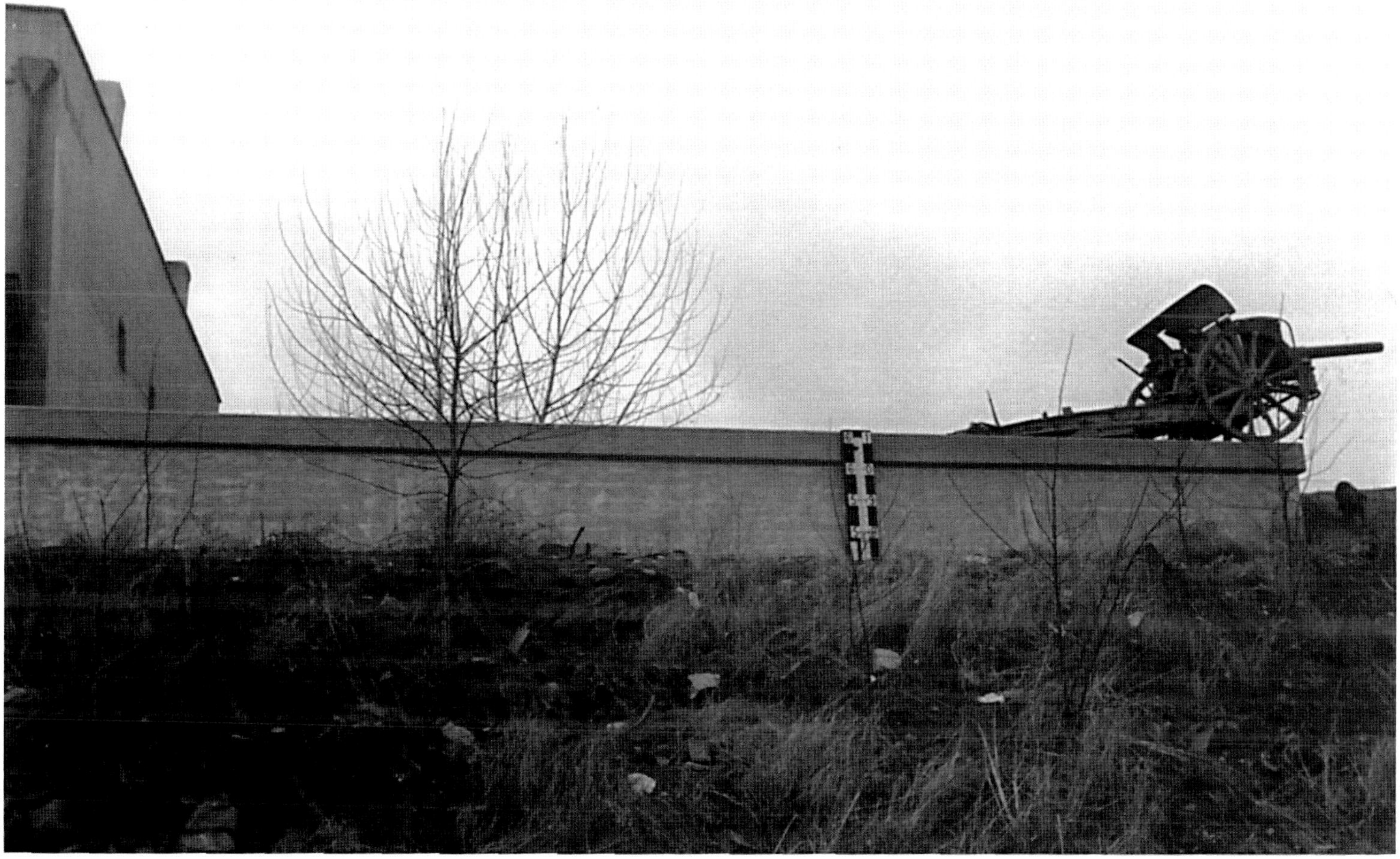

Levee and flood gauge.
Shawneetown. January, 1939.
Arthur Rothstein

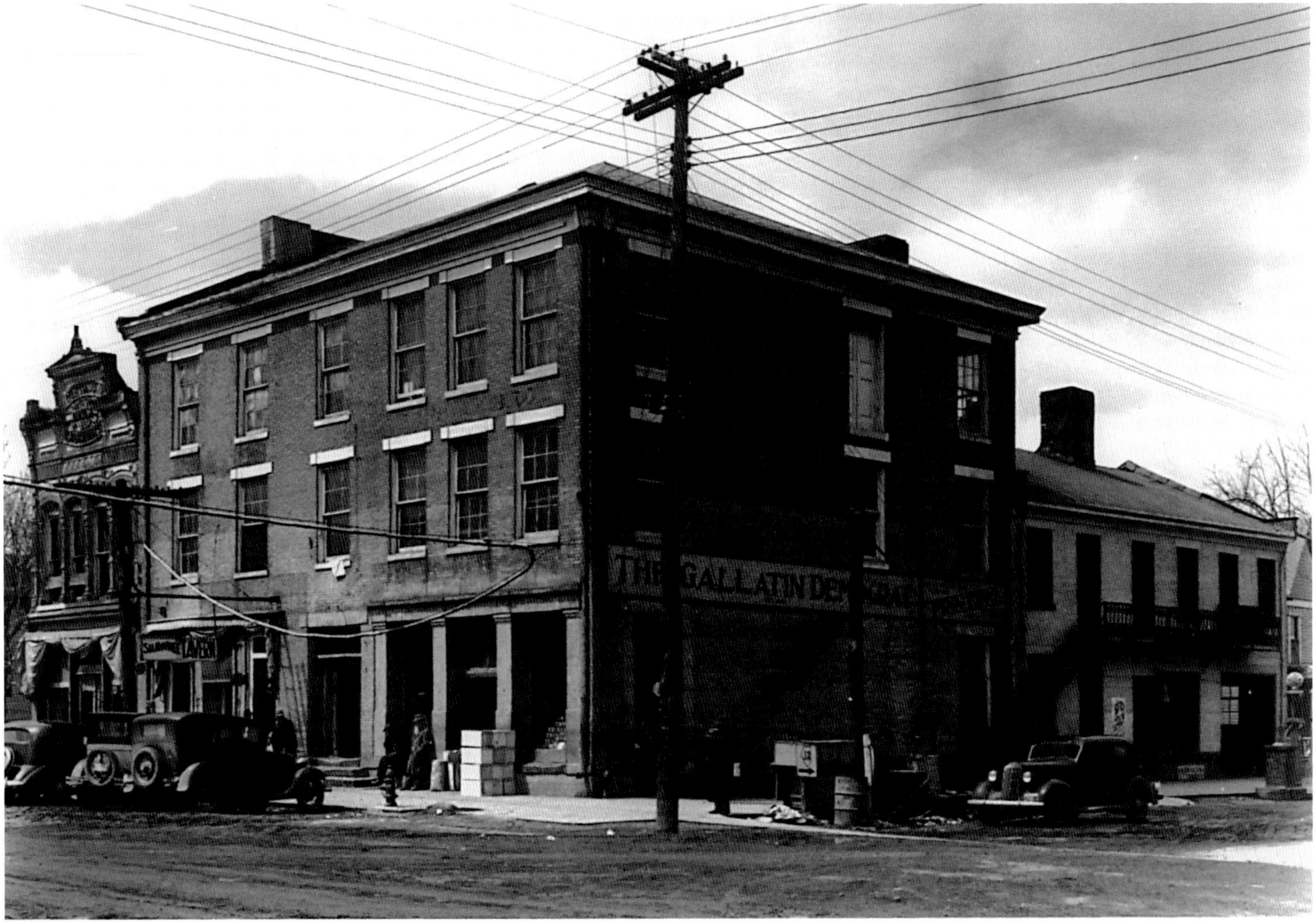

The Posey Building in which Abraham Lincoln and Robert
Ingersoll had law offices.
Shawneetown. April, 1937.
Russell Lee

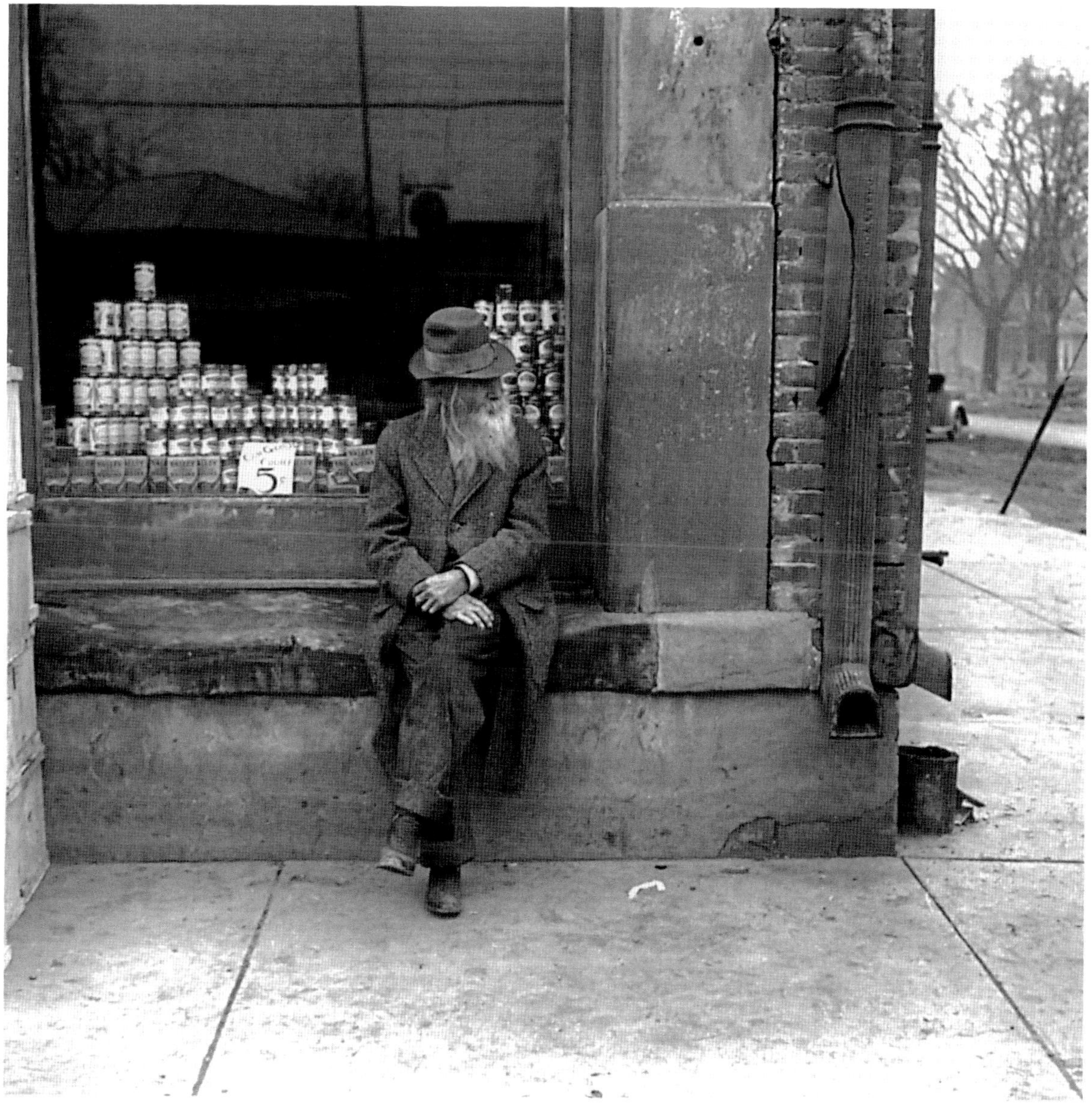

Old man on the street.
Shawneetown. April, 1937.
Russell Lee

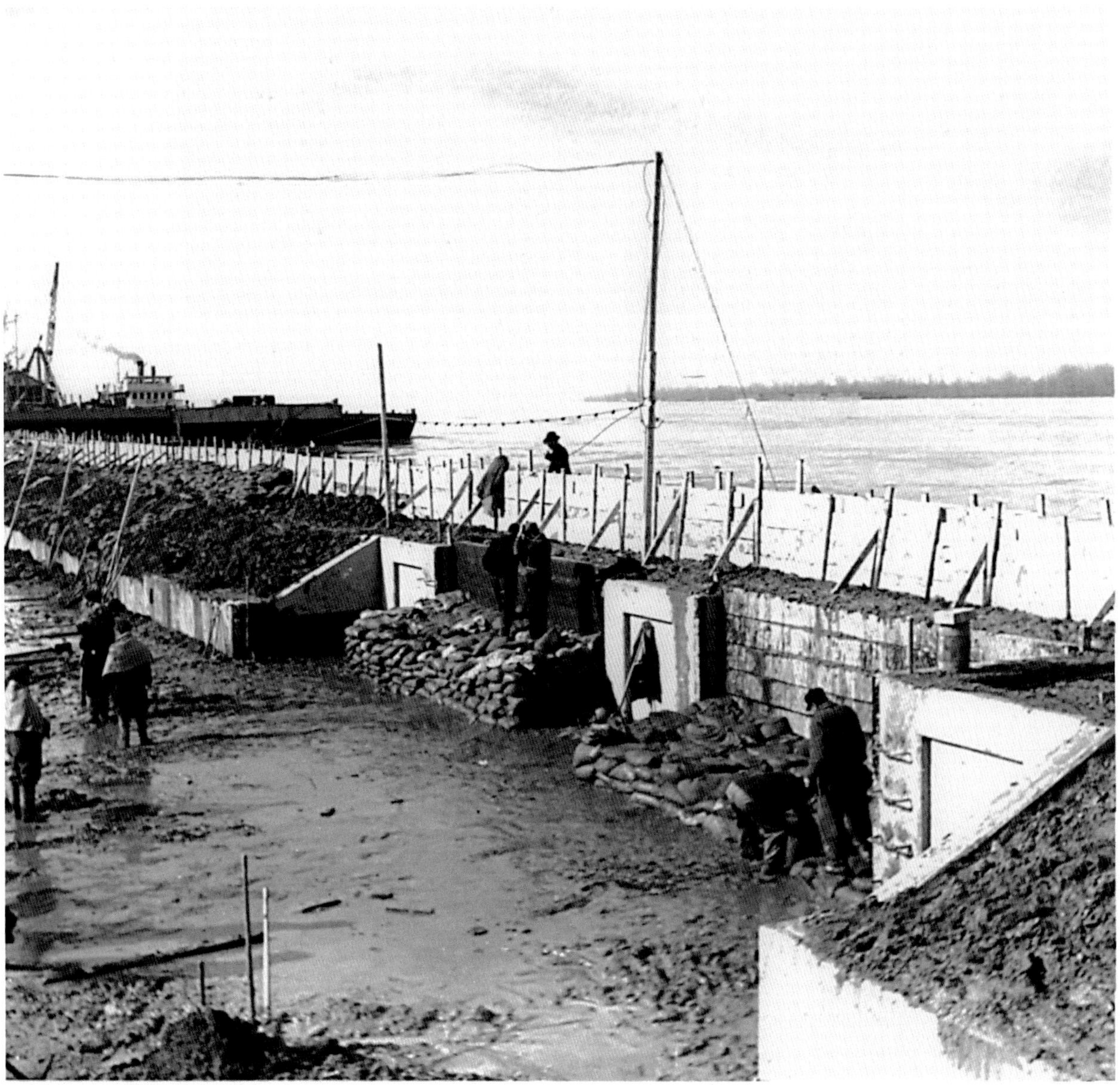

Piling sandbags along the levee during the height of the flood.
Cairo. February, 1937.
Russell Lee

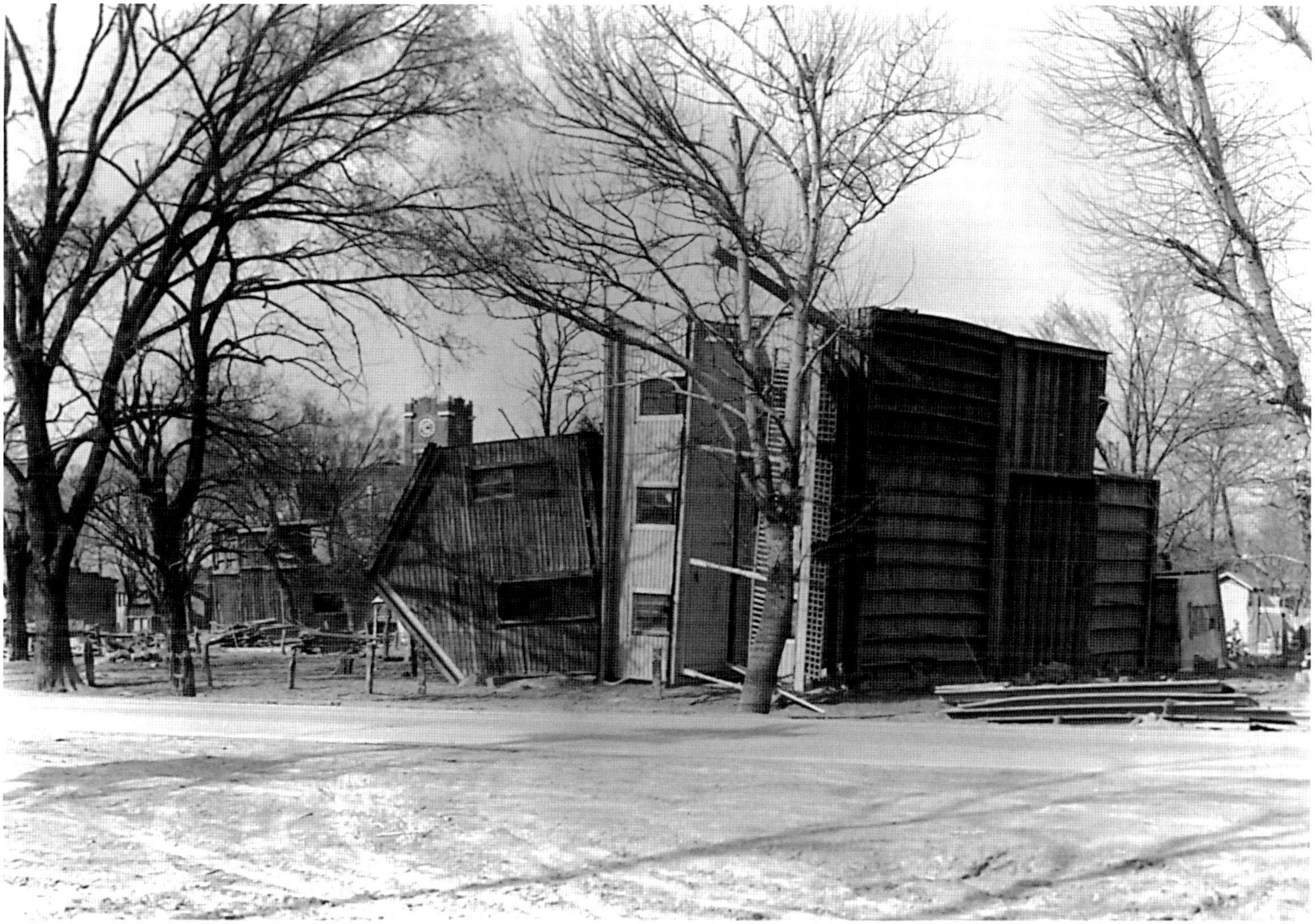

Houses overturned by the 1937 flood.
Shawneetown (vicinity). April, 1937.
Russell Lee

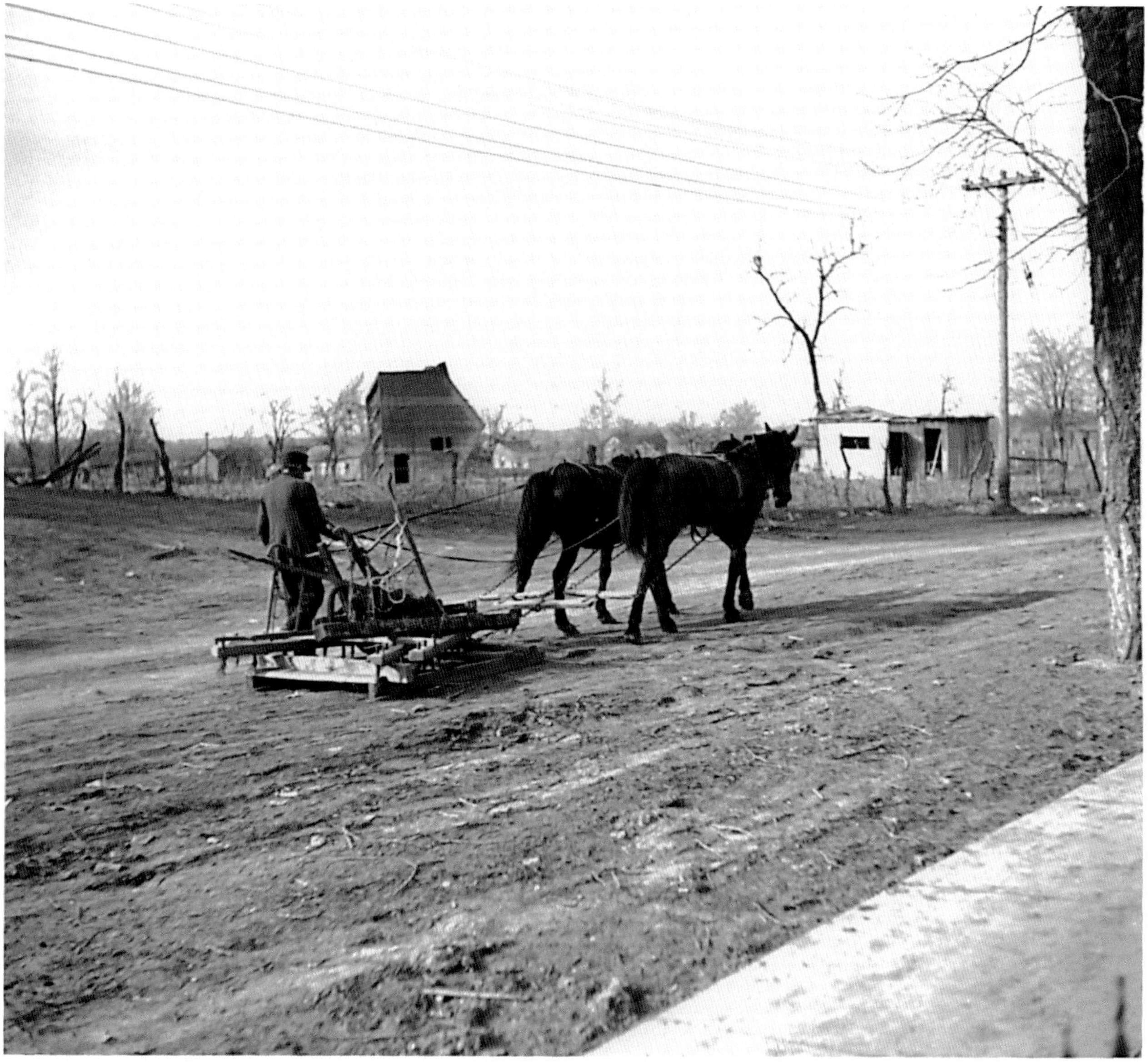

Horse-drawn mud sled in the 1937 flood area.
Shawneetown. April, 1937.
Russell Lee

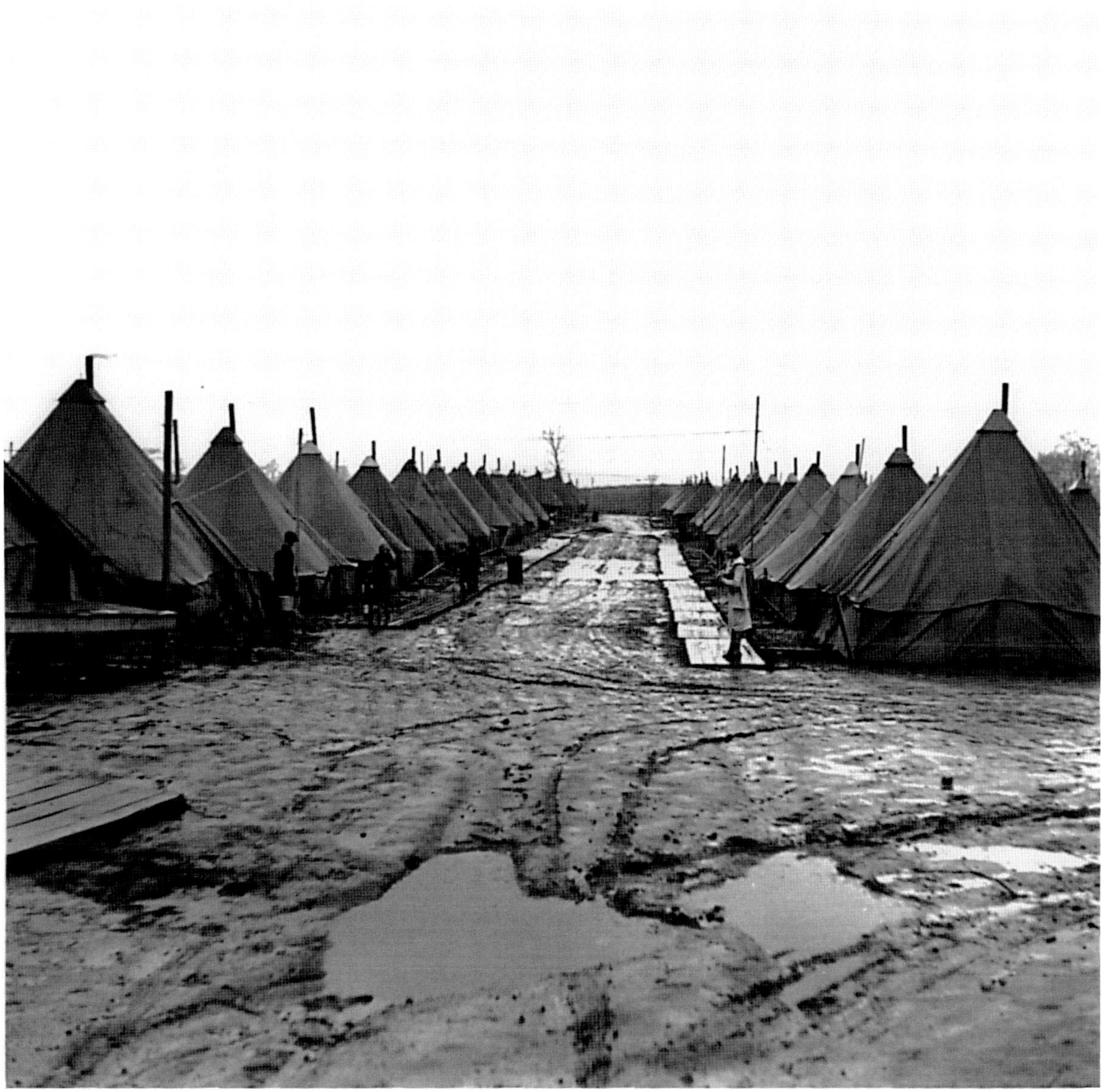

Tent city.
Shawneetown (vicinity). May, 1937.
Russell Lee

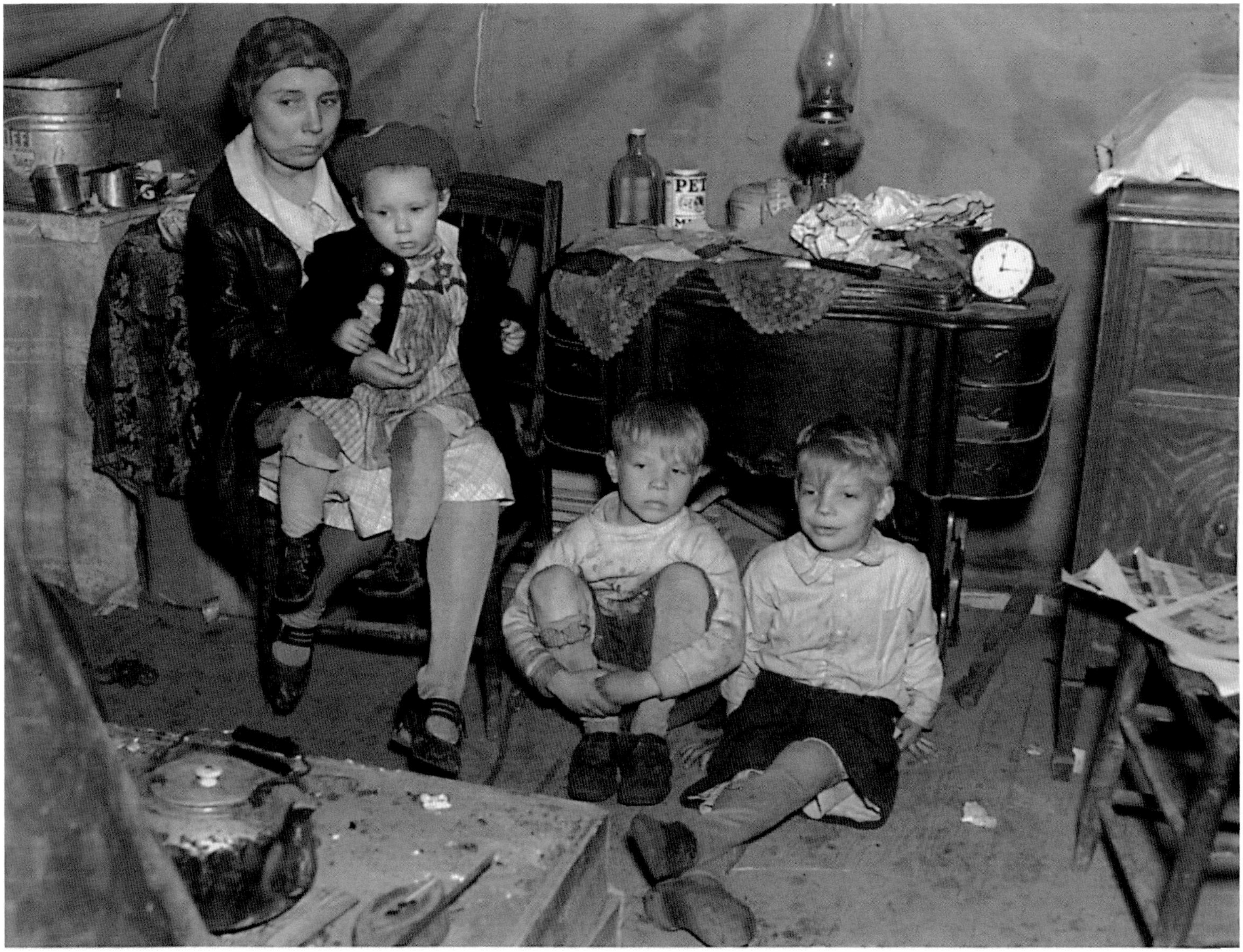

Part of a flood refugee family in a tent.
Tent City. April, 1937.
Russell Lee

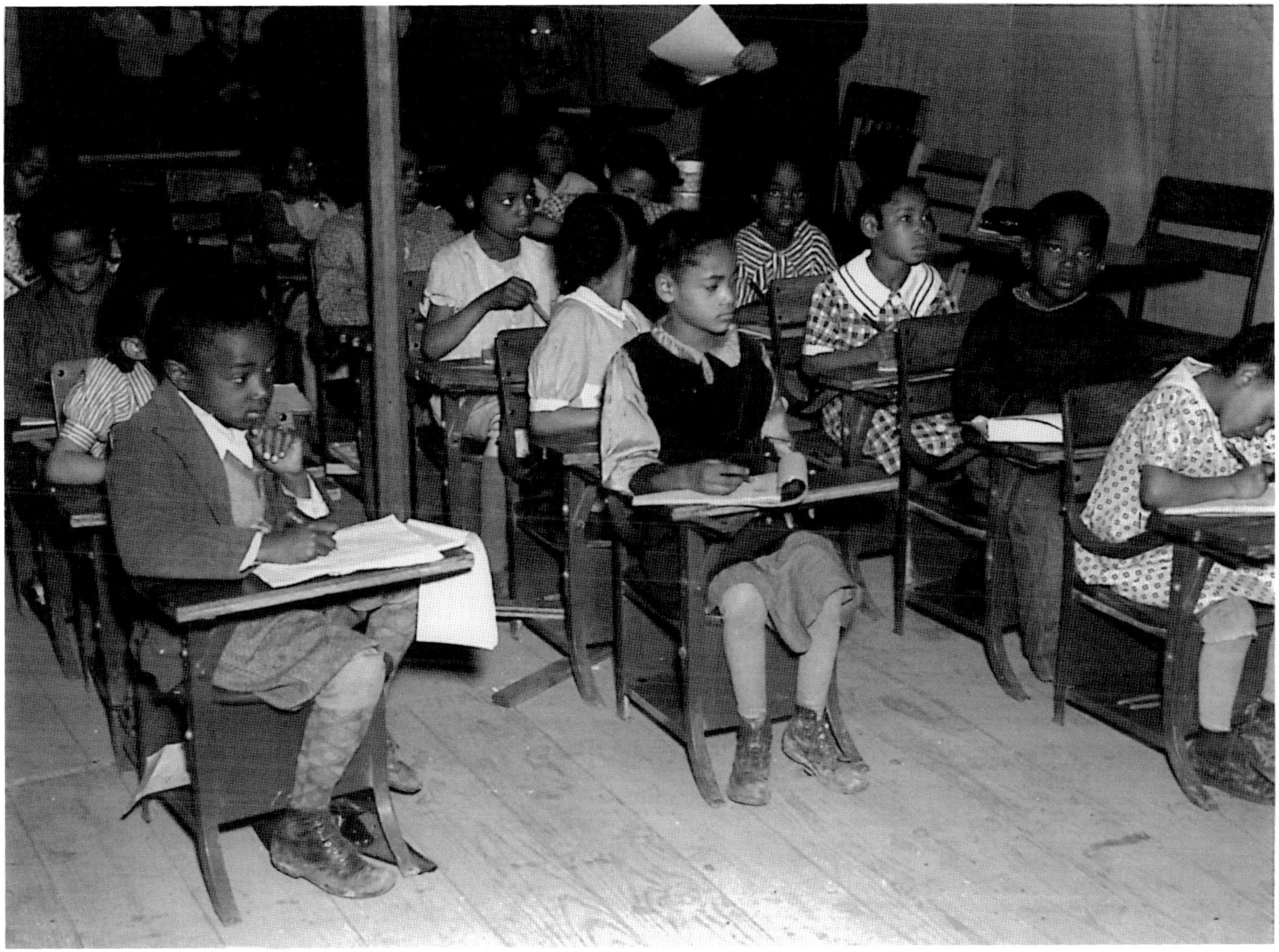

Negro school.
Tent City, Shawneetown (vicinity). April, 1937.
Russell Lee

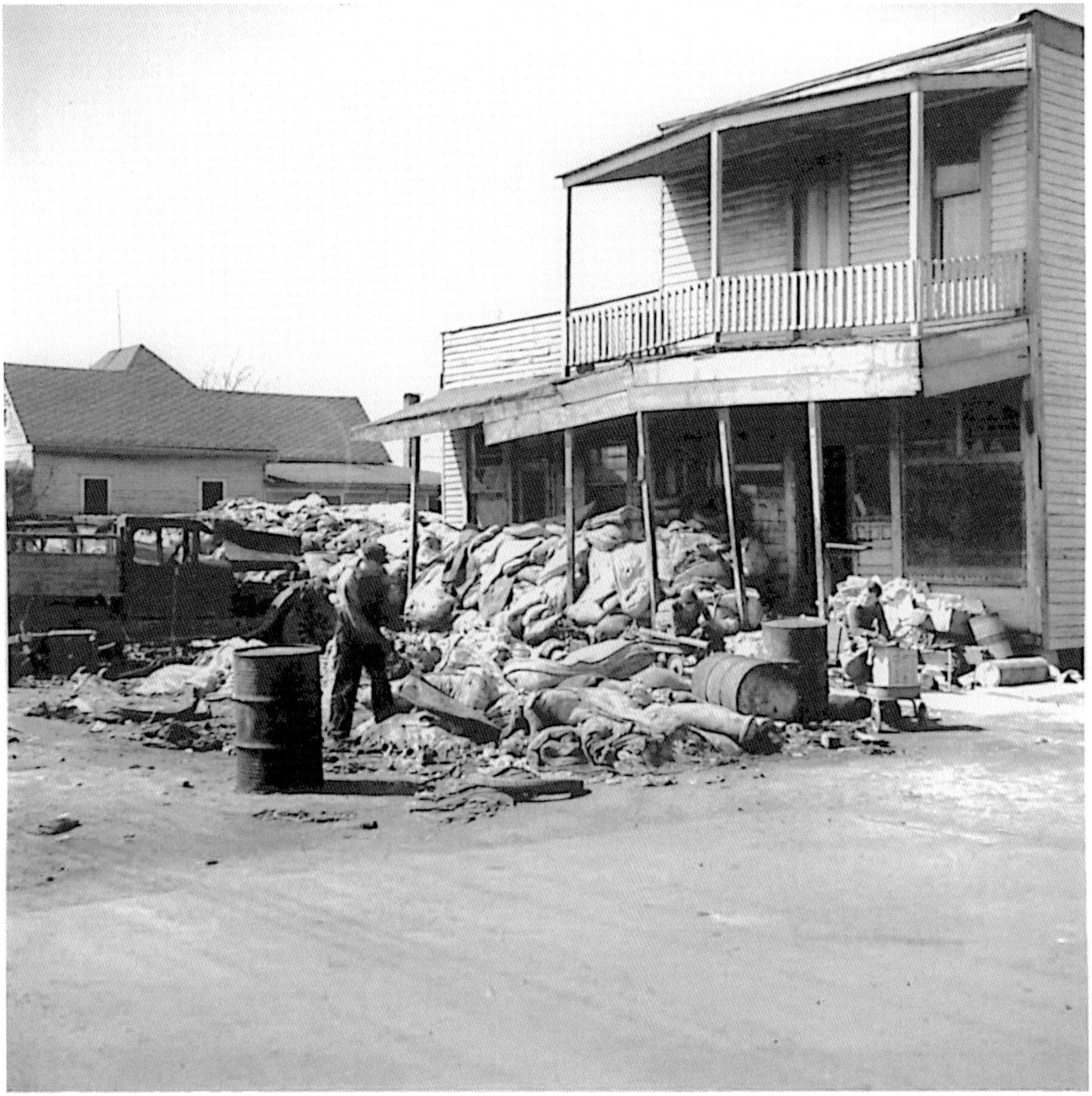

Debris from the flood.
Harrisburg. April, 1937
Russell Lee

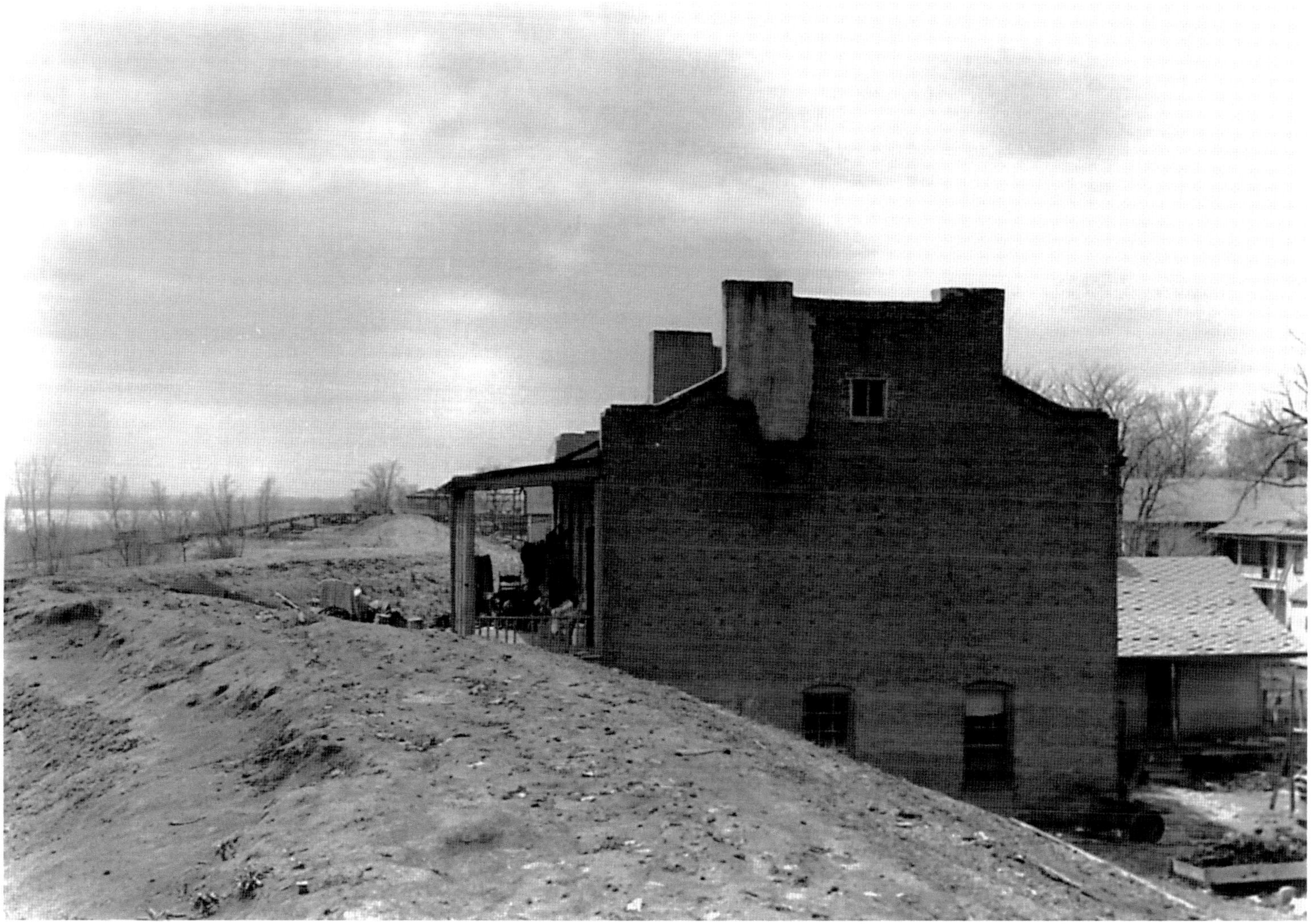

The first bank in Illinois territory. Note how the levee has been bowed out to protect the building. During the flood, the waters excavated some of the levee on each side of the bow, weakening it considerably. Shawneetown. April, 1937. Russell Lee

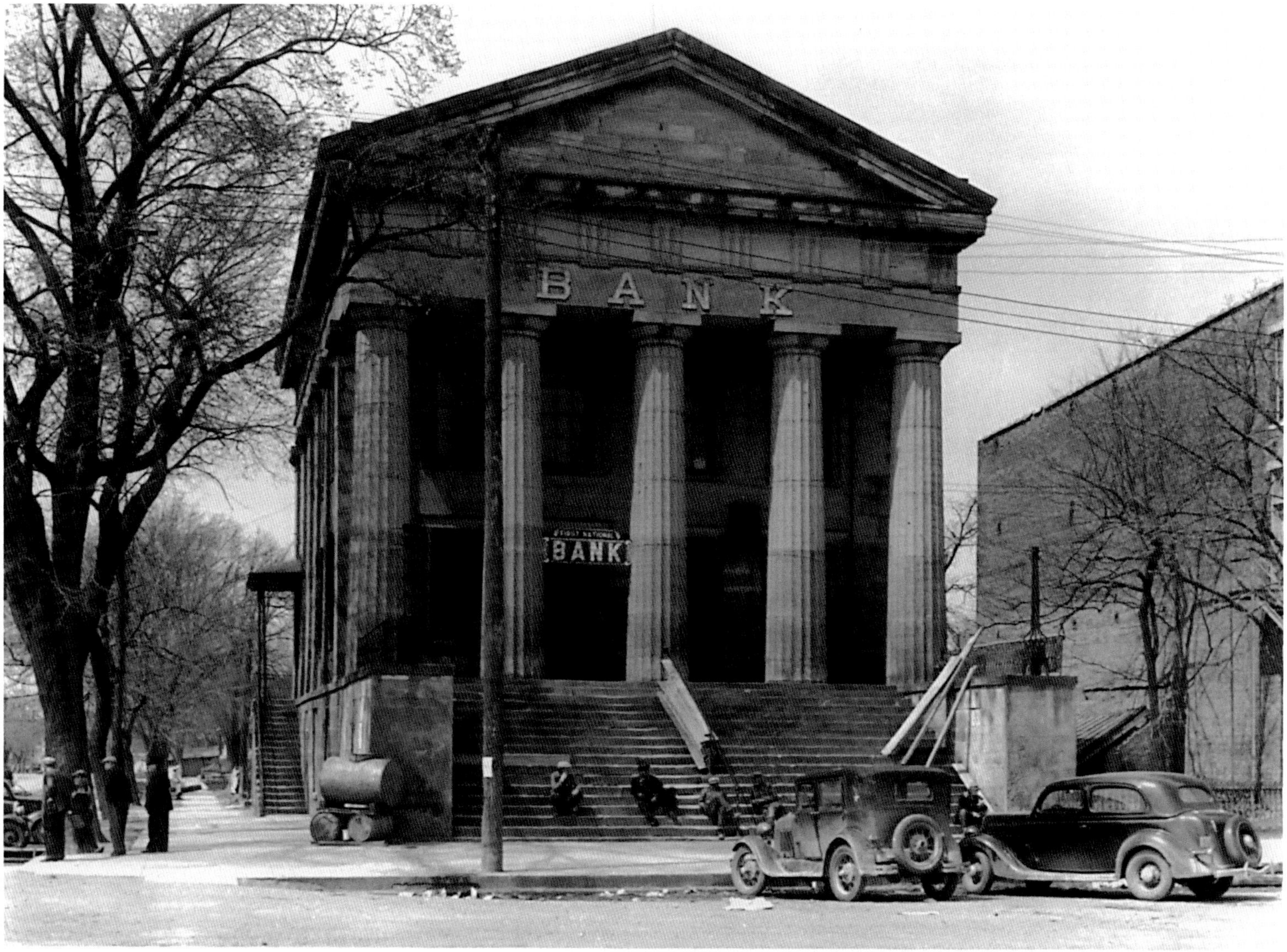

Bank built by the state in 1839. Note water tank for drinking
water on sidewalk.
Shawneetown. April, 1937.
Russell Lee

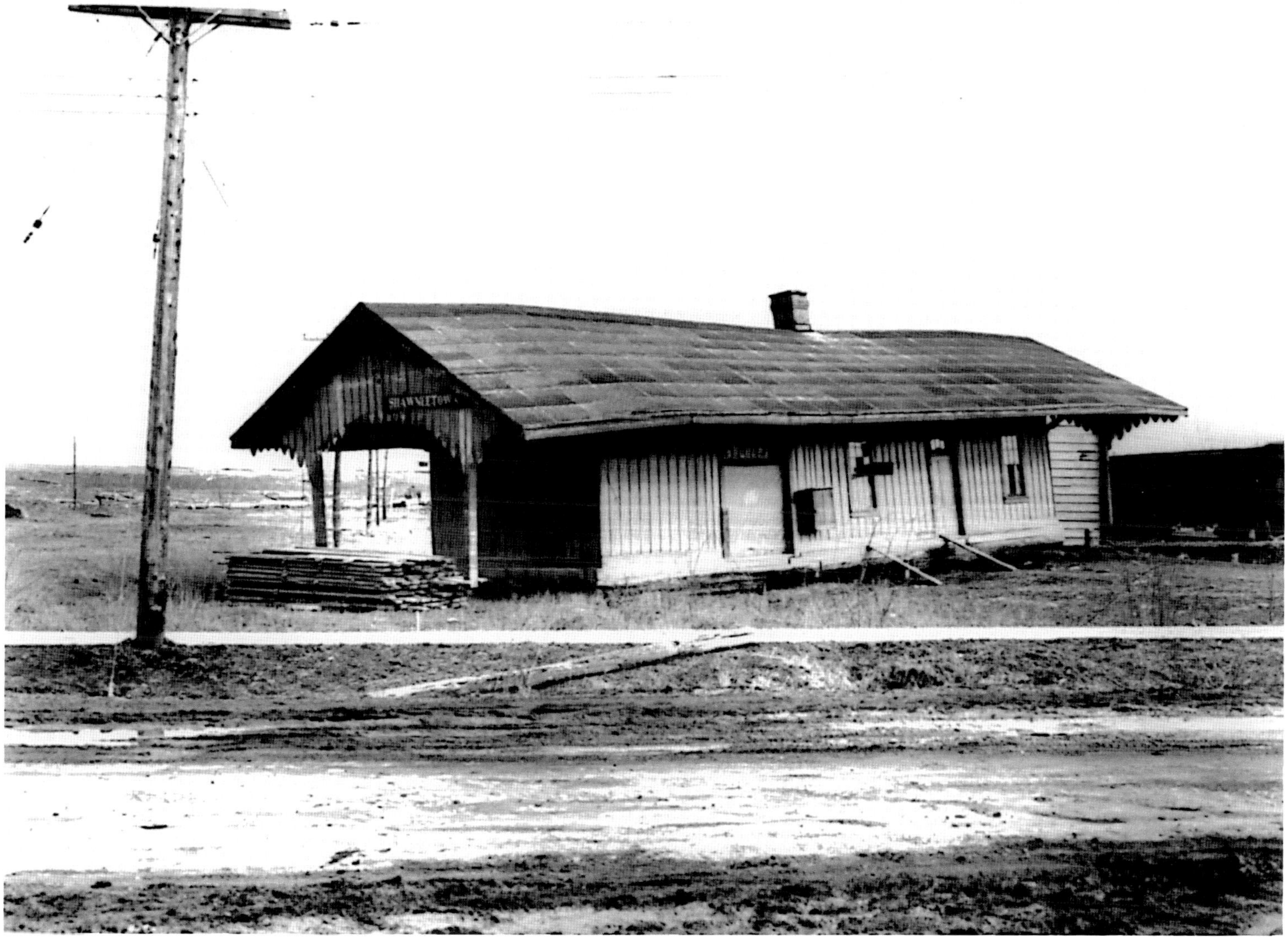

The old Louisville and Nashville railroad station after the flood. Note the flood marks on the building.
Shawneetown. April, 1937.
Russell Lee

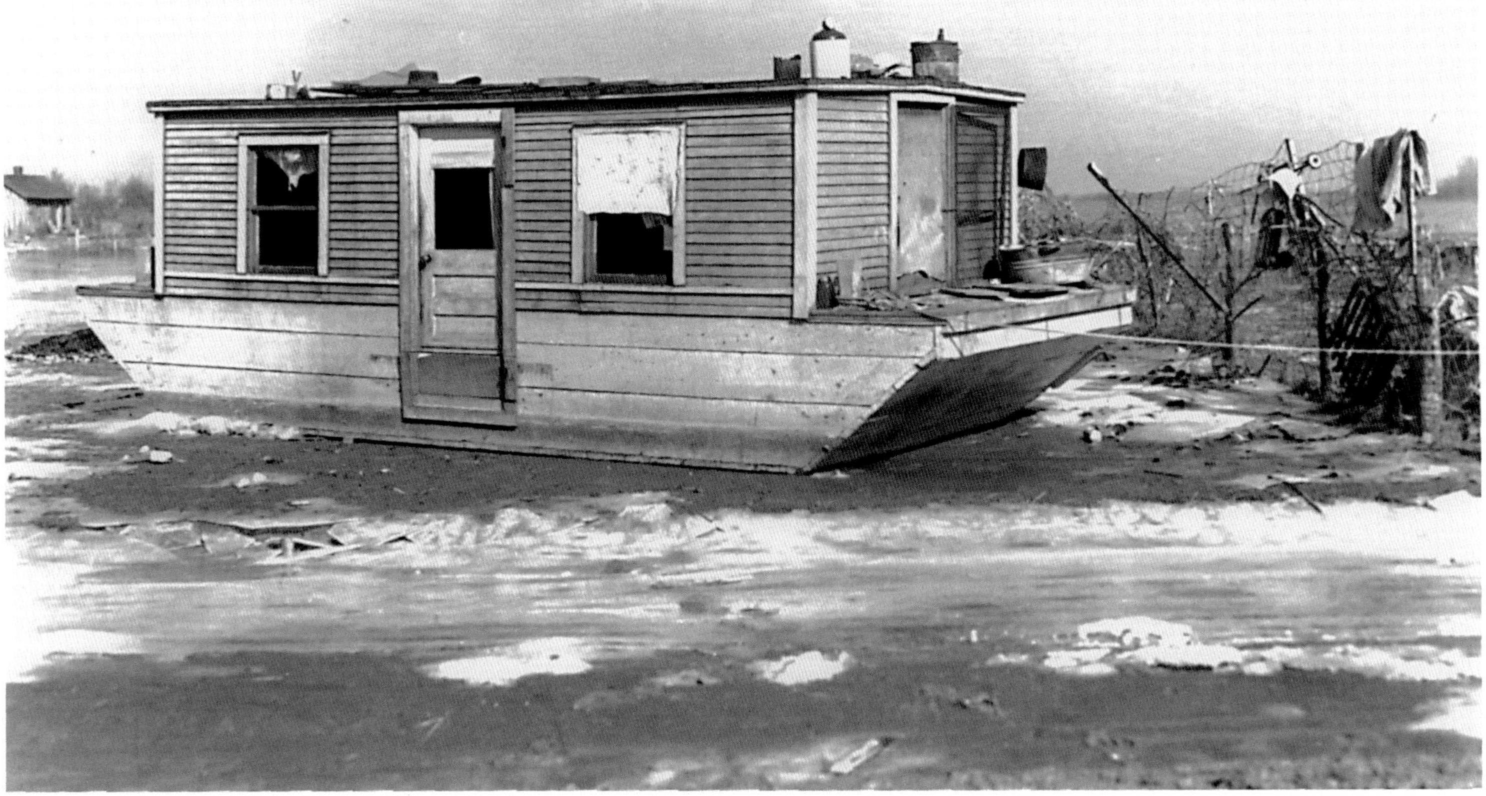

Houseboat washed high and dry amid debris in the flood area.
Maunie. February, 1937.
Russell Lee

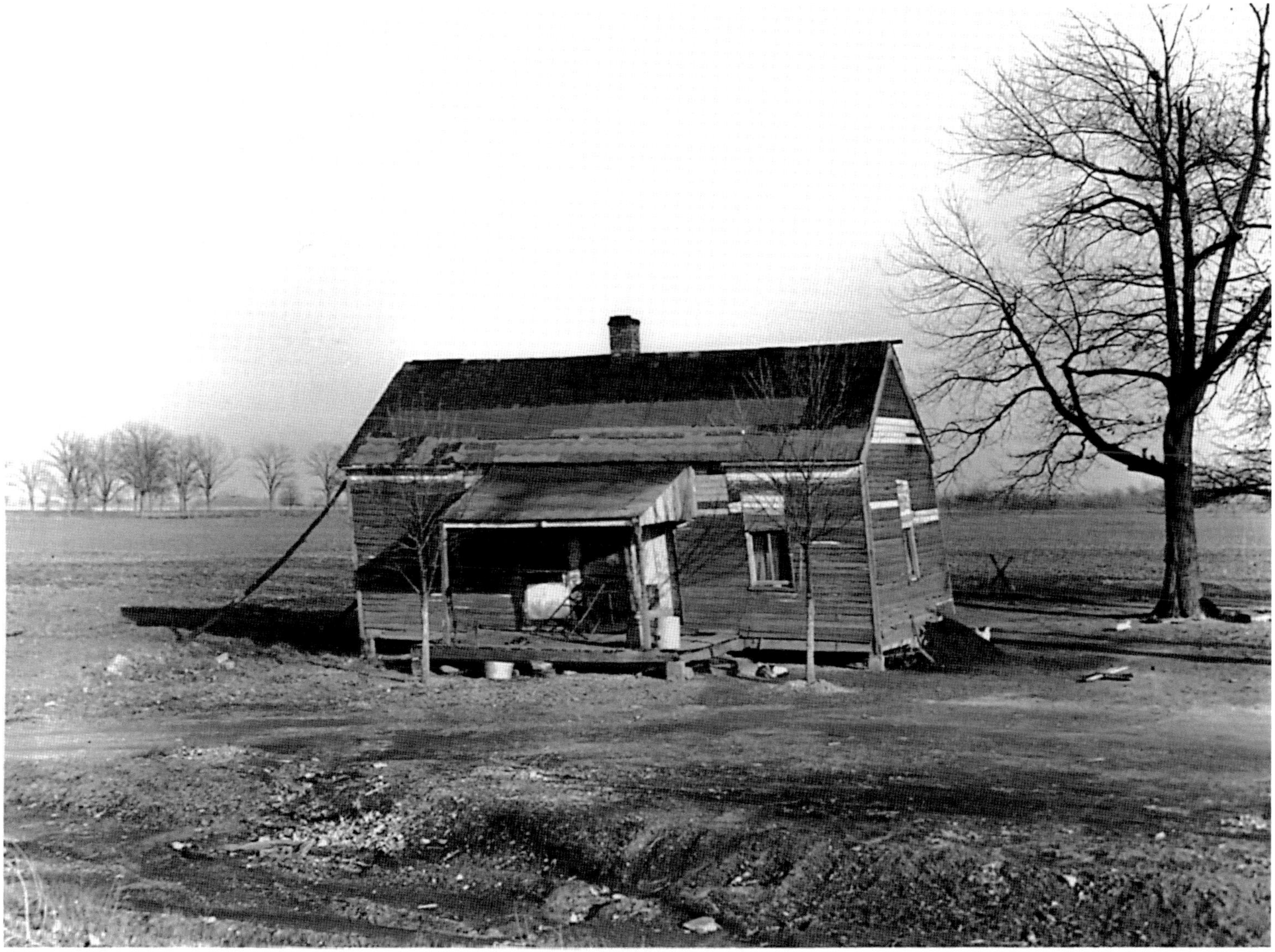

House damaged by the flood.
Saline County. January, 1939.
Arthur Rothstein

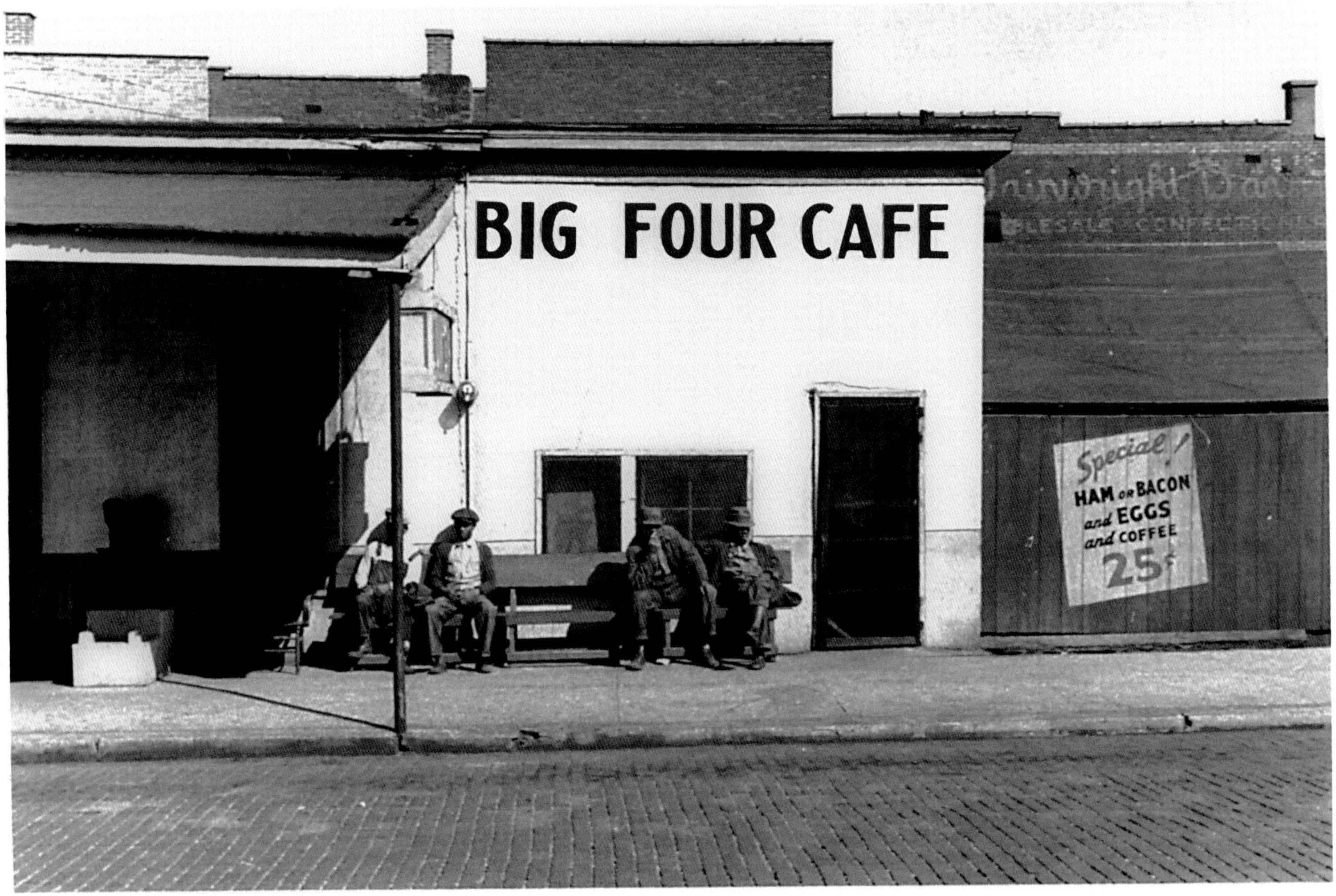

Big Four Cafe.
Cairo. May, 1940.
John Vachon

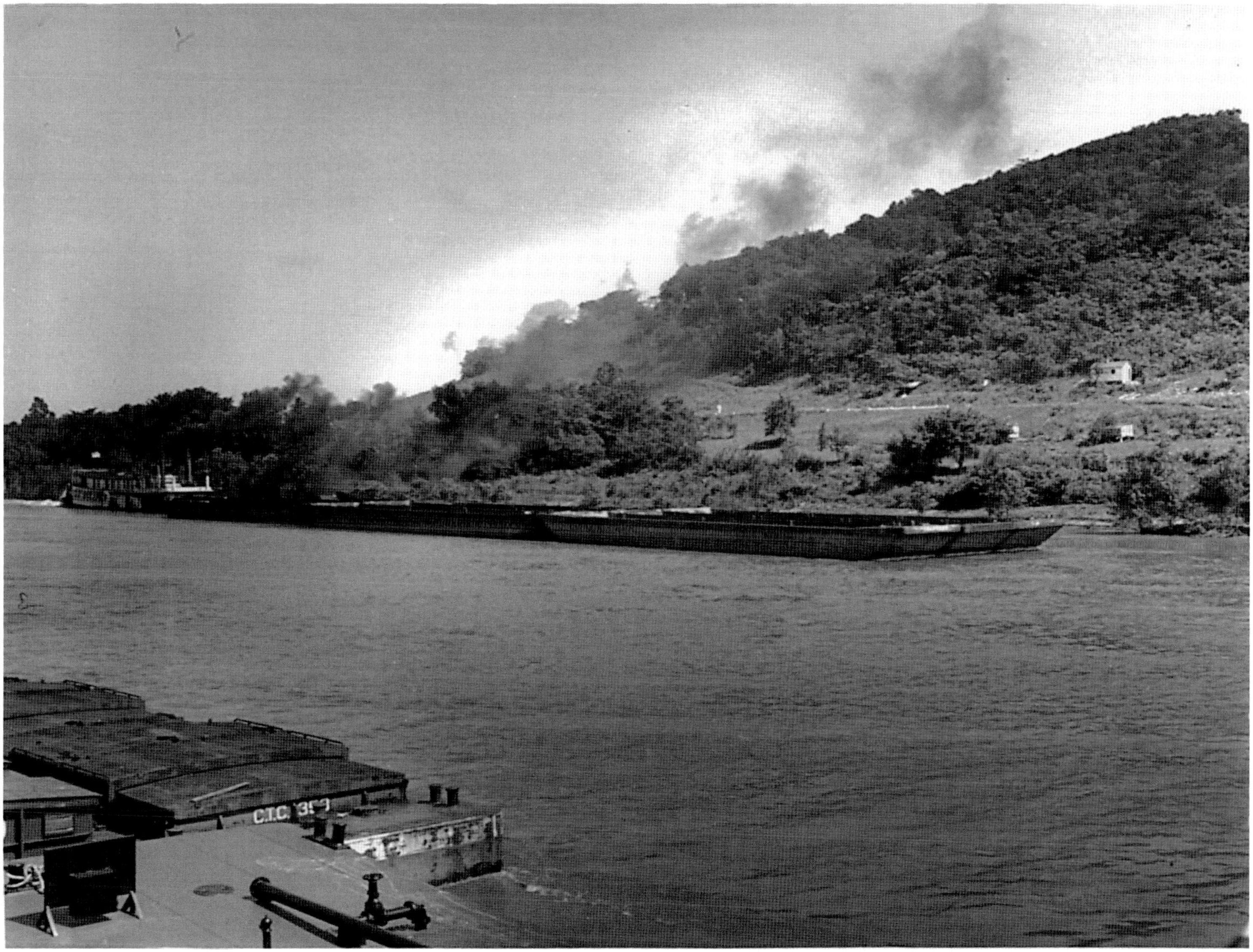

A tow of empty barges on the Ohio River.
June, 1943.
Arthur Siegel

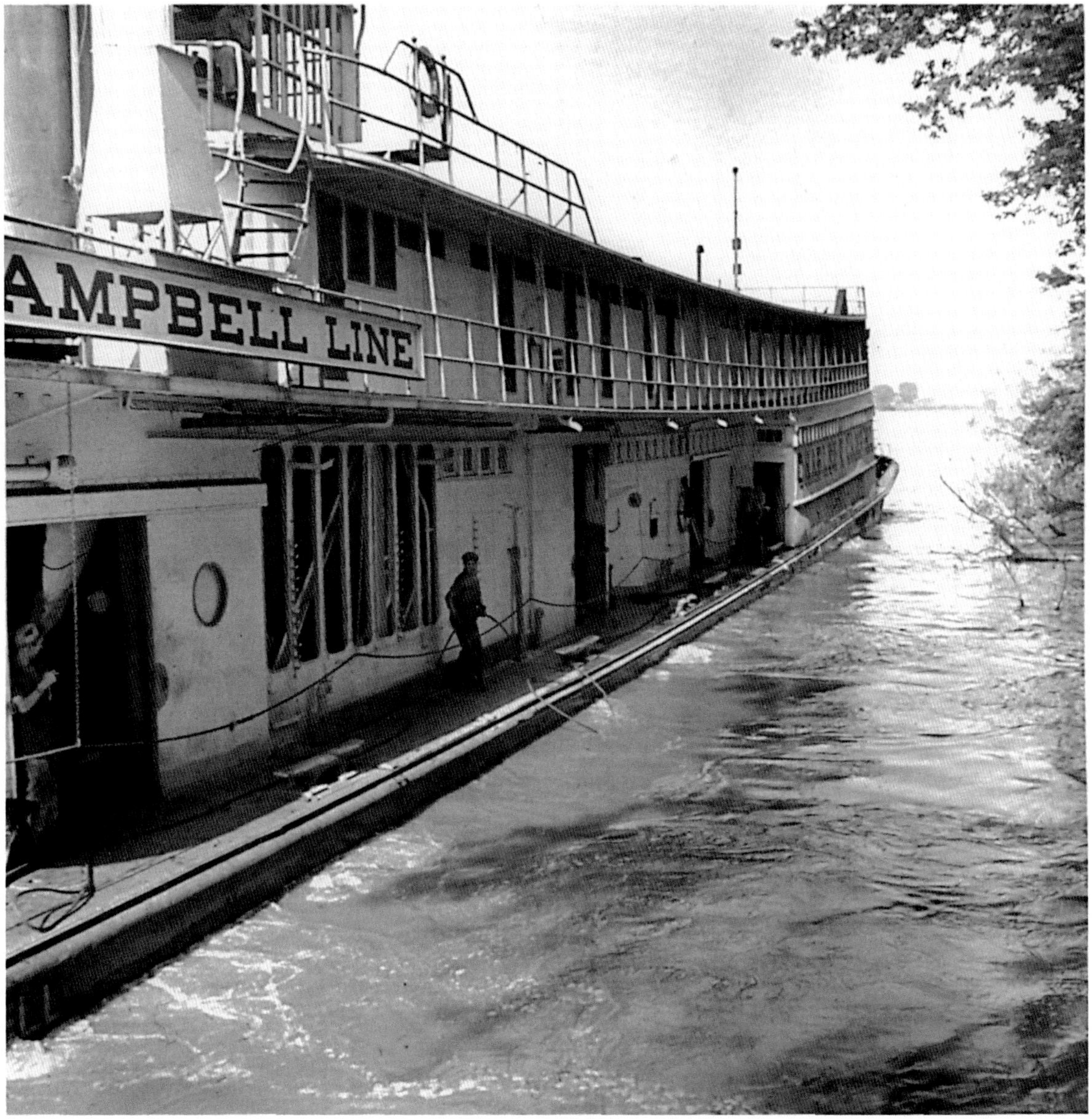

The side of the *Charles T. Campbell,* a towboat, on the Ohio River.
June, 1943.
Arthur Siegel

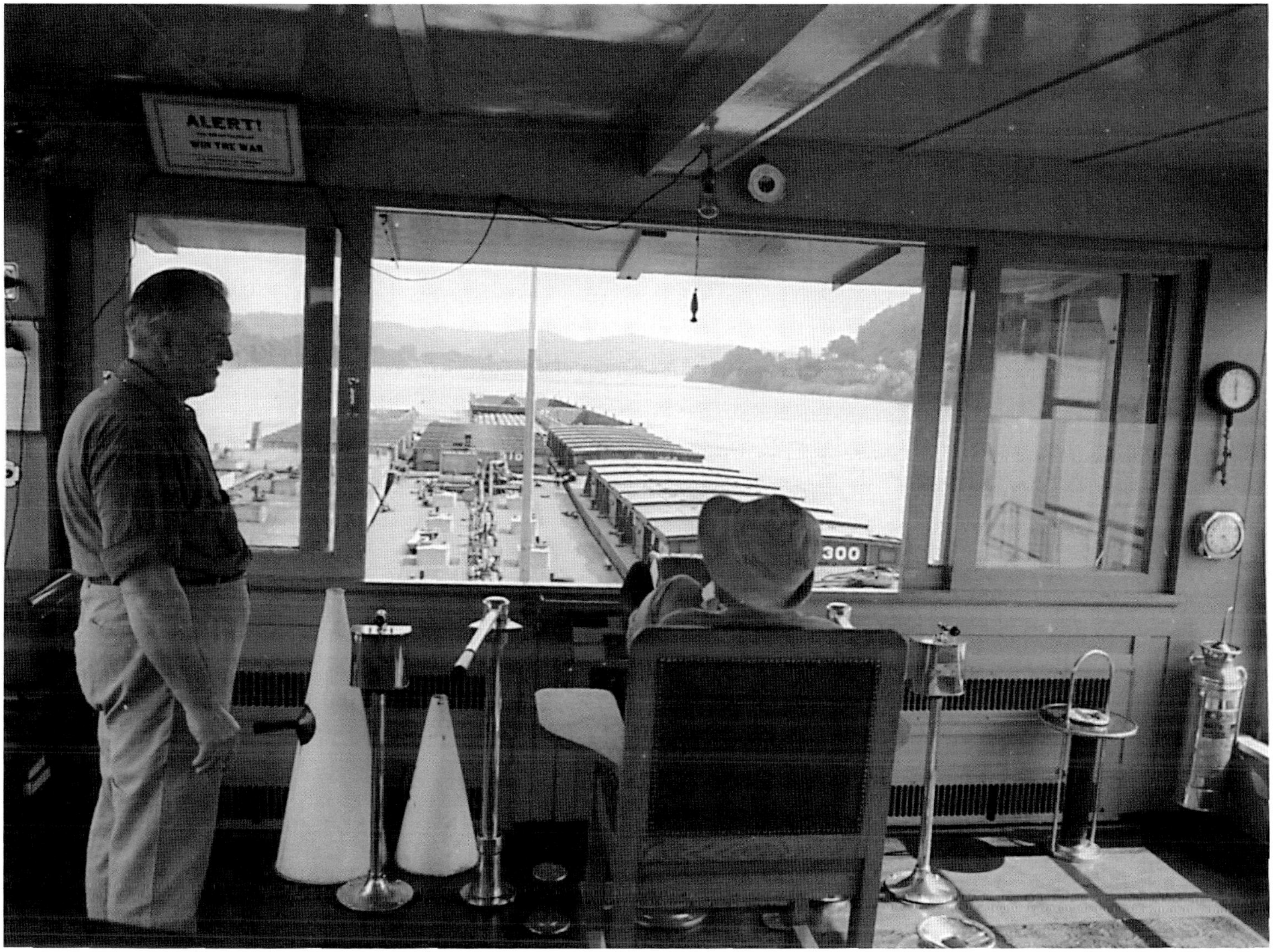

The pilot of the *Charles T. Campbell*, a towboat, sitting on the "throne," going down the Ohio River.
June, 1943.
Arthur Siegel

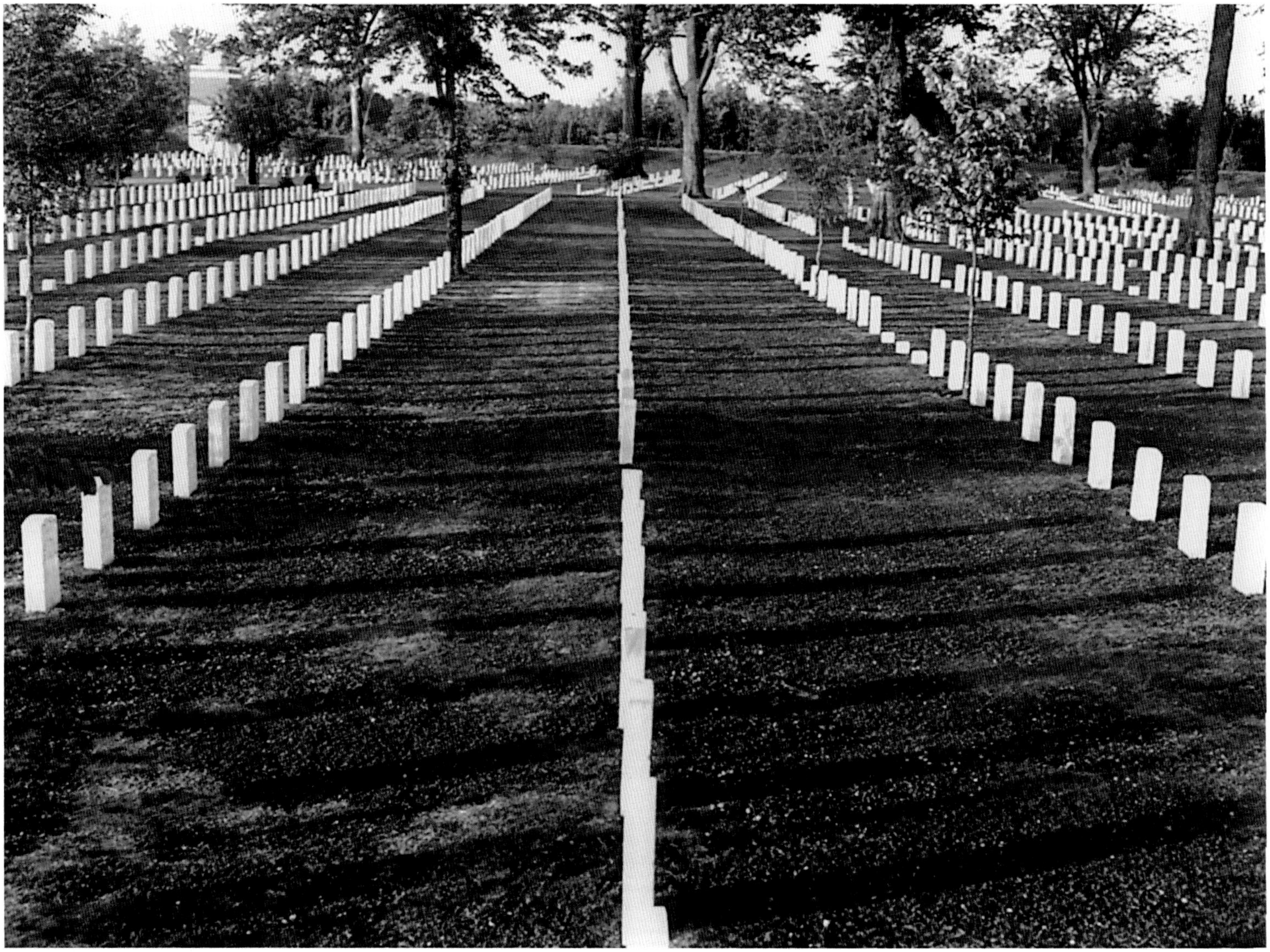

National cemetery.
Cairo. May, 1940.
John Vachon

RECREATION AND RELIGION

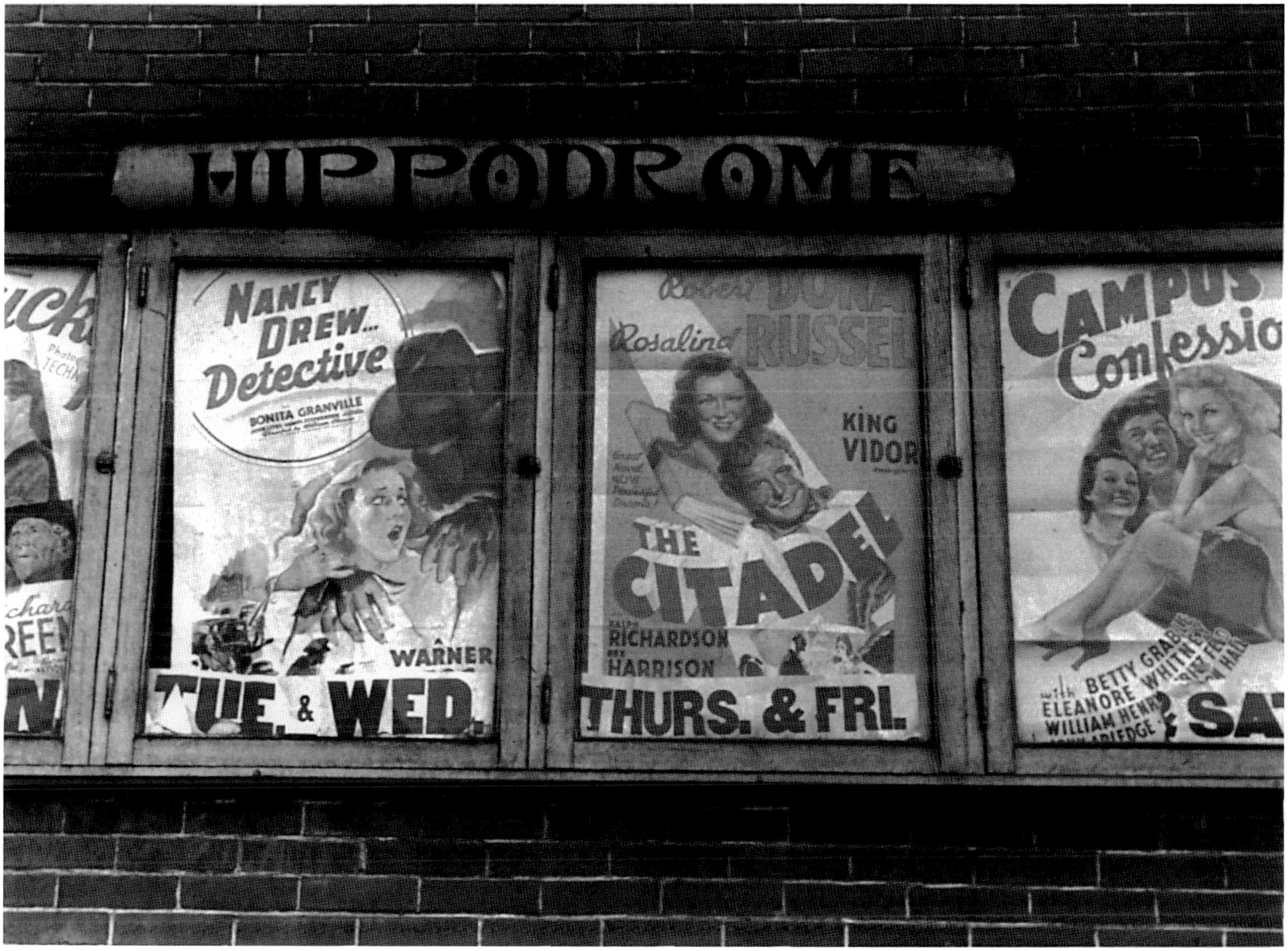

Movie advertisements.
Herrin. January, 1939.
Arthur Rothstein

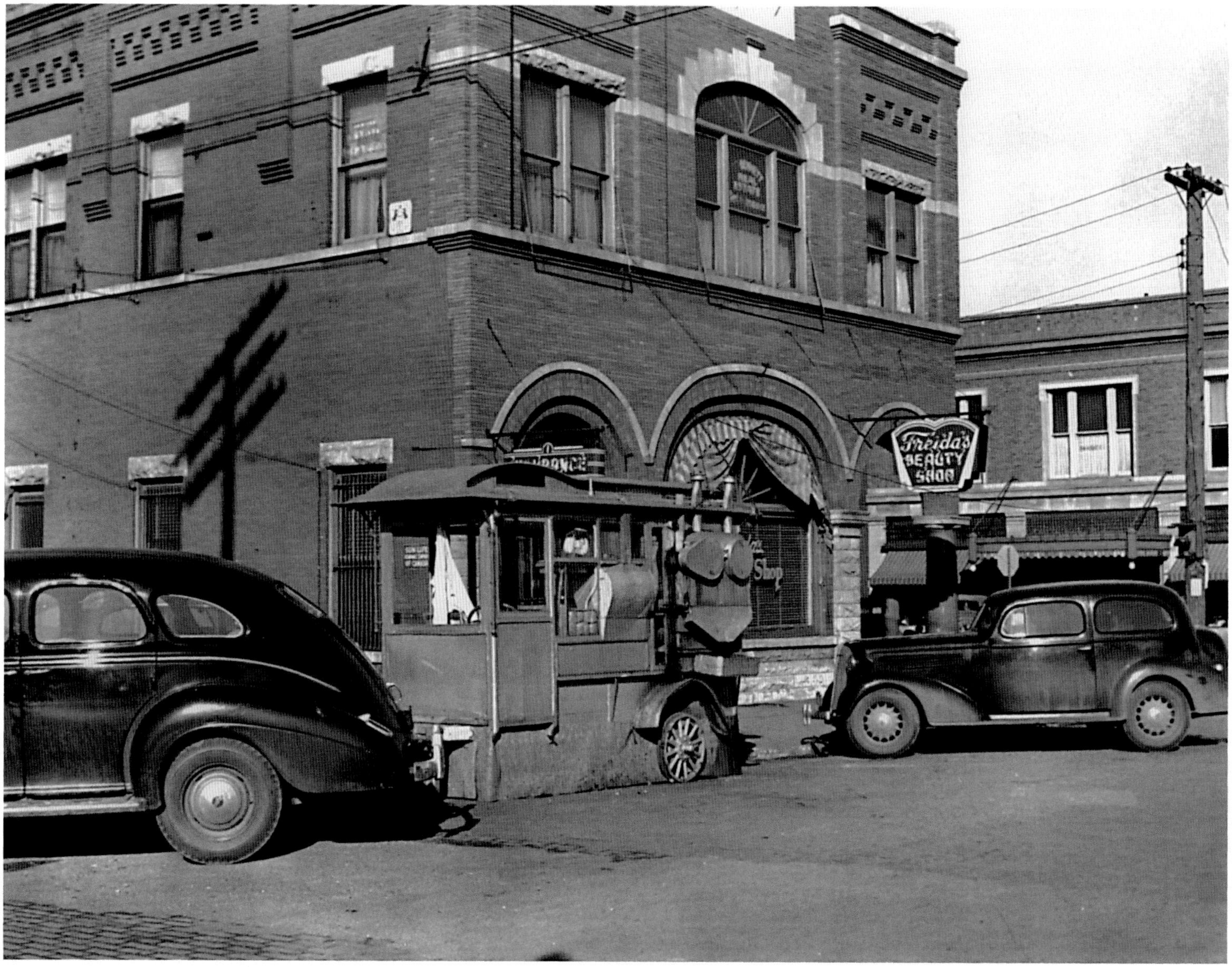

Popcorn stand on main street.
Herrin. January, 1939.
Arthur Rothstein

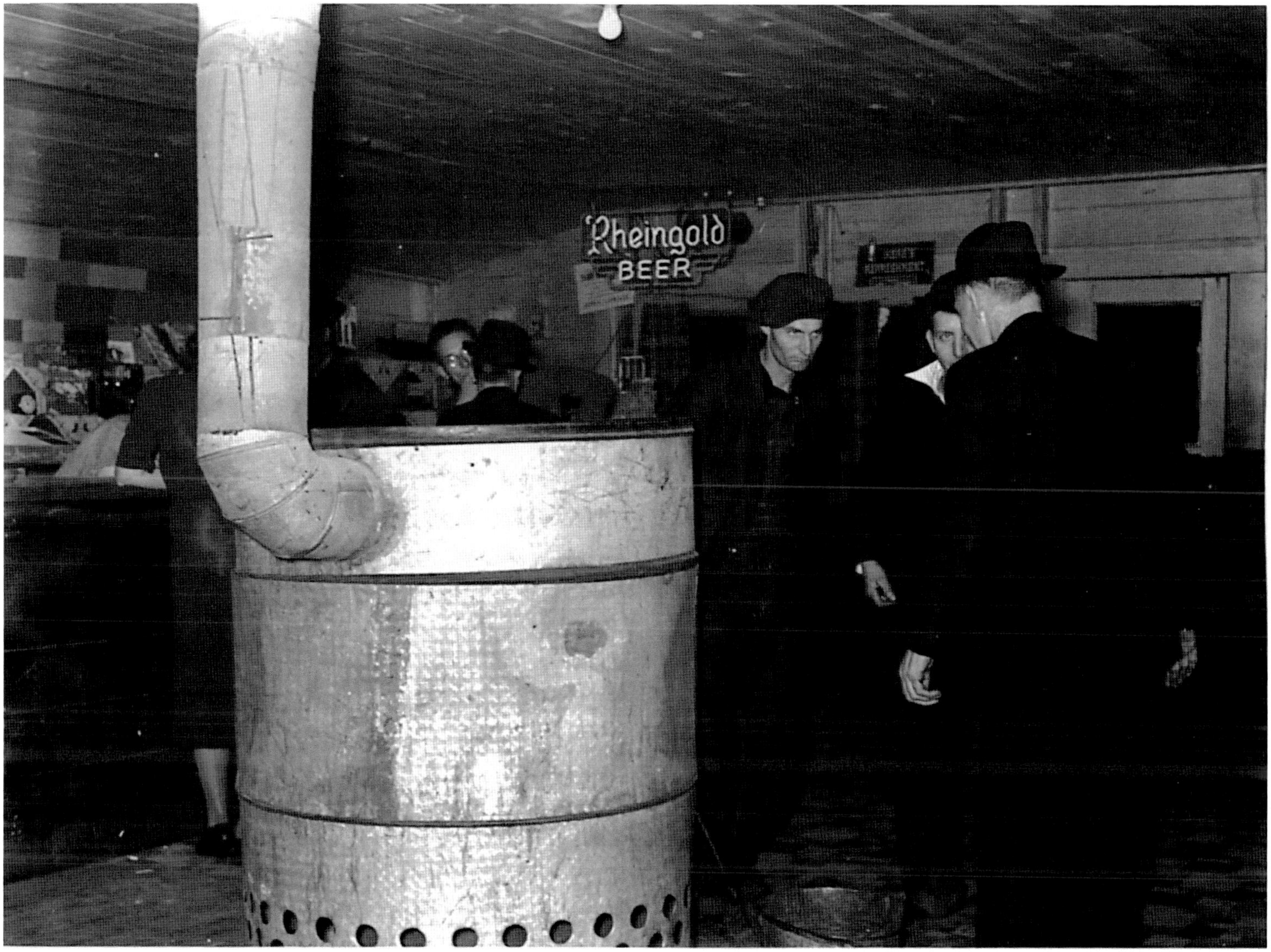

Miners and farmers in the Oke Doke dance hall.
Williamson County, January, 1939.
Arthur Rothstein

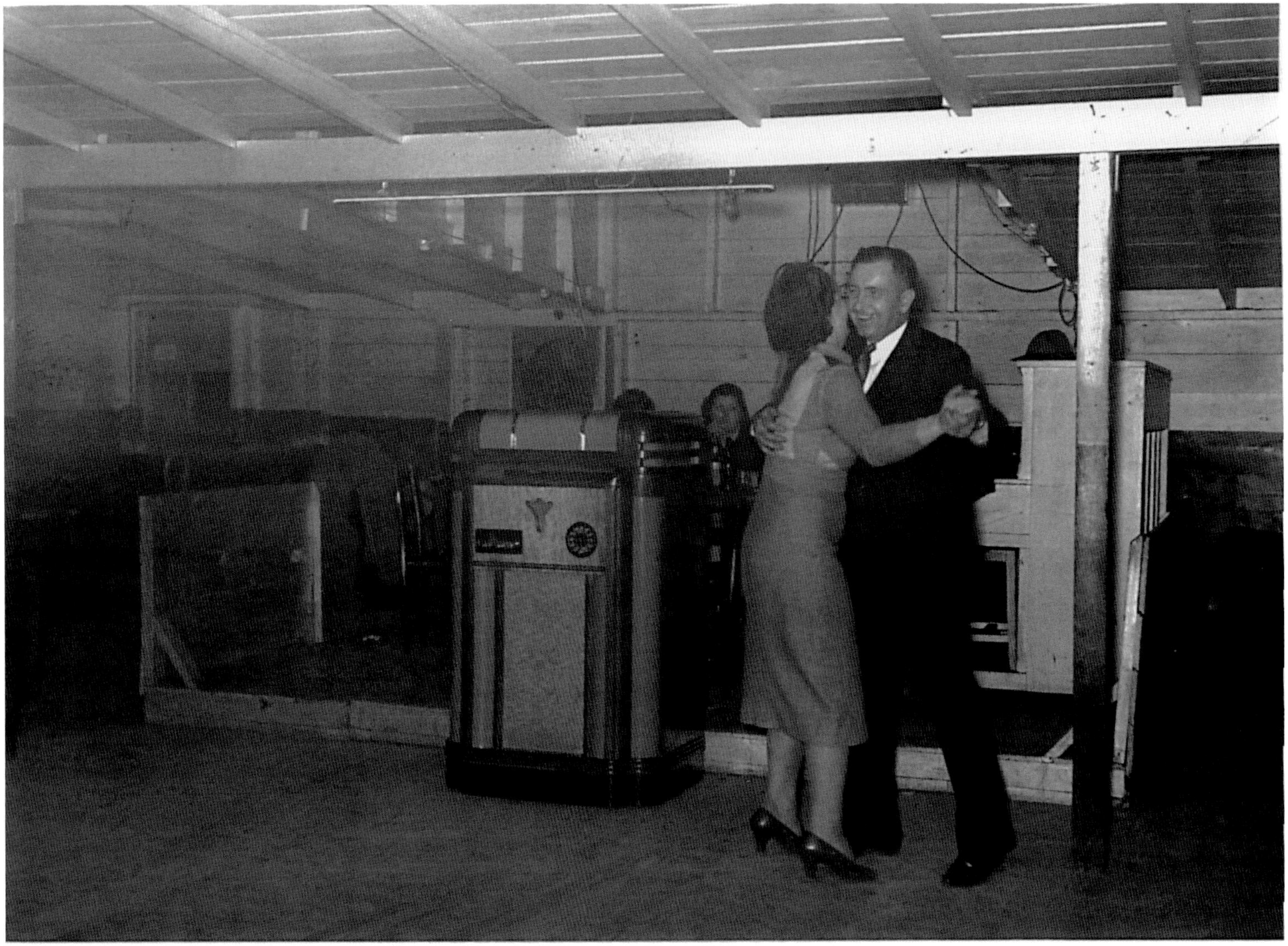

Interior of the Oke Doke dance hall patronized by farmers
and miners.
Williamson County. January, 1939.
Arthur Rothstein

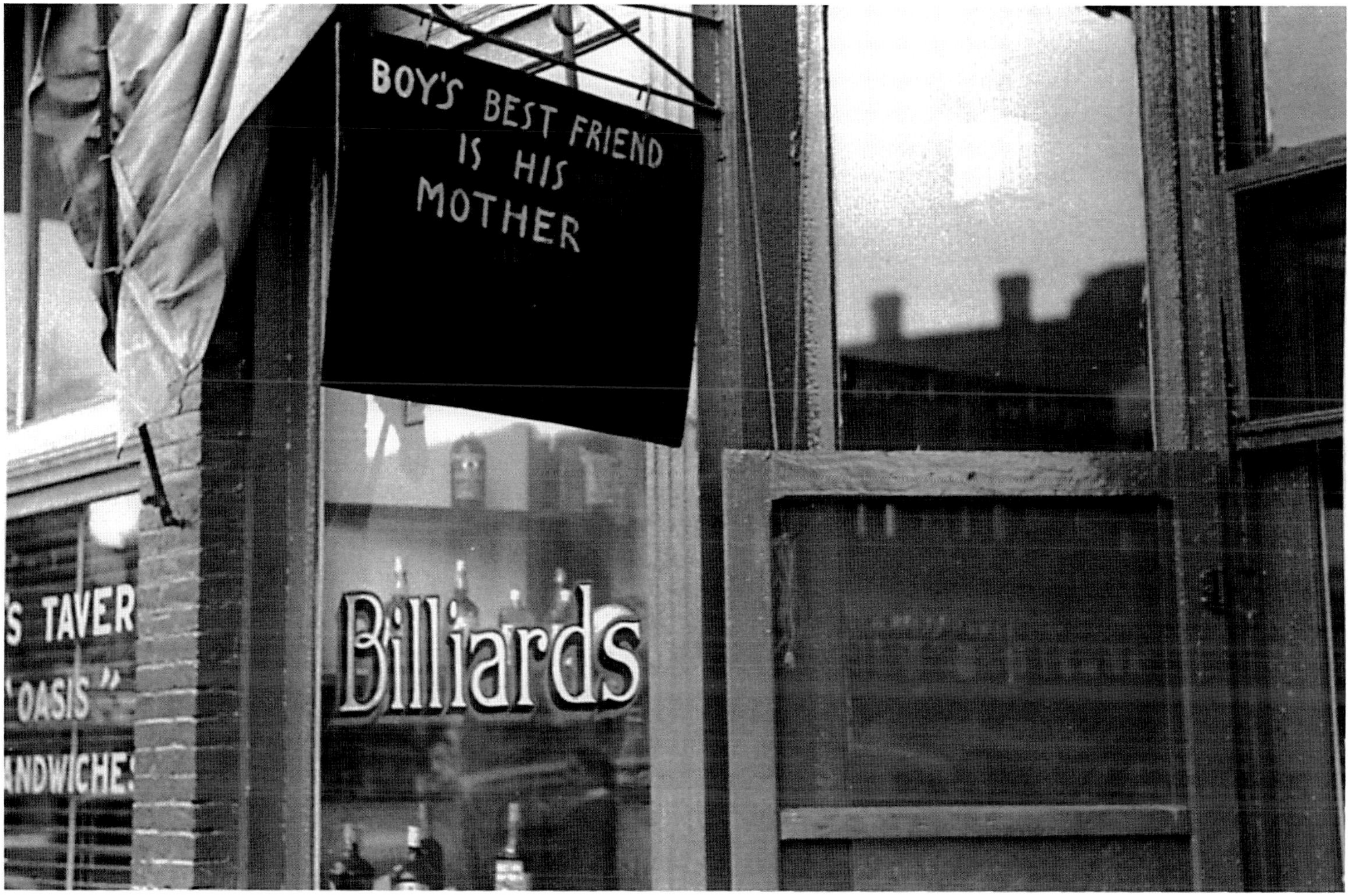

Poolroom.
Grayville. May, 1940.
John Vachon

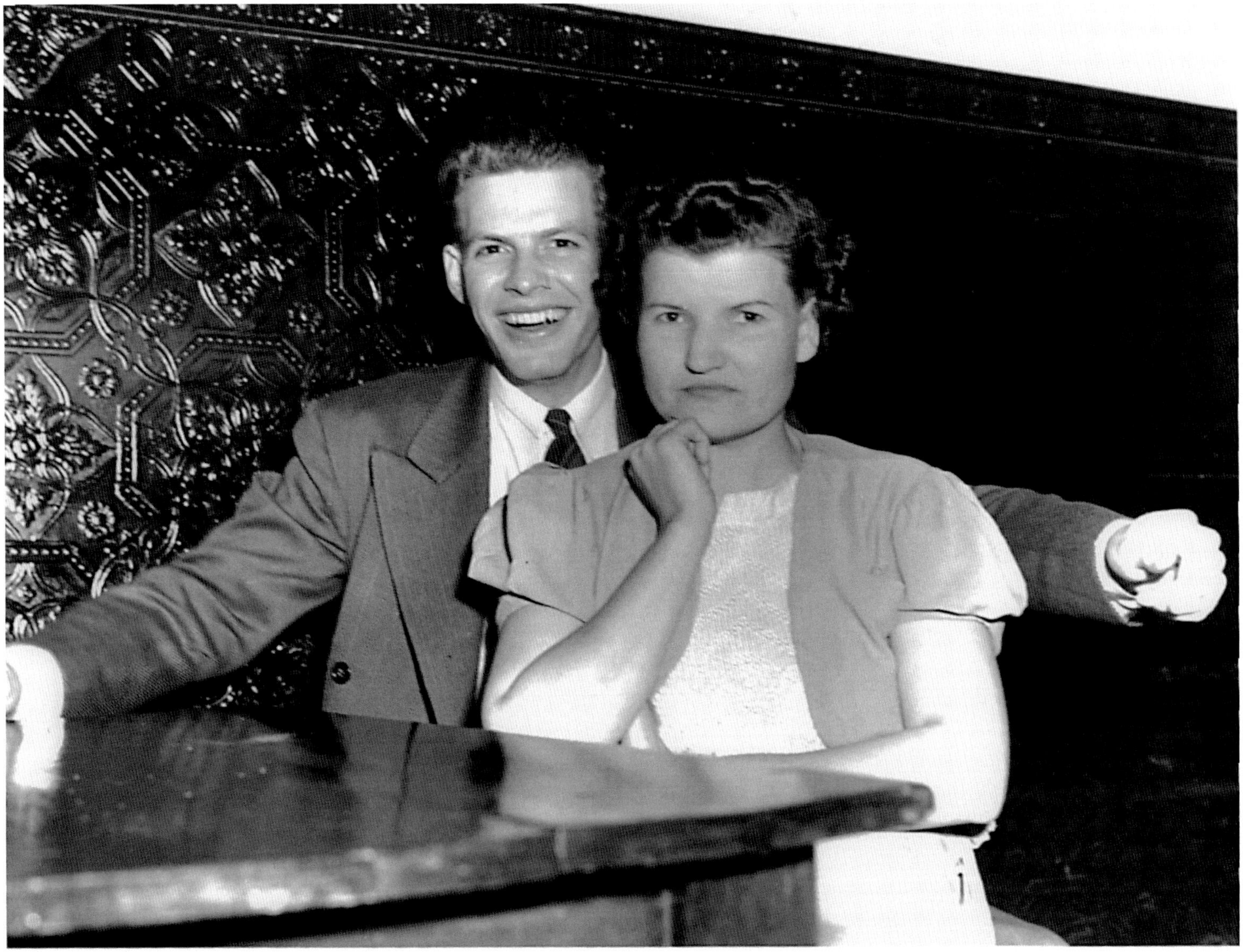

Young couple in a beer parlor.
Cairo. May, 1940.
John Vachon

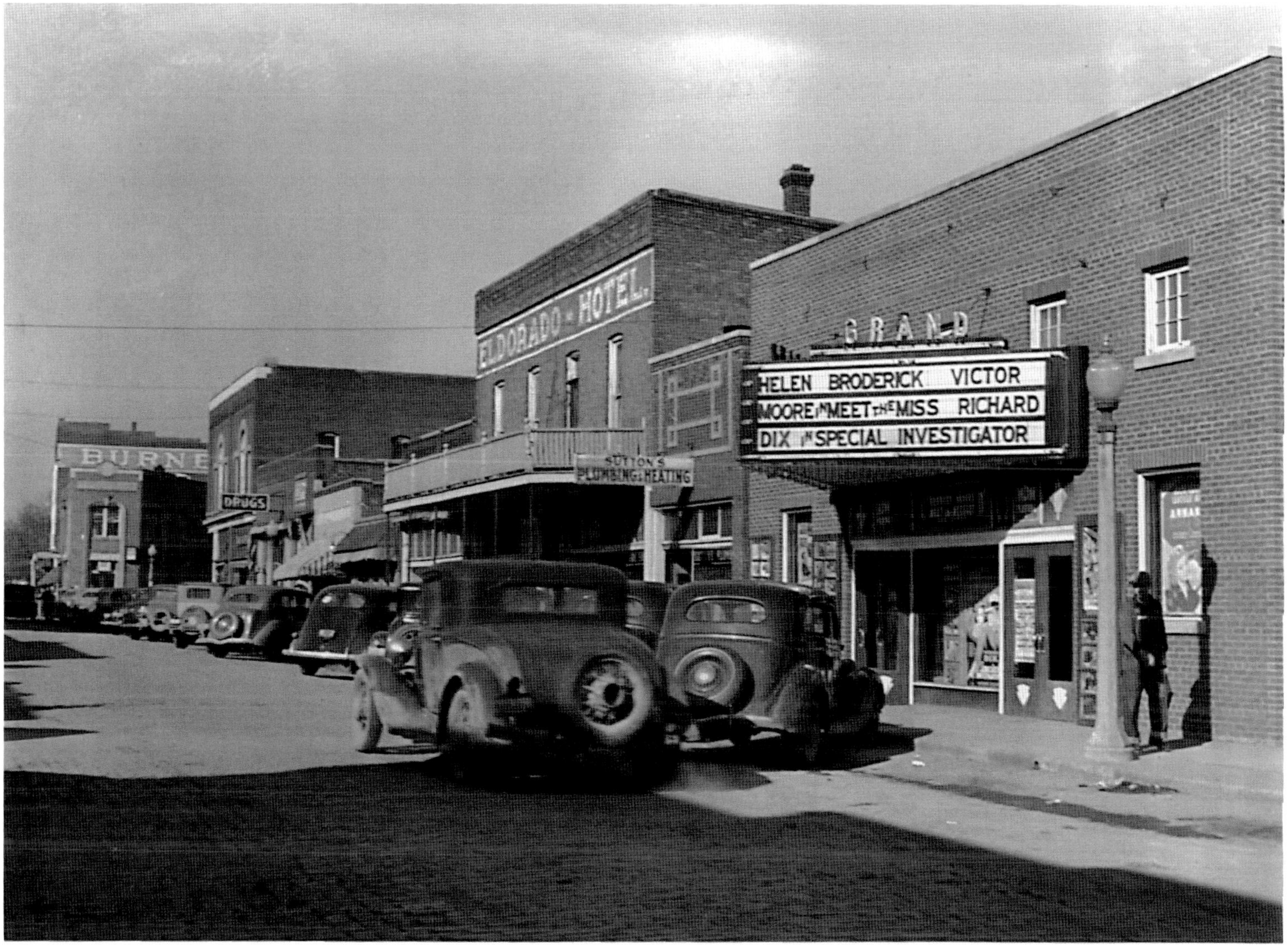

Shopping center.
Eldorado. January, 1939.
Arthur Rothstein

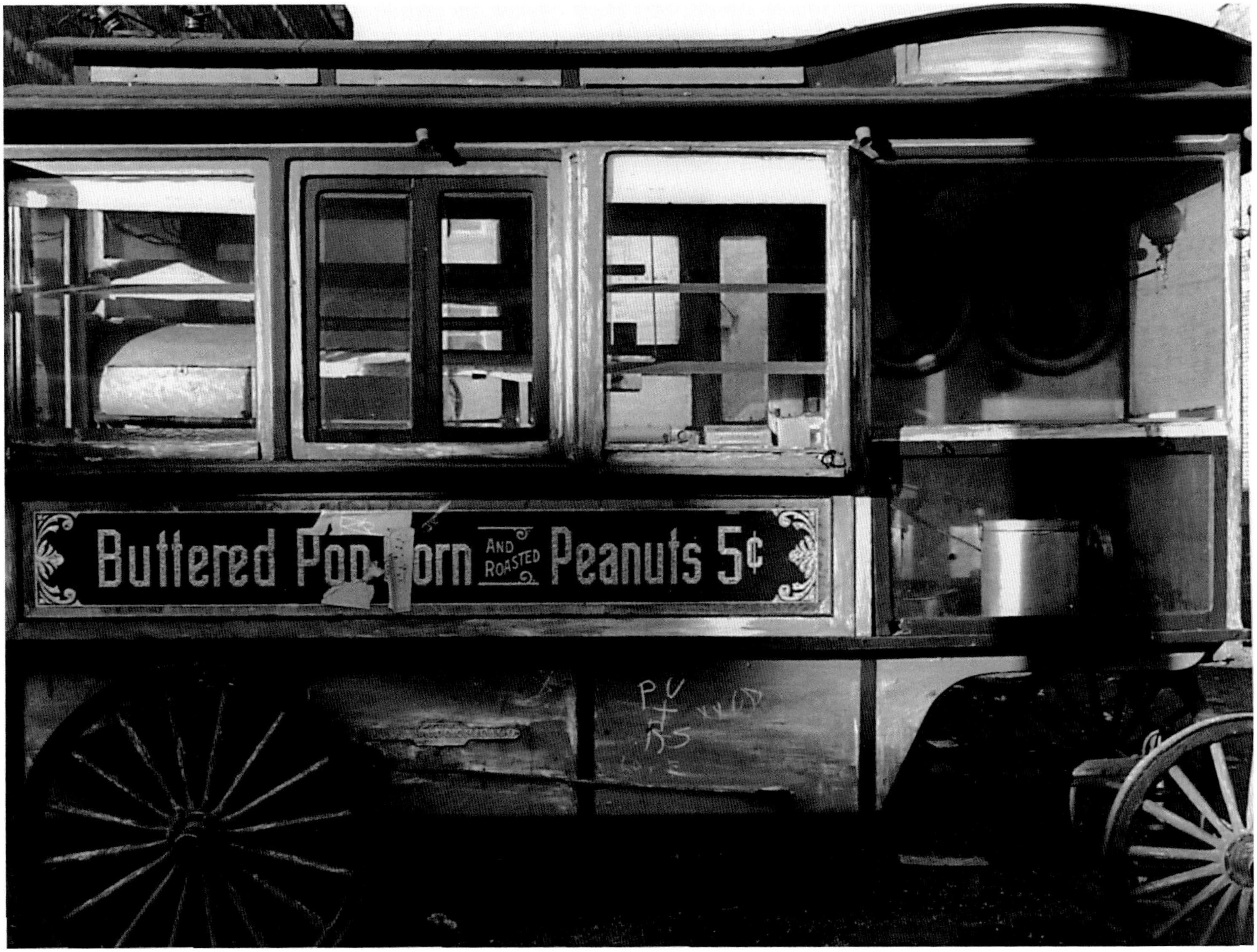

A popcorn stand.
Johnston City. January, 1939.
Arthur Rothstein

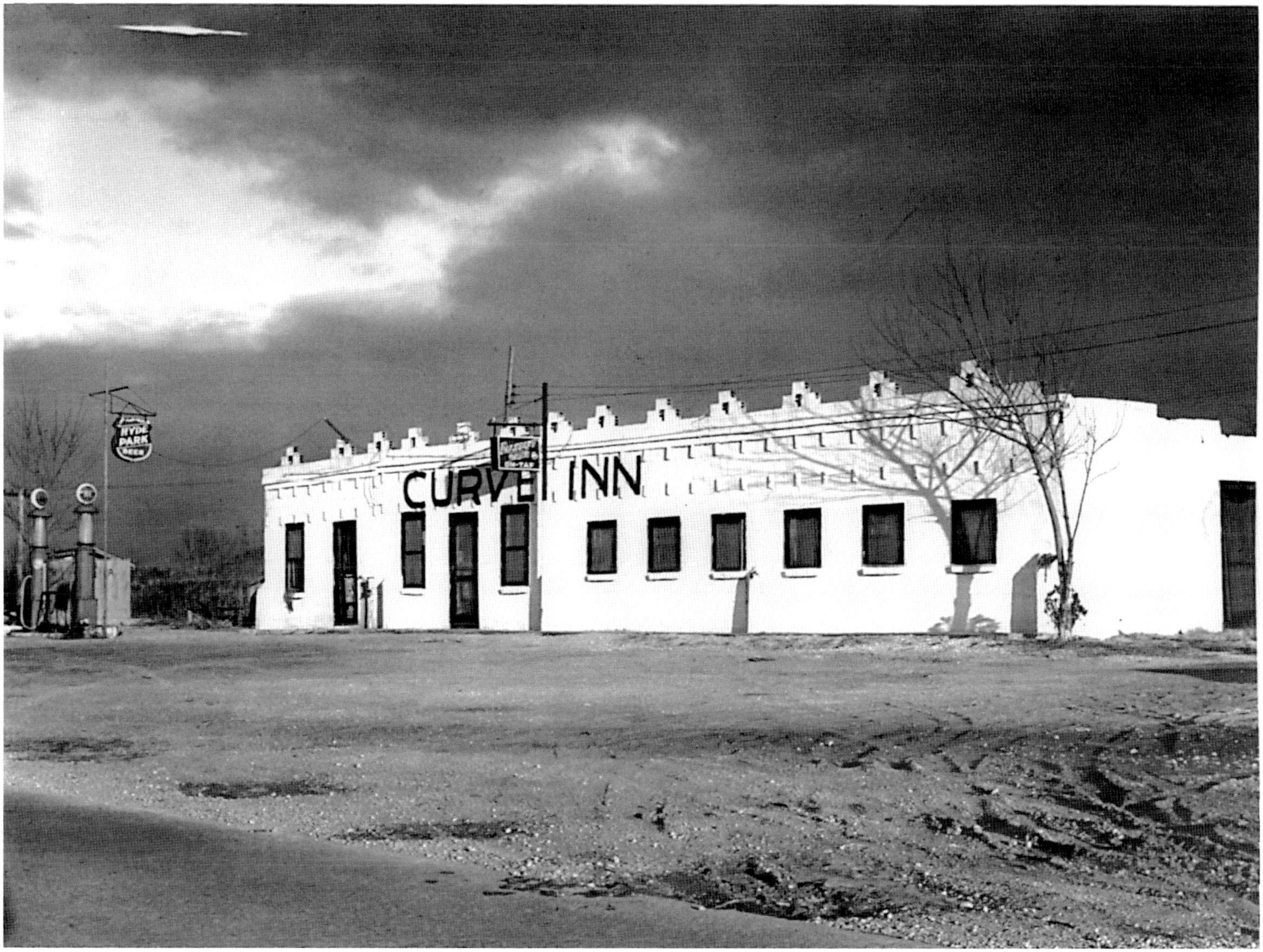

Roadhouse.
Union County. February, 1942.
John Vachon

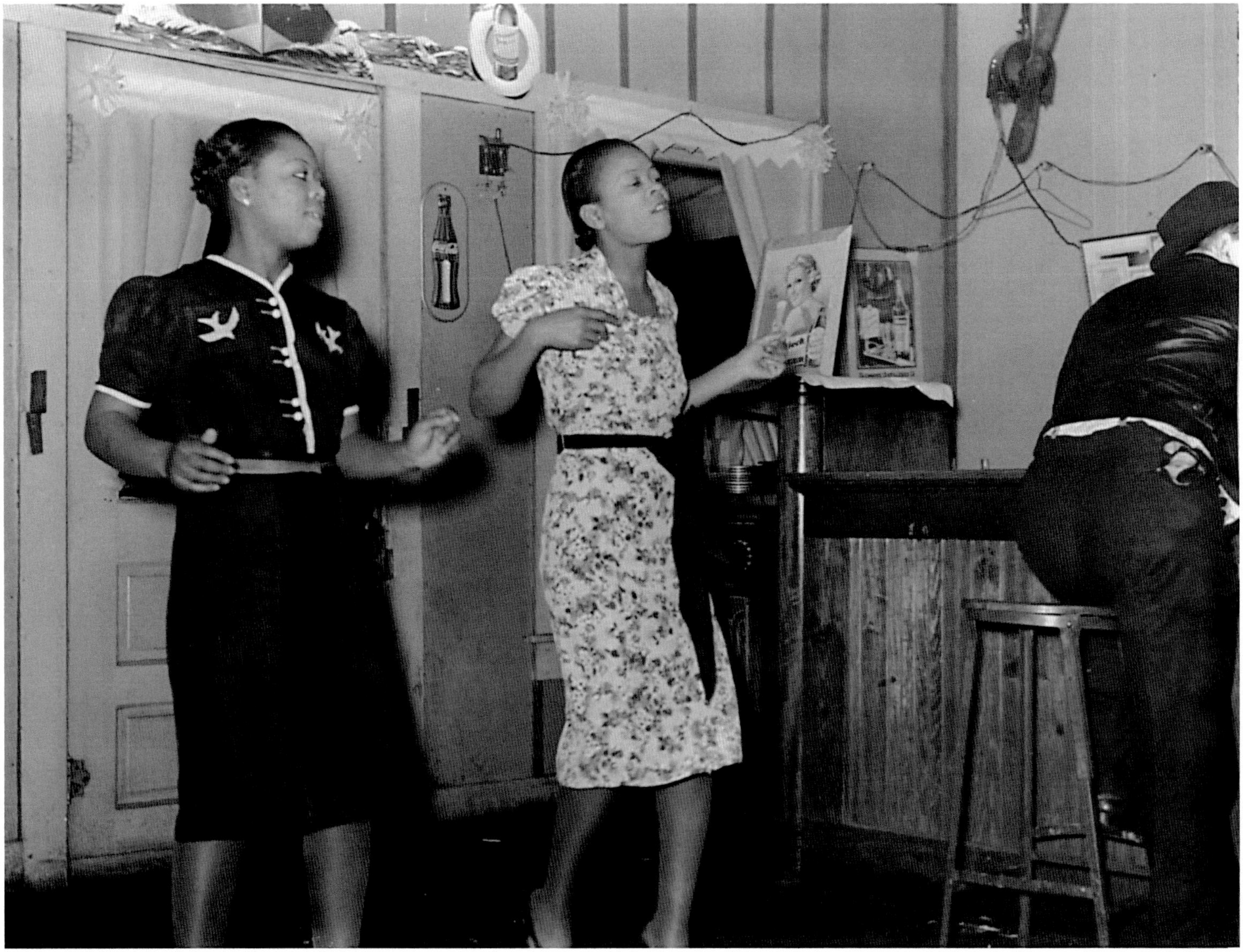

Girls dancing in a tavern.
Colp. January, 1939.
Arthur Rothstein

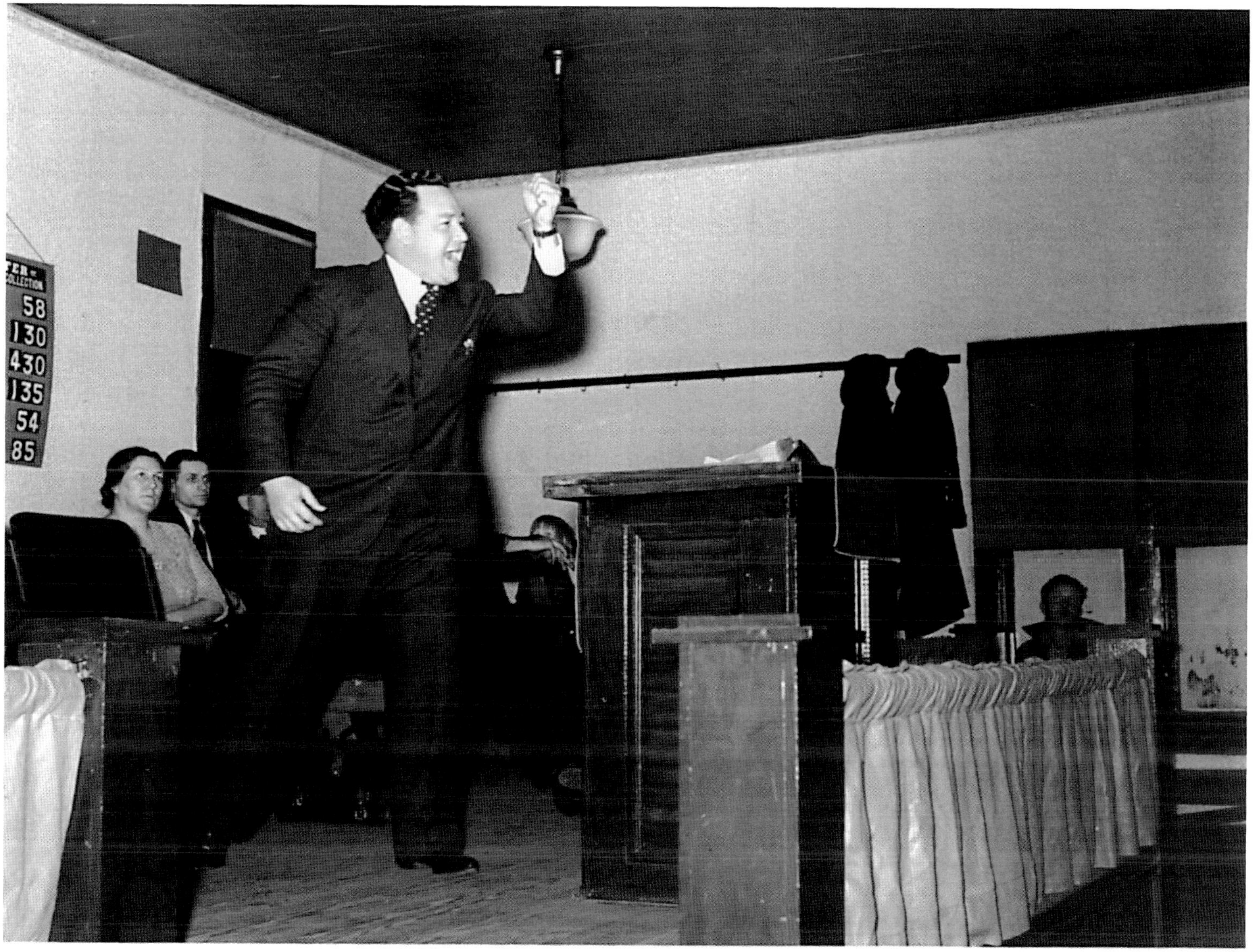

Evangelist preaching sermon, Pentecostal Church, Cambria. January, 1939.
Arthur Rothstein

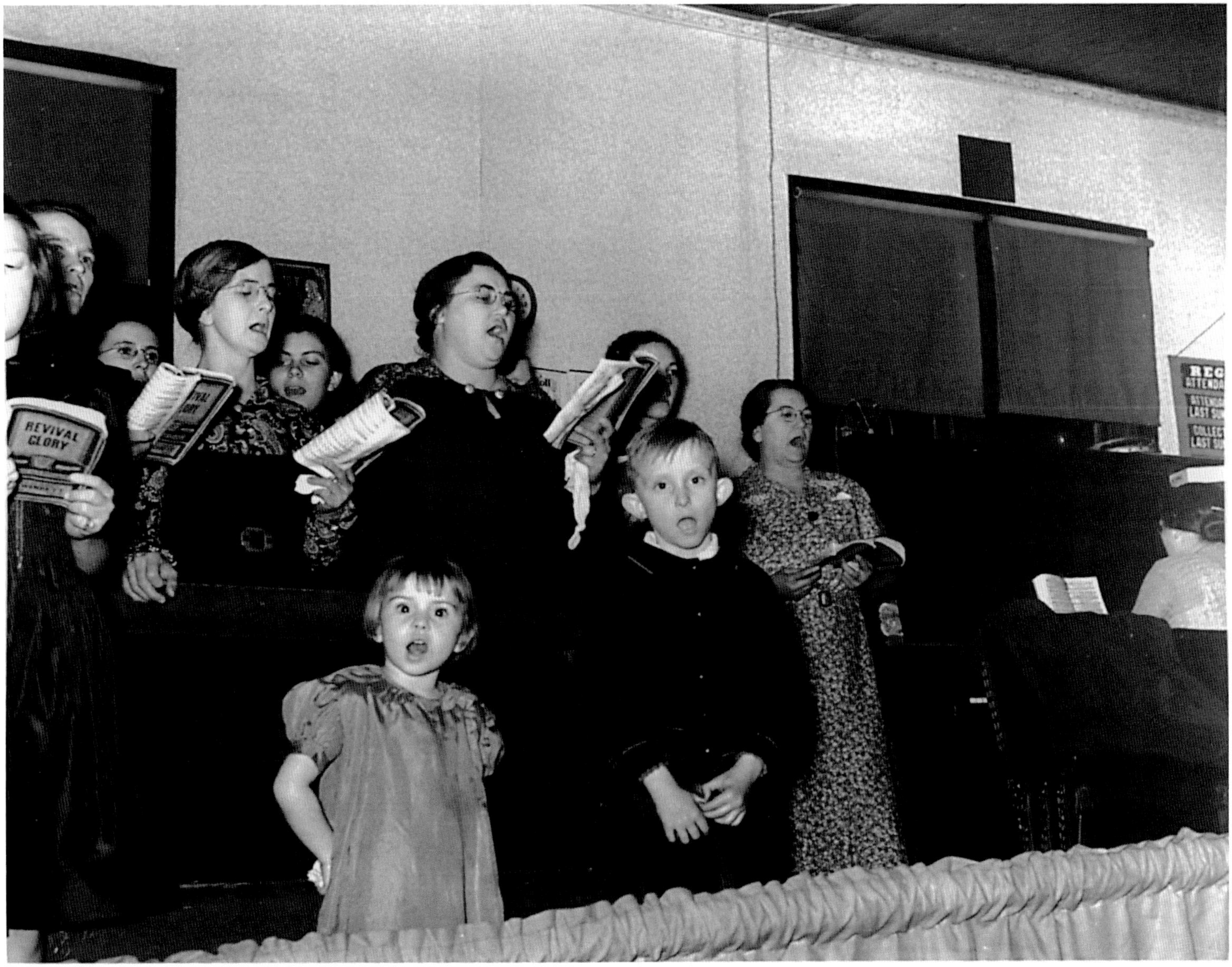

Choir singing at revival meeting in Pentecostal Church.
Cambria. January, 1939.
Arthur Rothstein

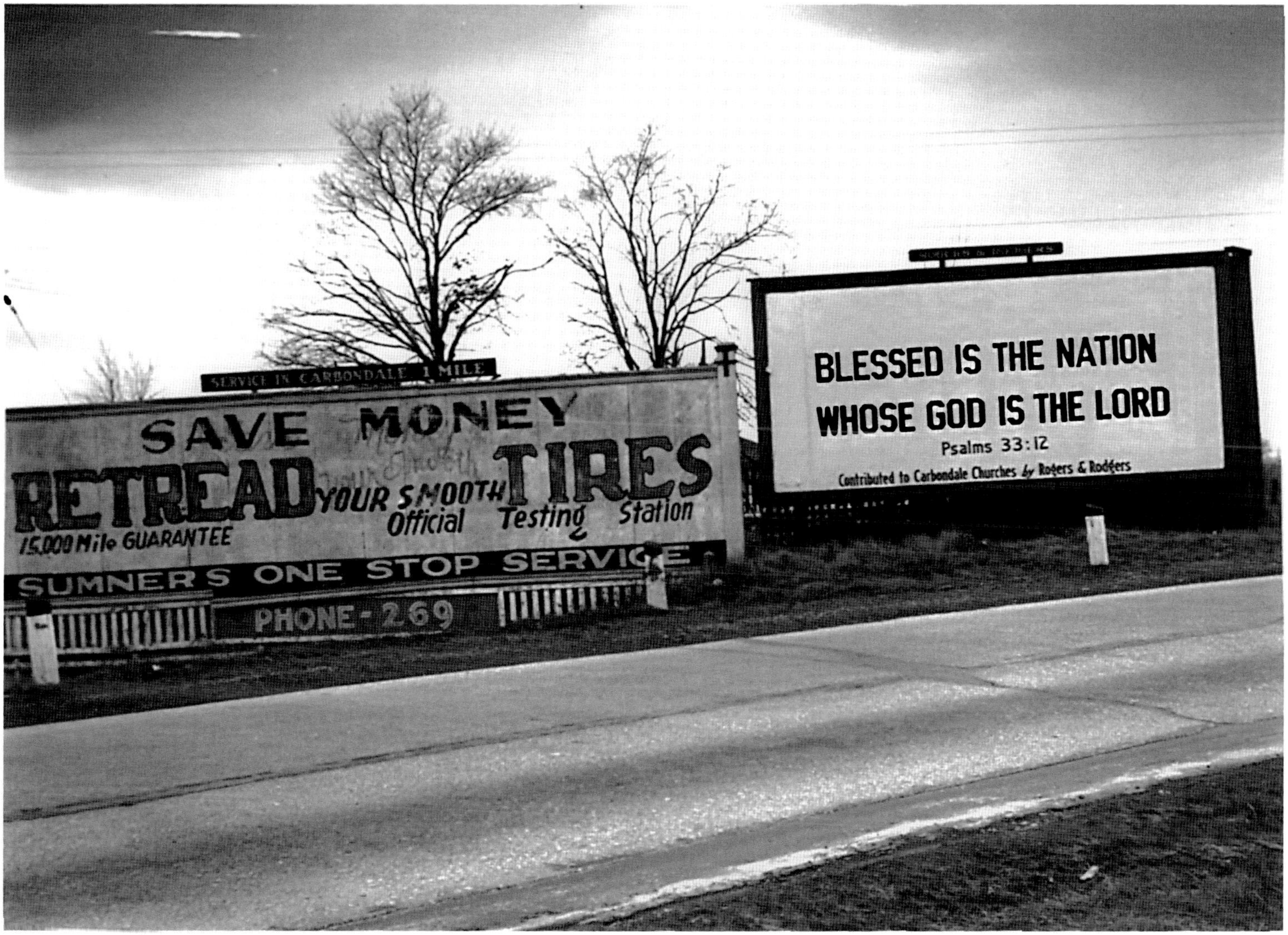

Signs.
Carbondale (vicinity). February, 1942.
John Vachon

SIGNS OF THE TIMES

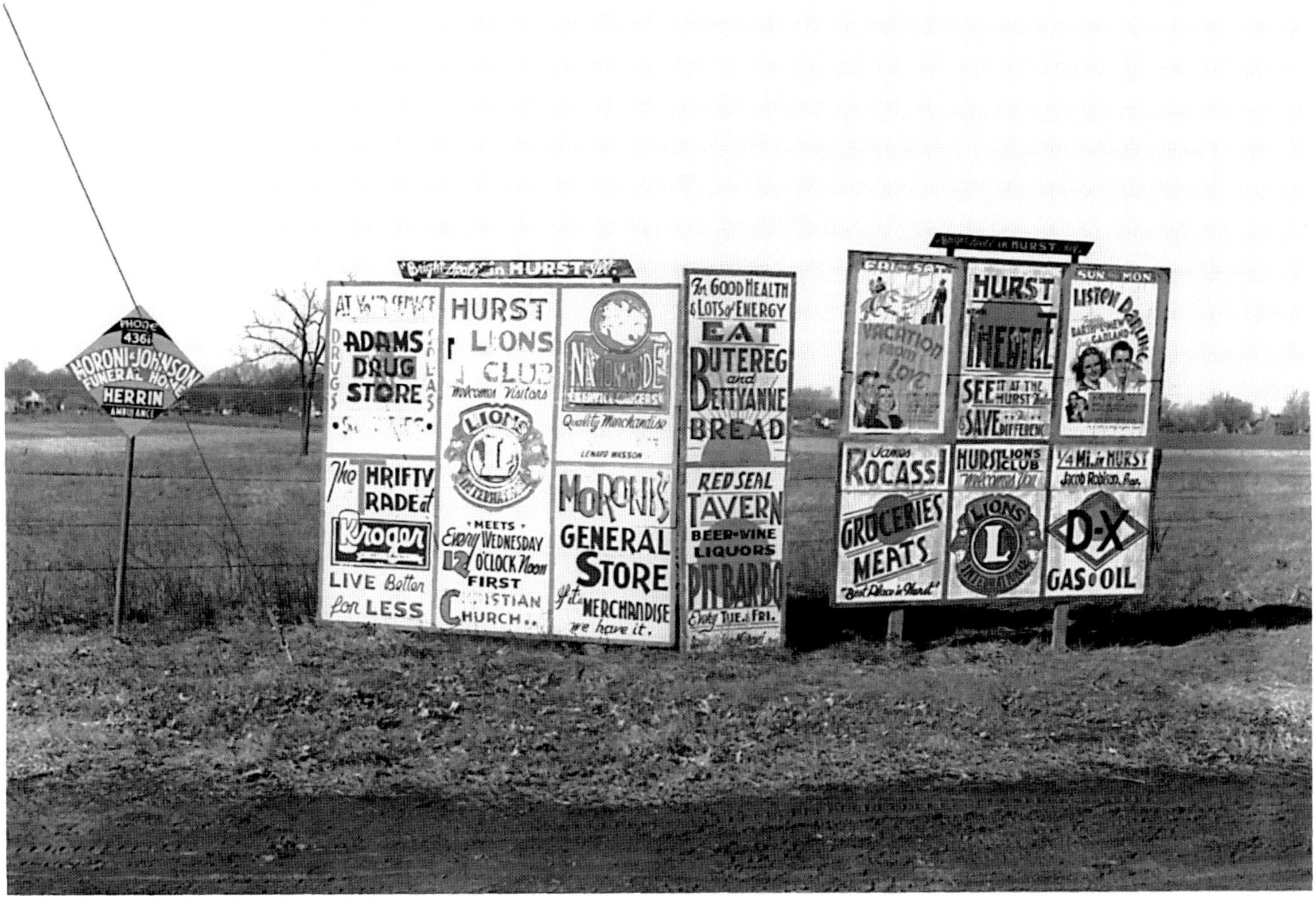

Signs along highway approaching Hurst.
Williamson County. January, 1939.
Arthur Rothstein

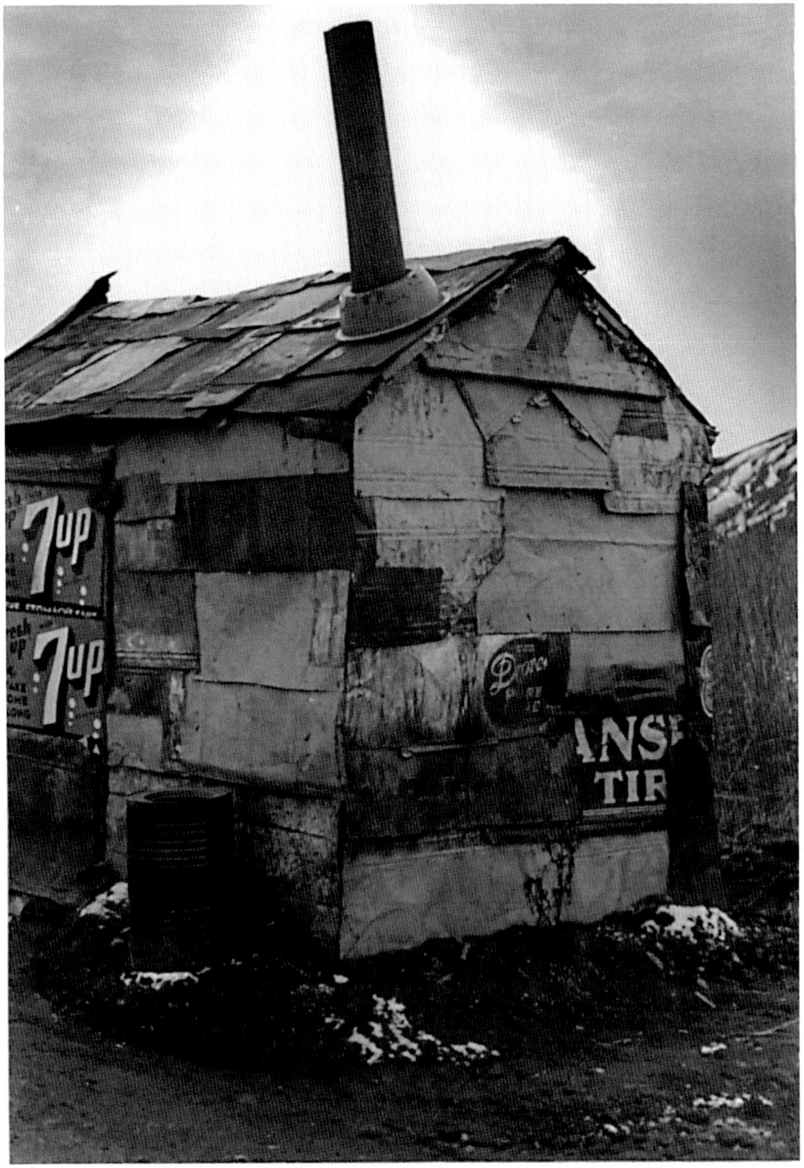

A shanty built of refuse near the Sunnyside slack pile.
Herrin. January, 1939.
Arthur Rothstein

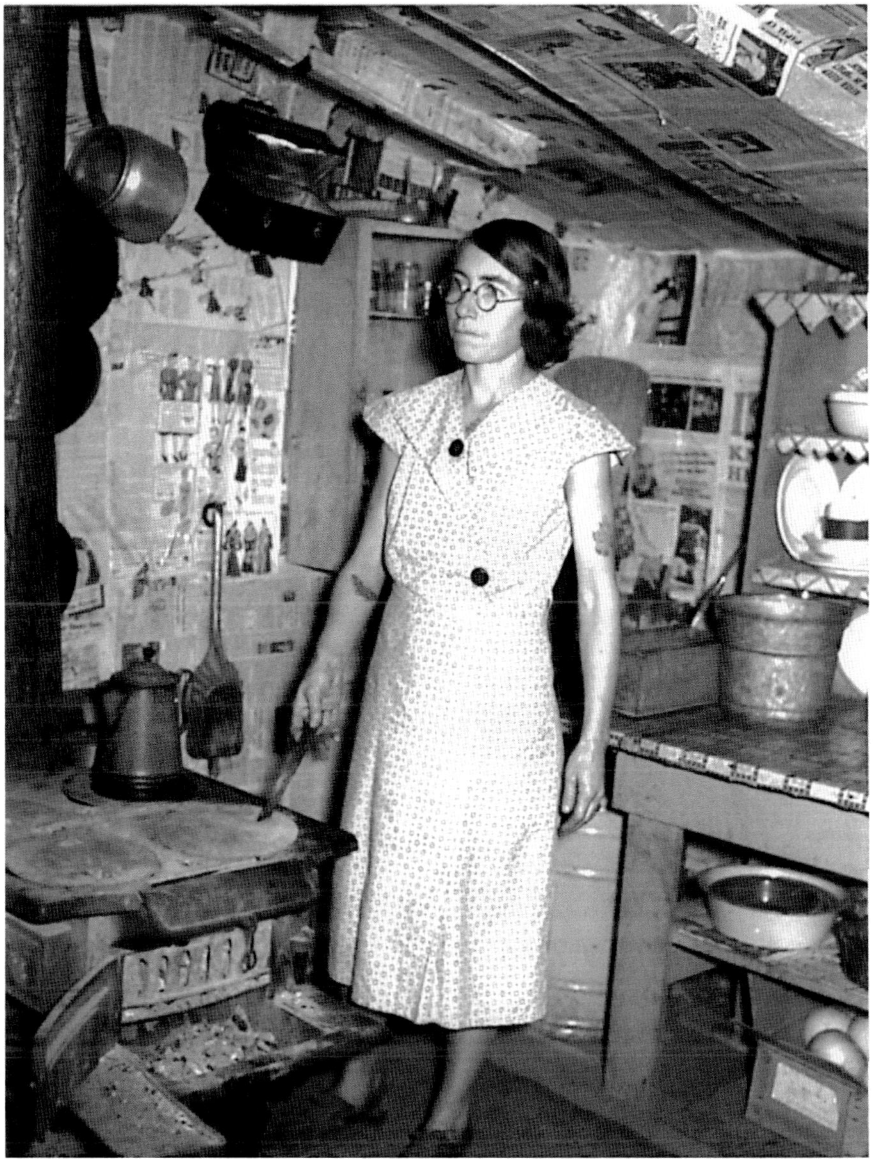

The wife of a man who is on relief.
Herrin. January, 1939.
Arthur Rothstein

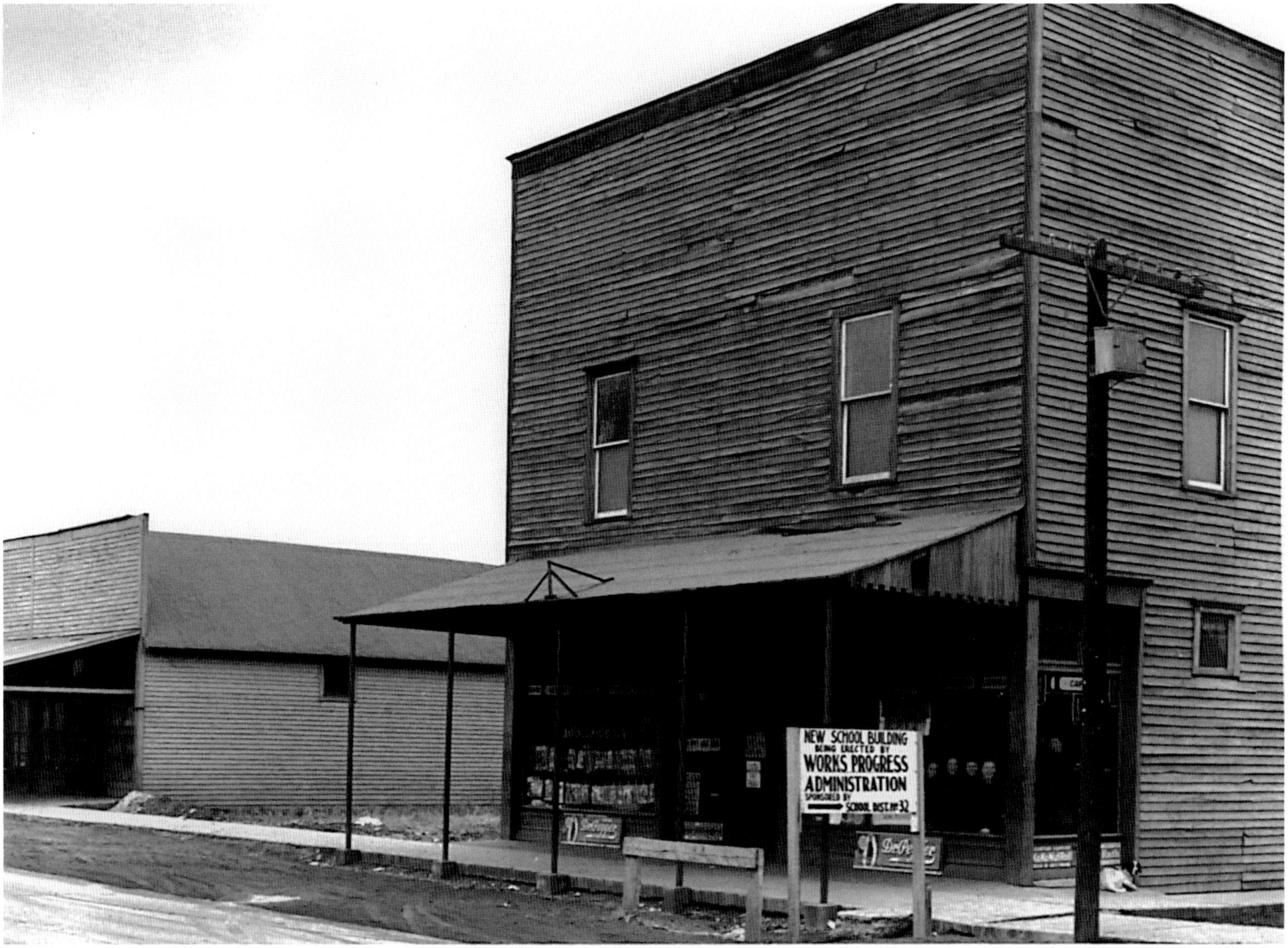

Works Progress Administration project.
Cambria. January, 1939.
Arthur Rothstein

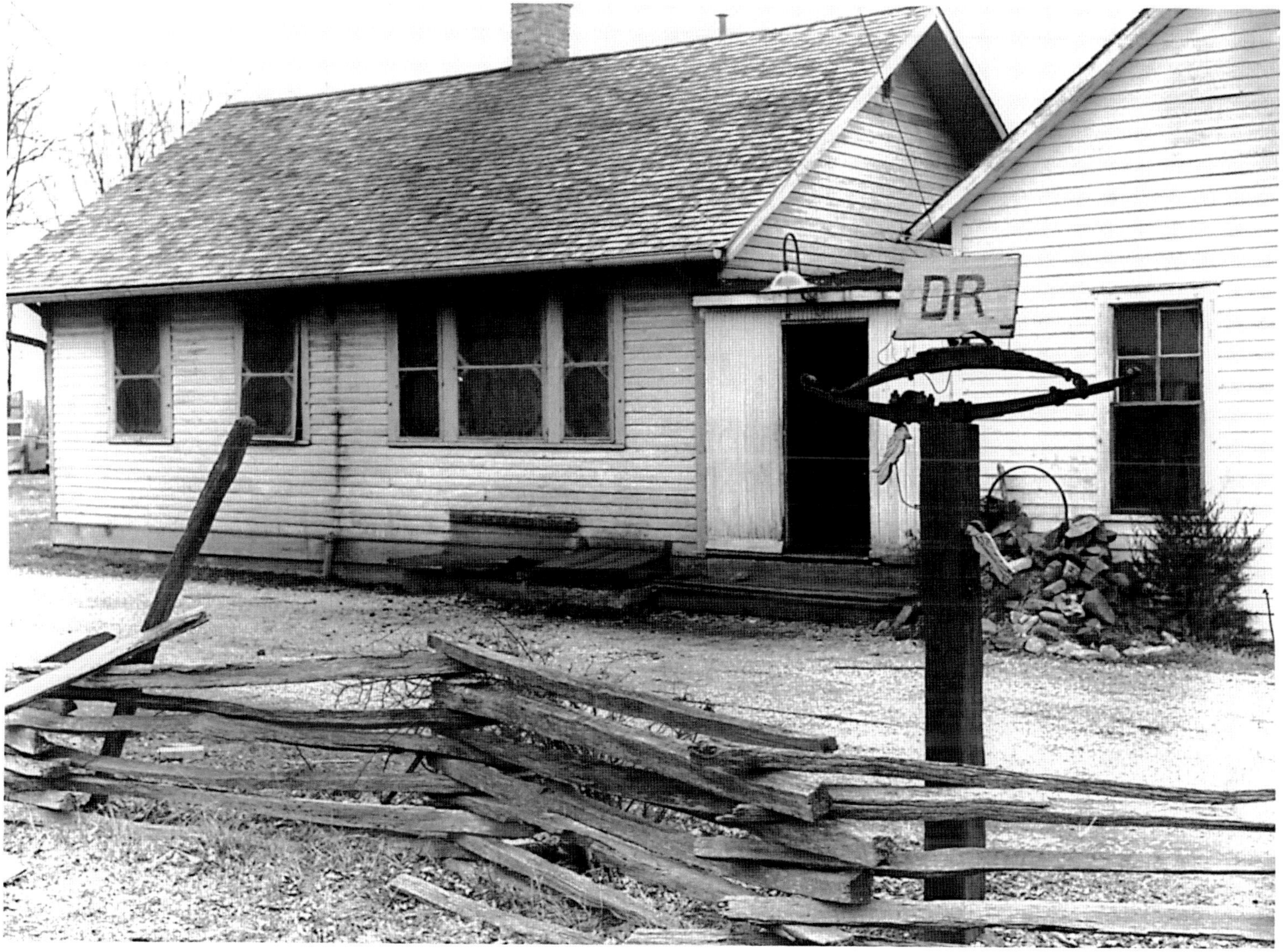

Dr. Spring's office.
Colp. January, 1939.
Arthur Rothstein

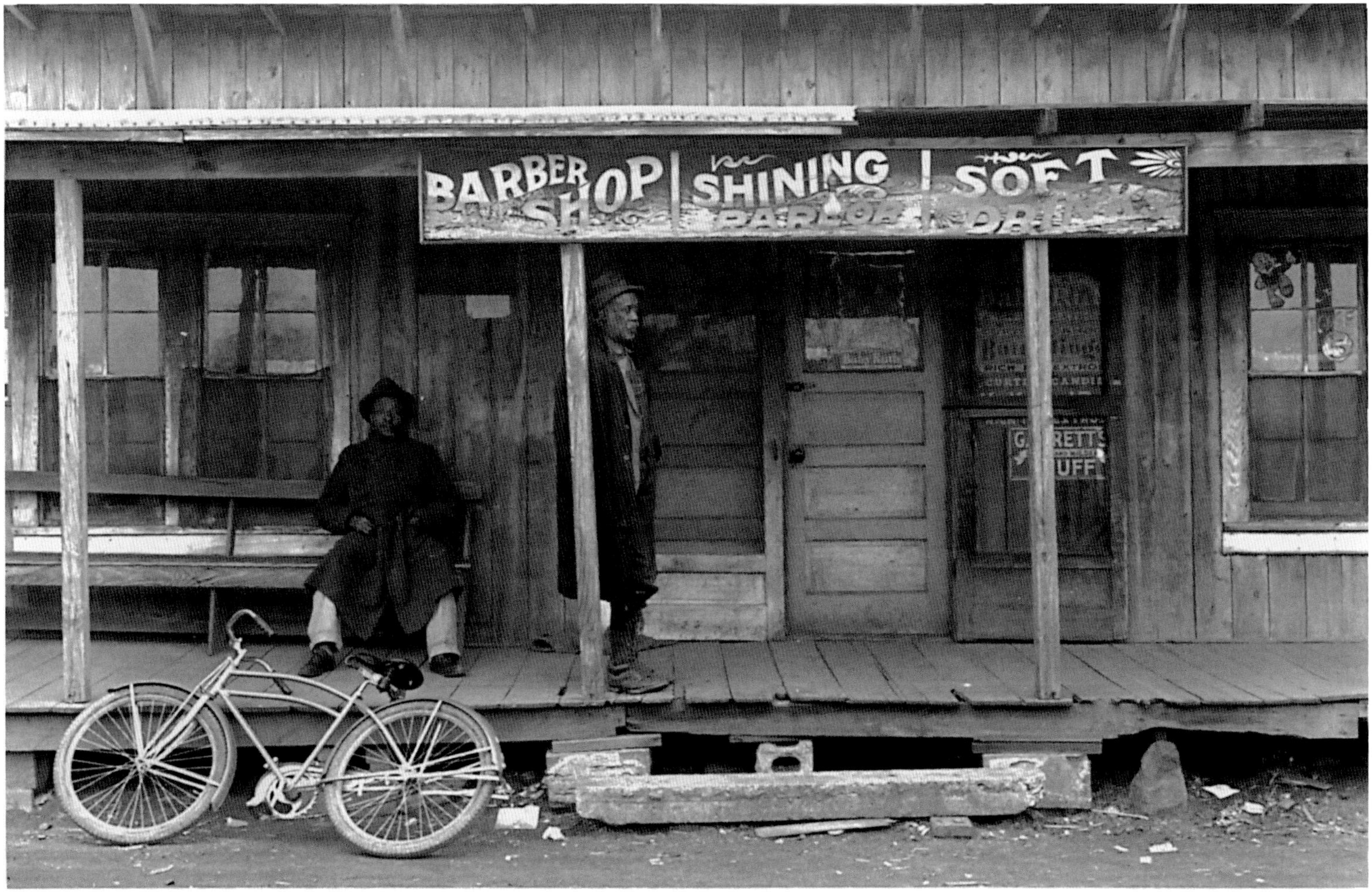

Business center.
Colp. January, 1939.
Arthur Rothstein

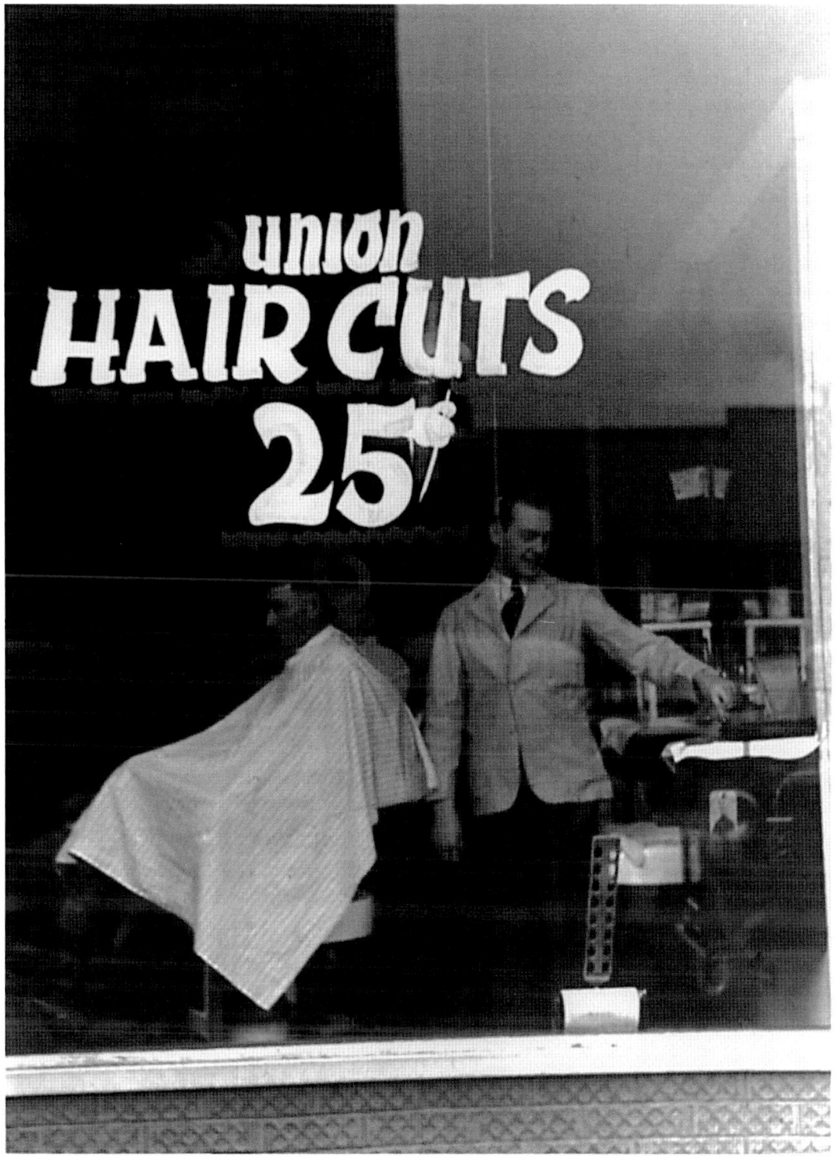

Union barbershop.
Herrin. January, 1939.
Arthur Rothstein

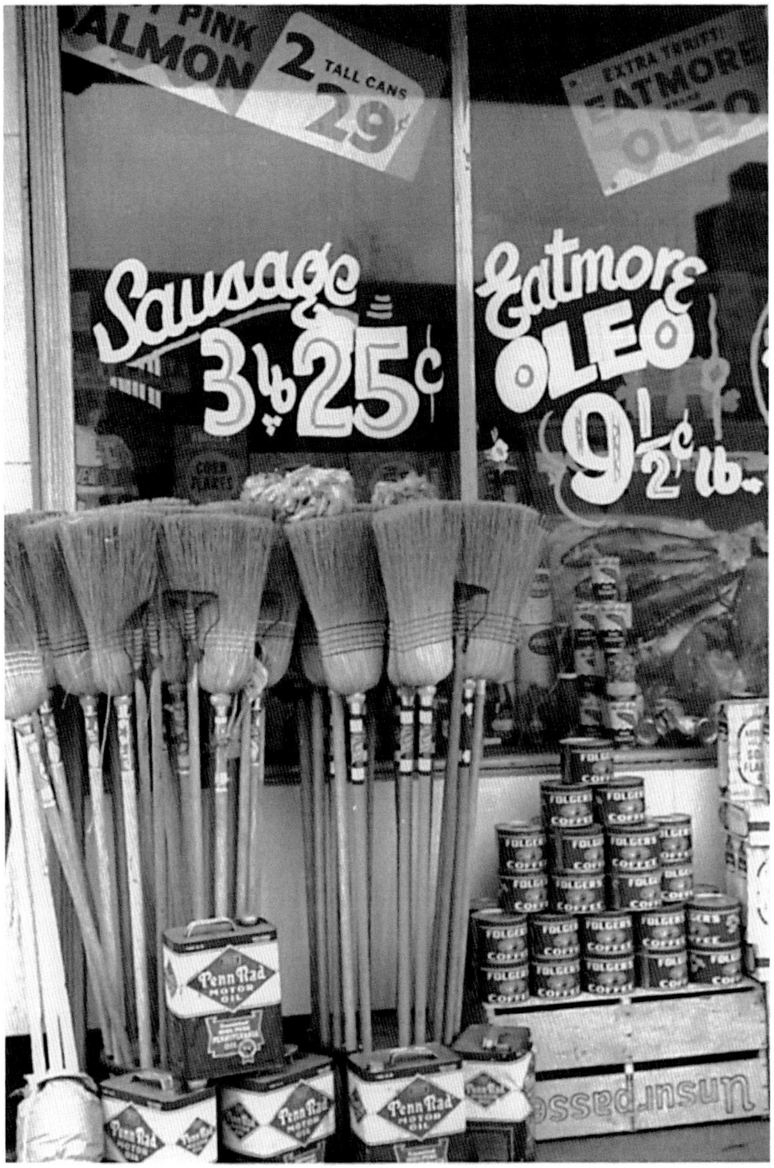

Salem. February, 1940.
Arthur Rothstein

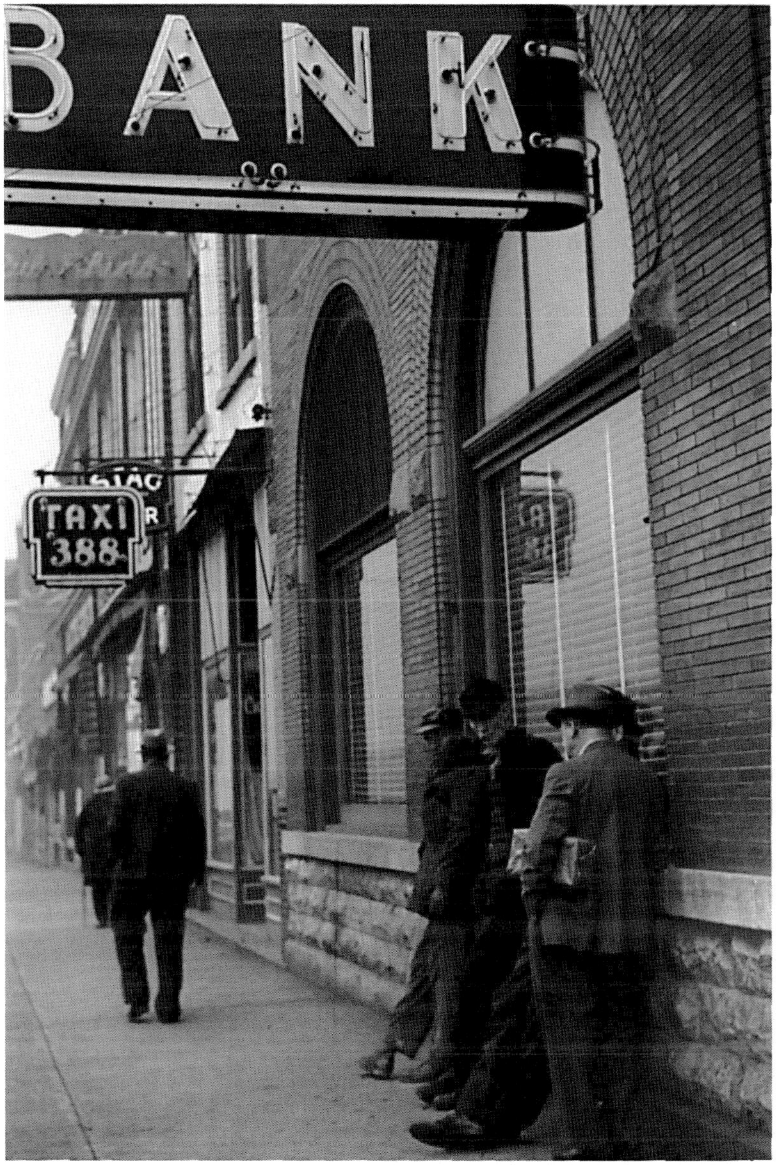

Unemployed miners.
Herrin. January, 1939.
Arthur Rothstein

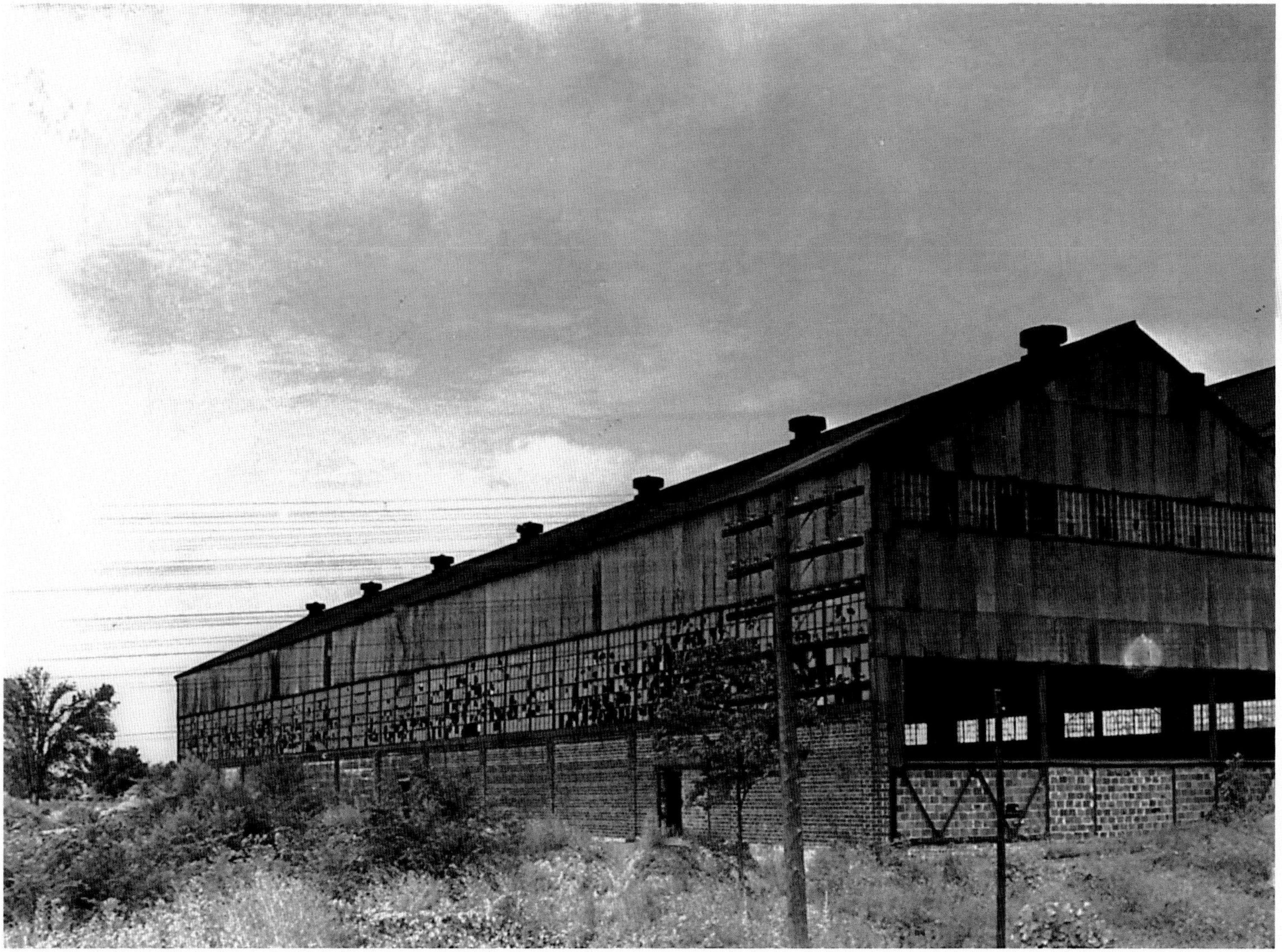

"For sale."
Murphysboro (vicinity). [No date.]
C. William Horrell

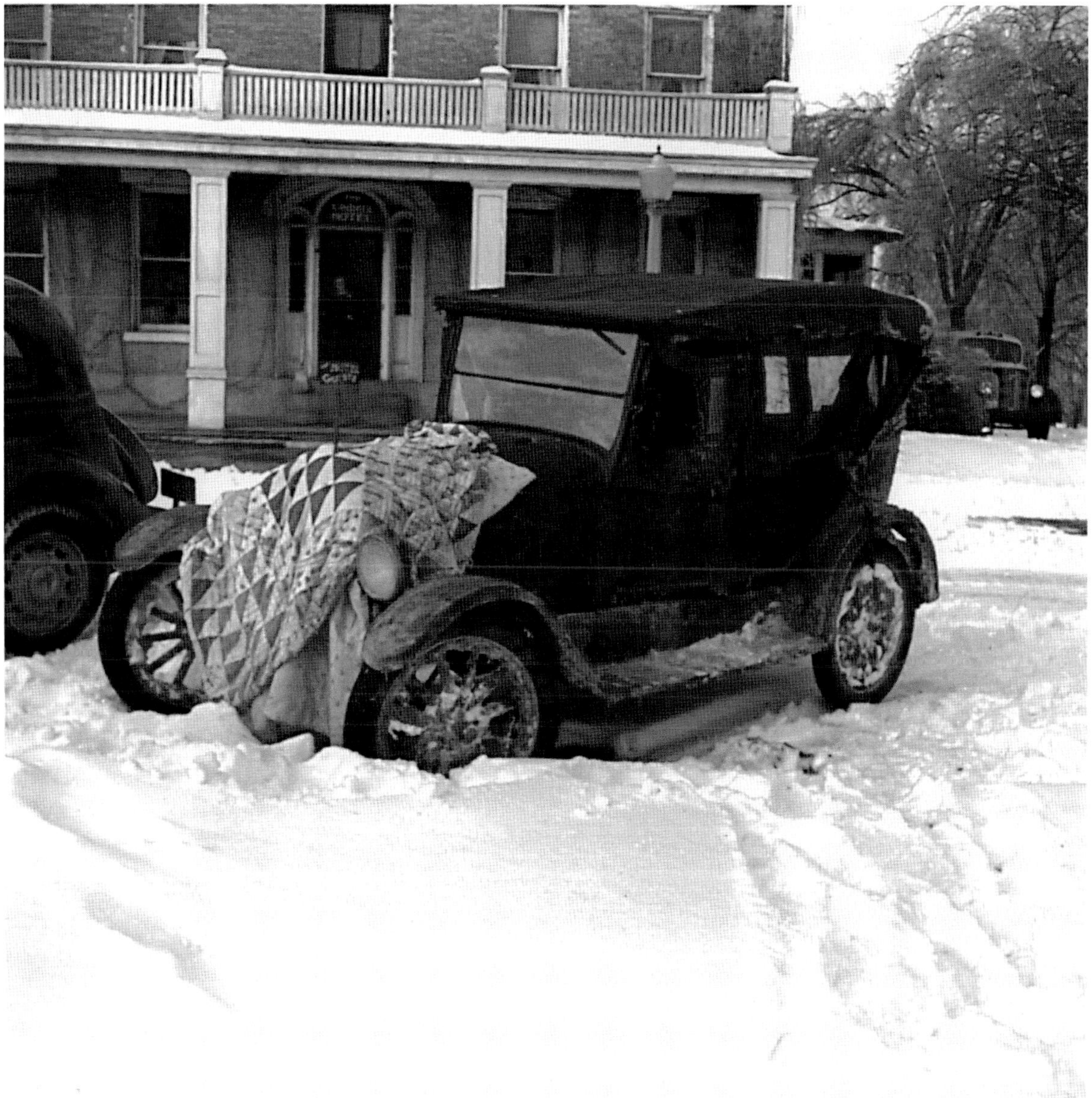

Automobile owned by a Southern Illinois farmer.
McLeansboro. February, 1937.
Russell Lee

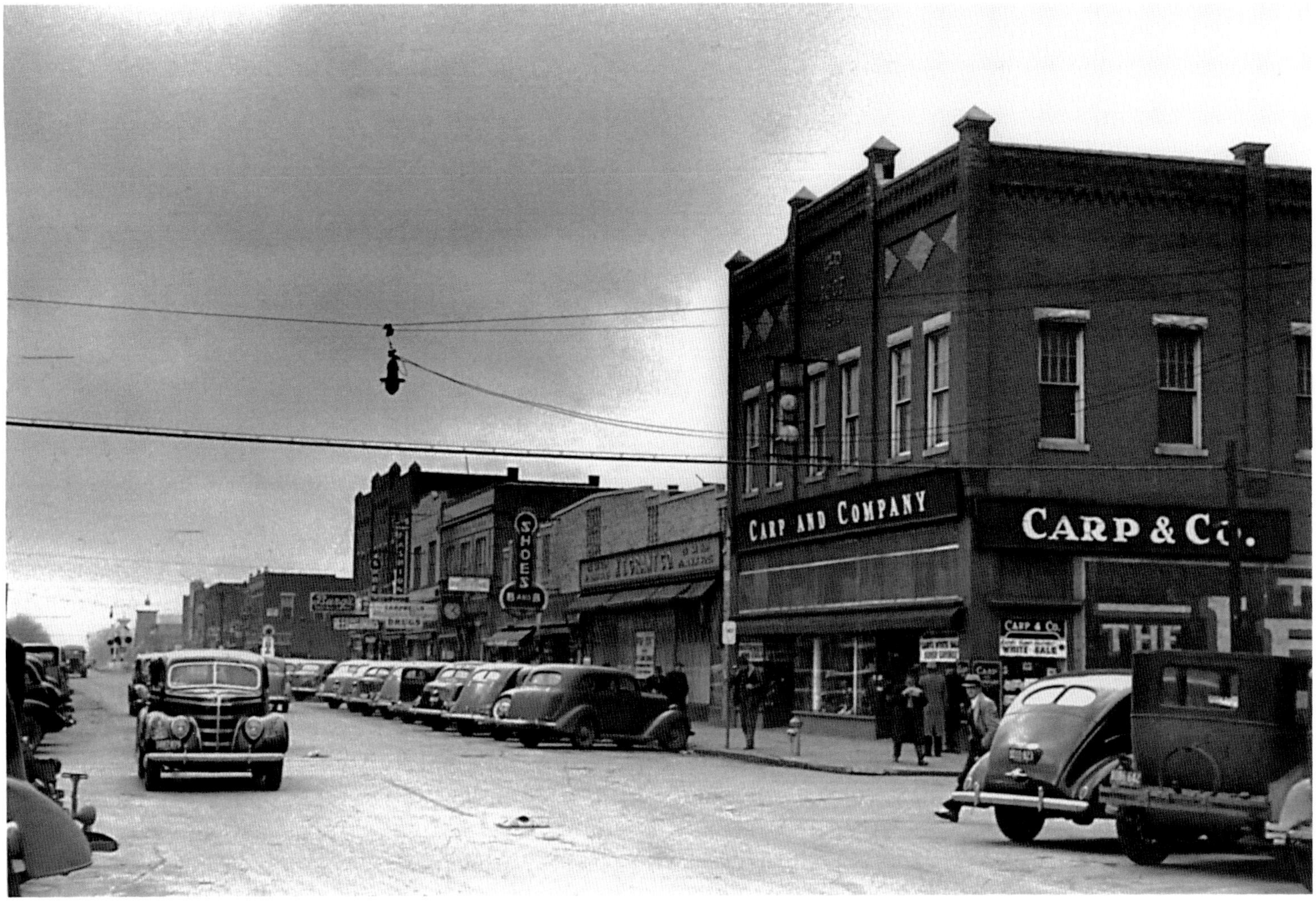

Main Street.
West Frankfort. January, 1939.
Arthur Rothstein

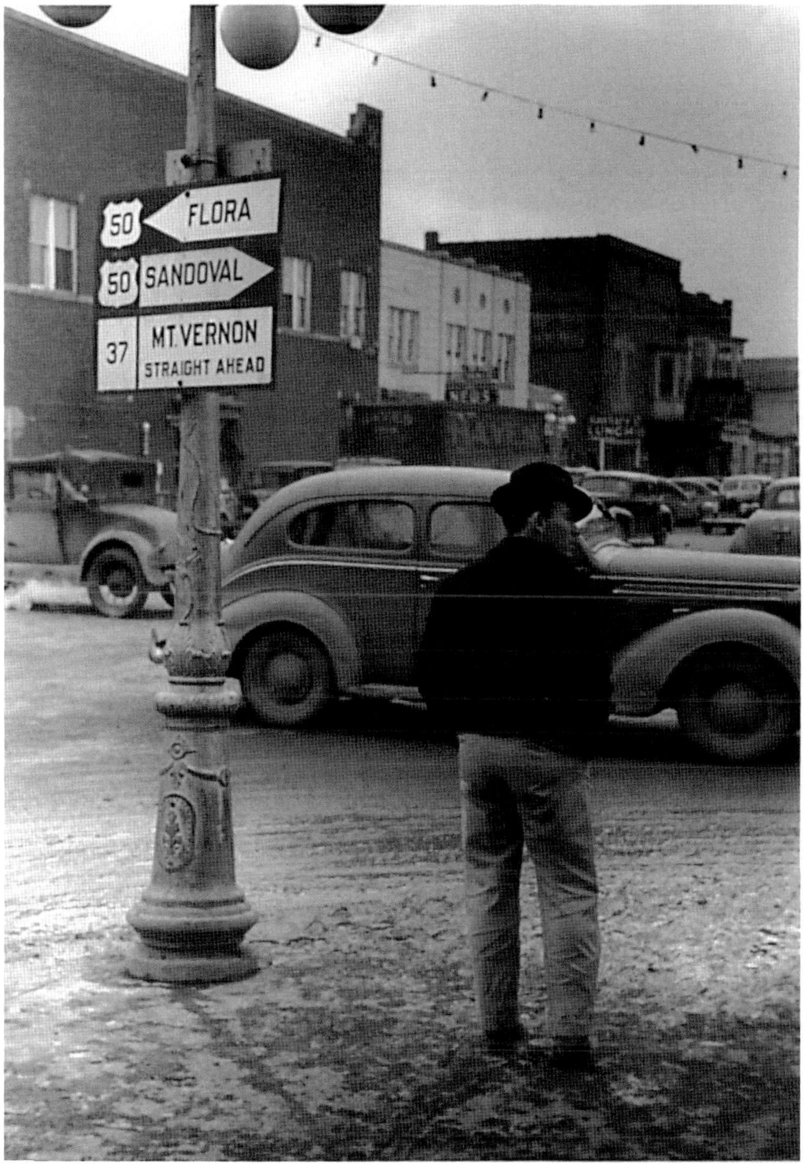

Oil worker.
Salem. February, 1940.
Arthur Rothstein

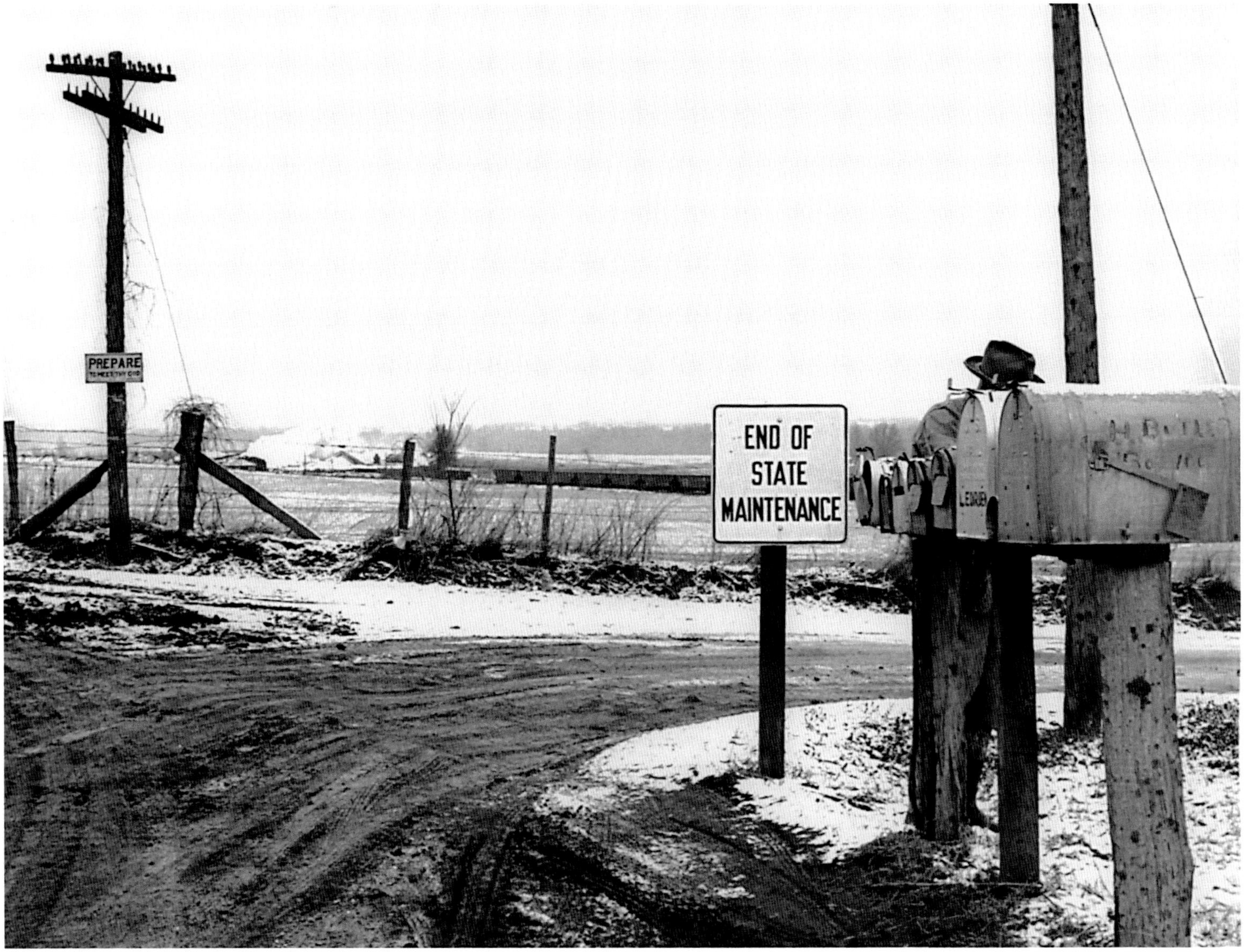

Highway.
Franklin County. January, 1939.
Arthur Rothstein

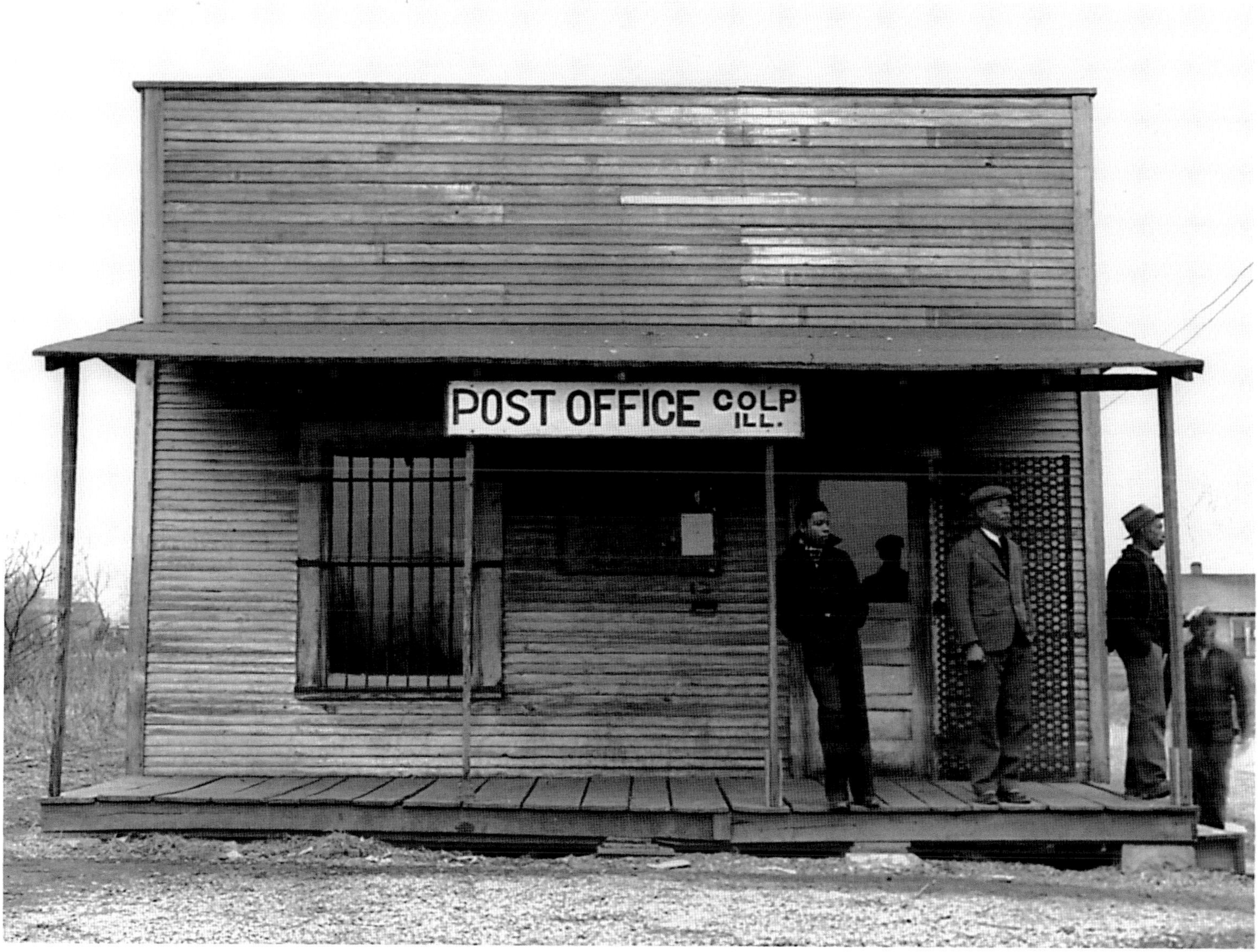

Post office.
Colp. January, 1939.
Arthur Rothstein

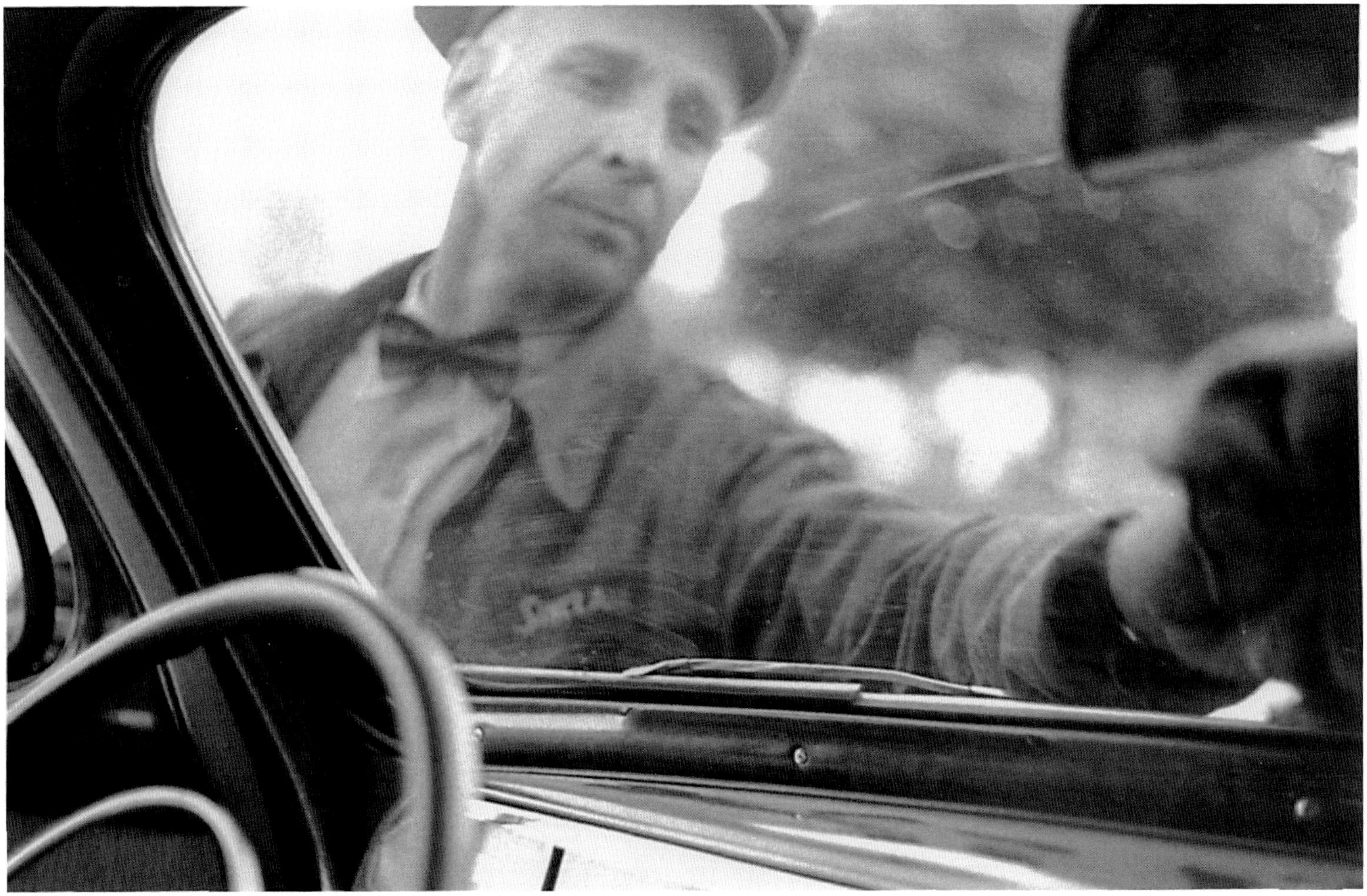

Wiping off a windshield in a service station.
Cairo. May, 1940.
Arthur Rothstein

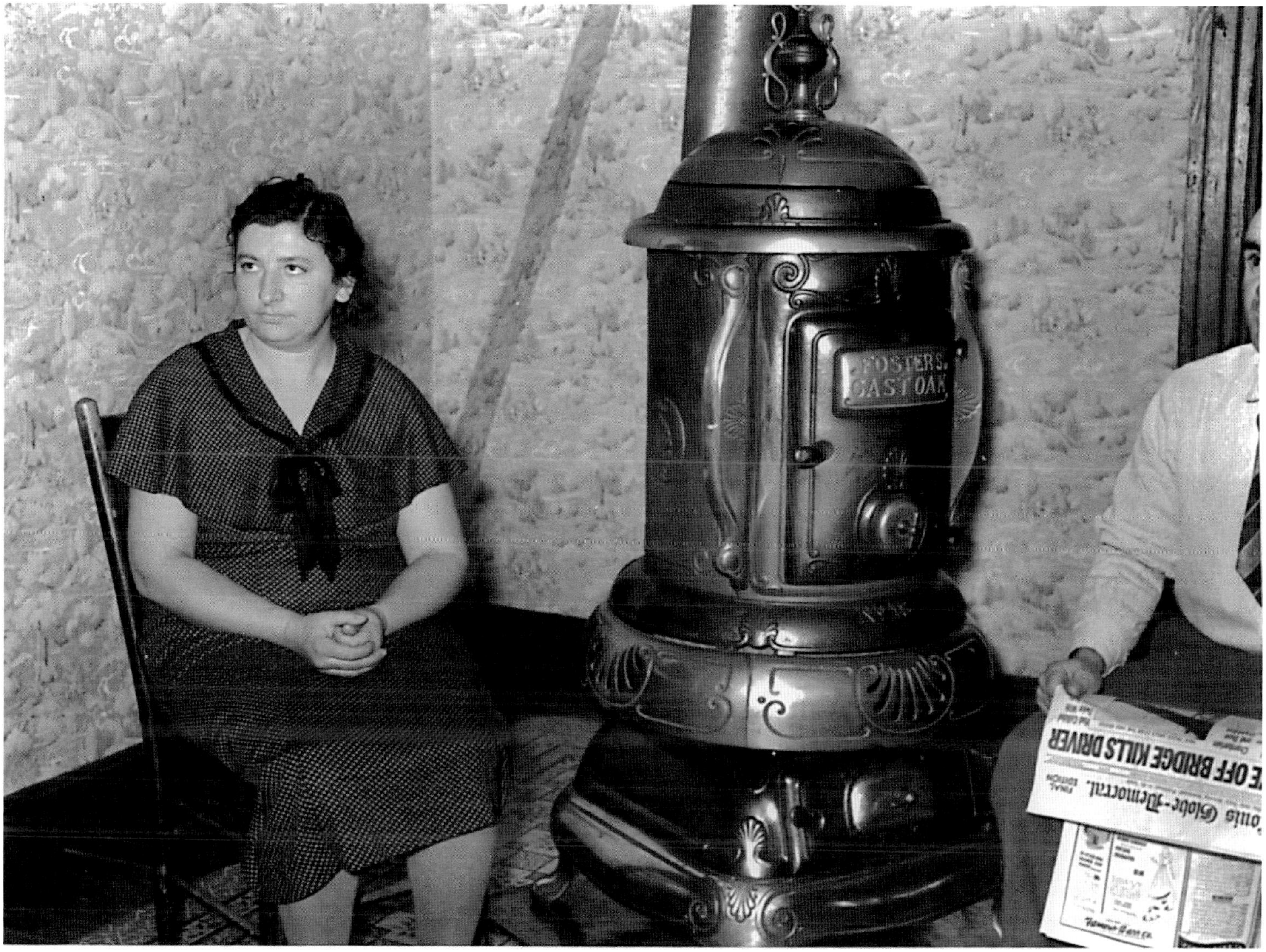

Wife of Works Progress Administration worker.
Bush. January, 1939.
Arthur Rothstein

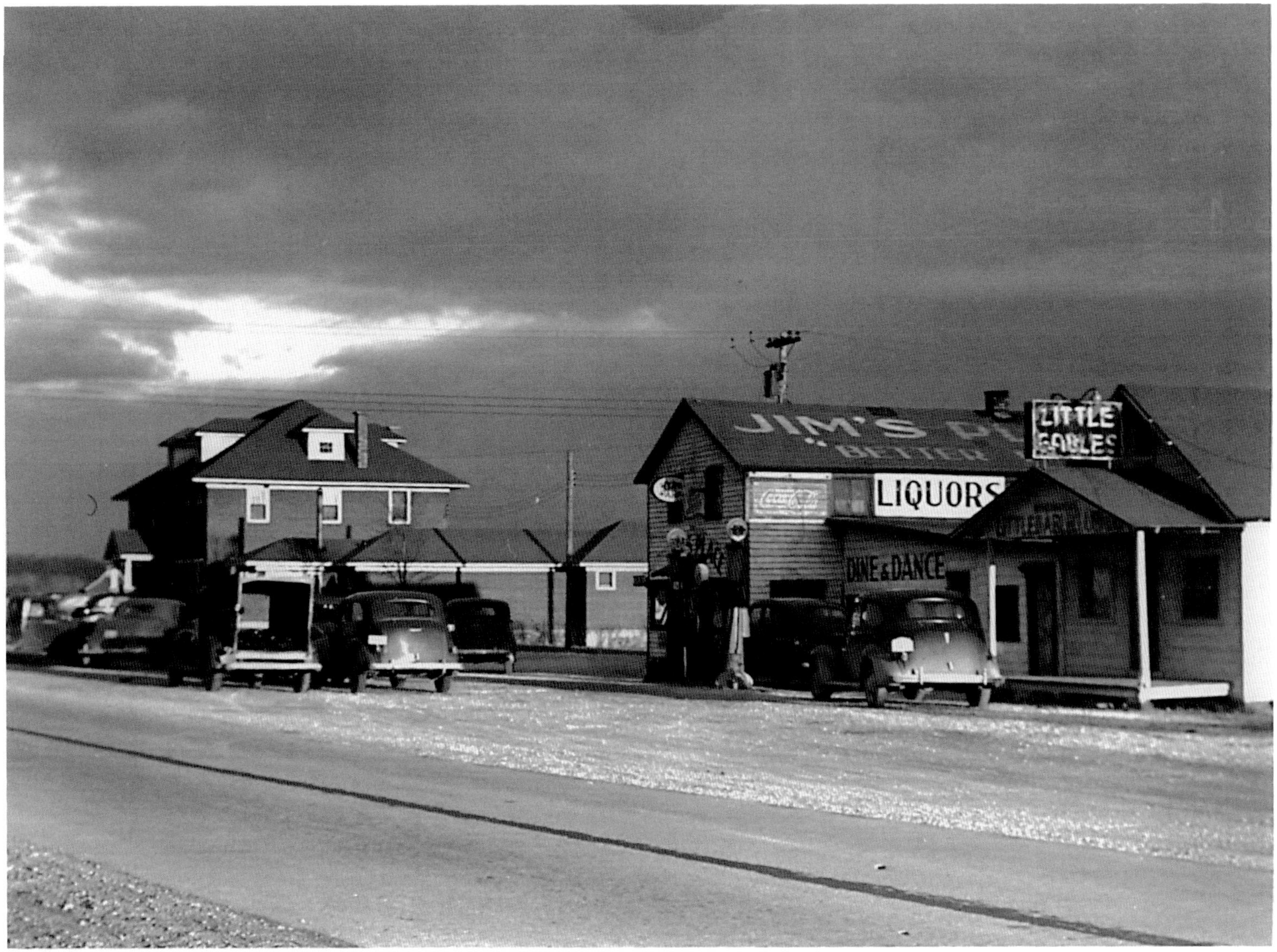

Gas station and roadhouse.
Union County. February, 1942.
John Vachon

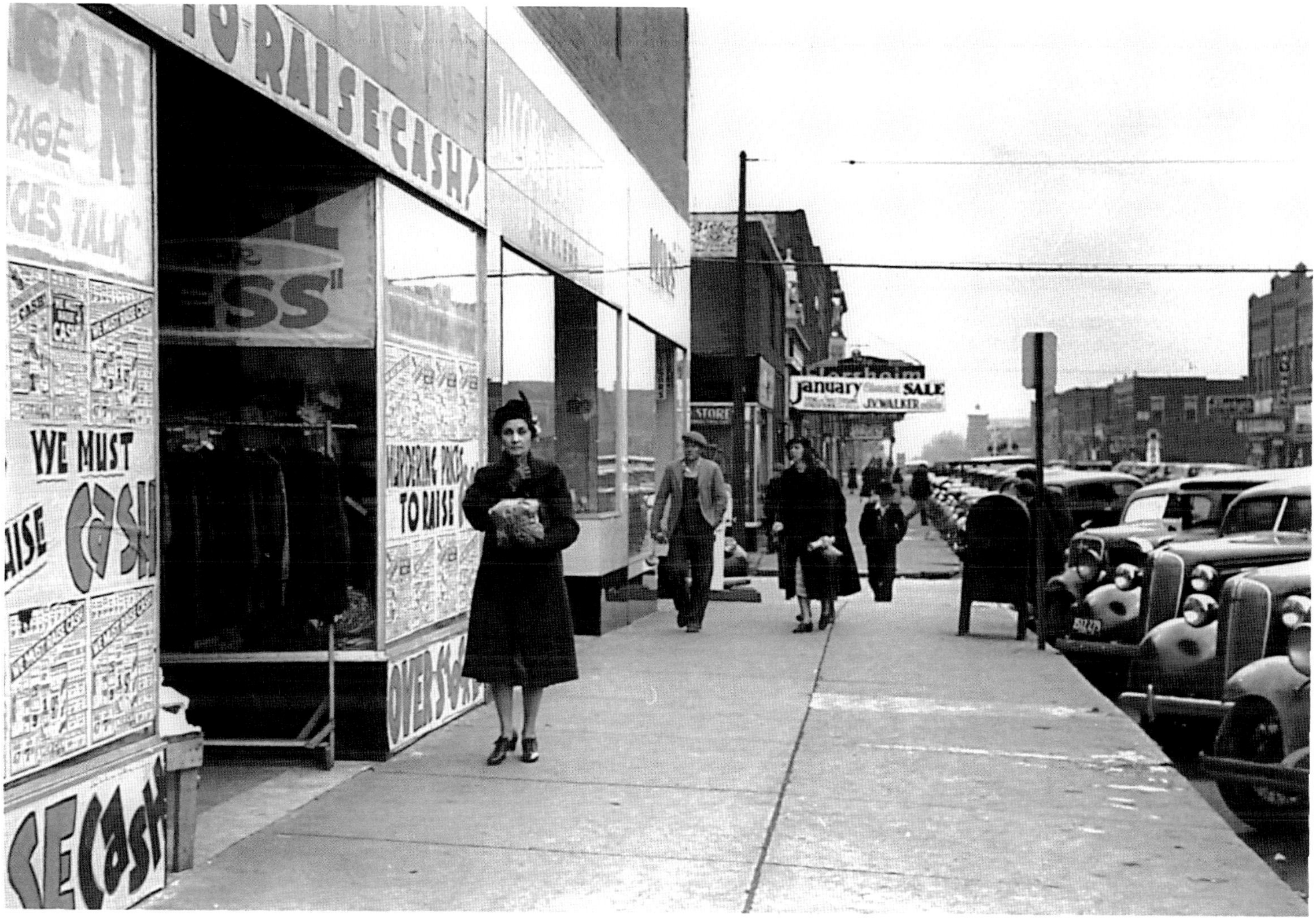

Main Street.
West Frankfort. January, 1939.
Arthur Rothstein

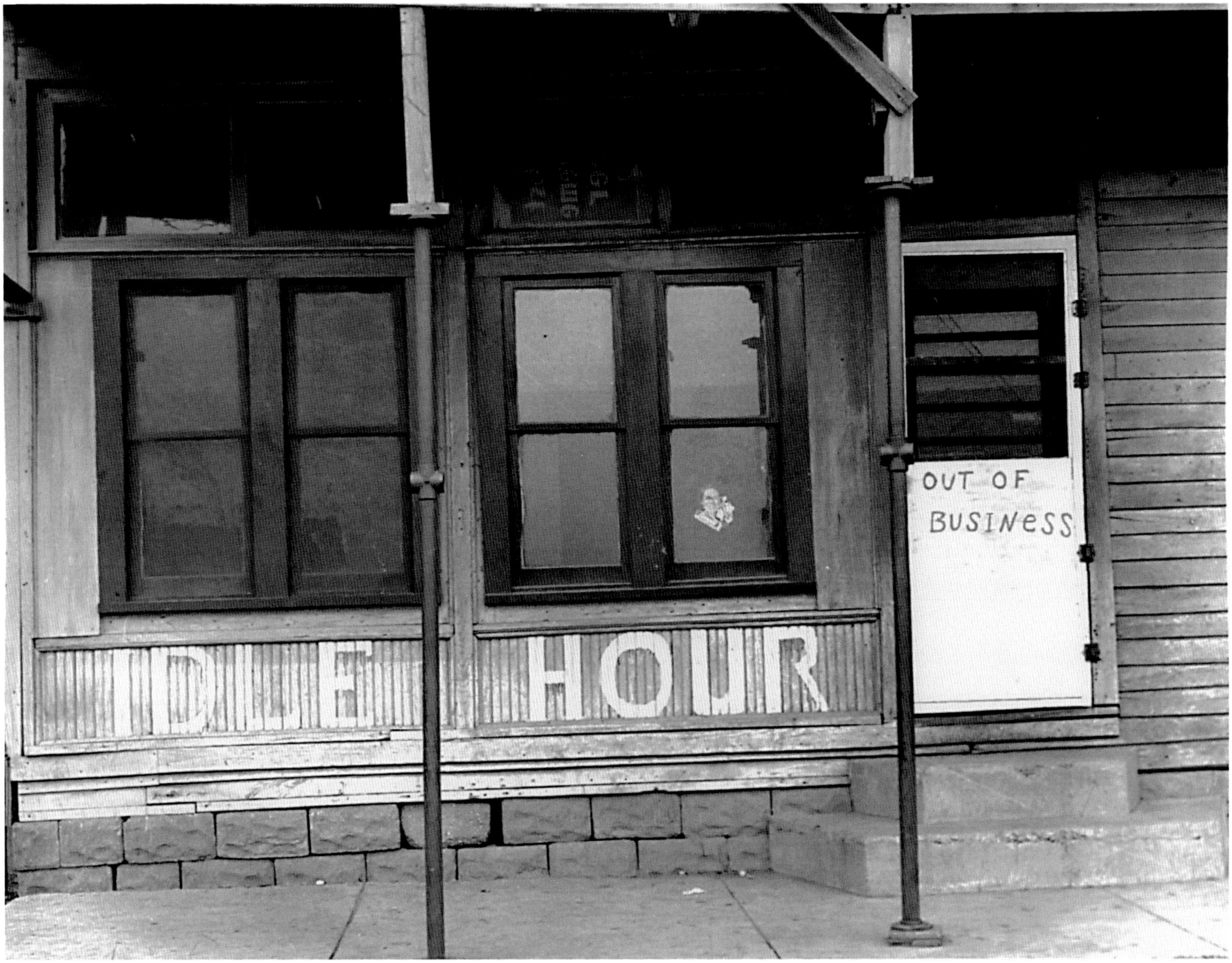

Closed pool hall.
Colp. January, 1939.
Arthur Rothstein

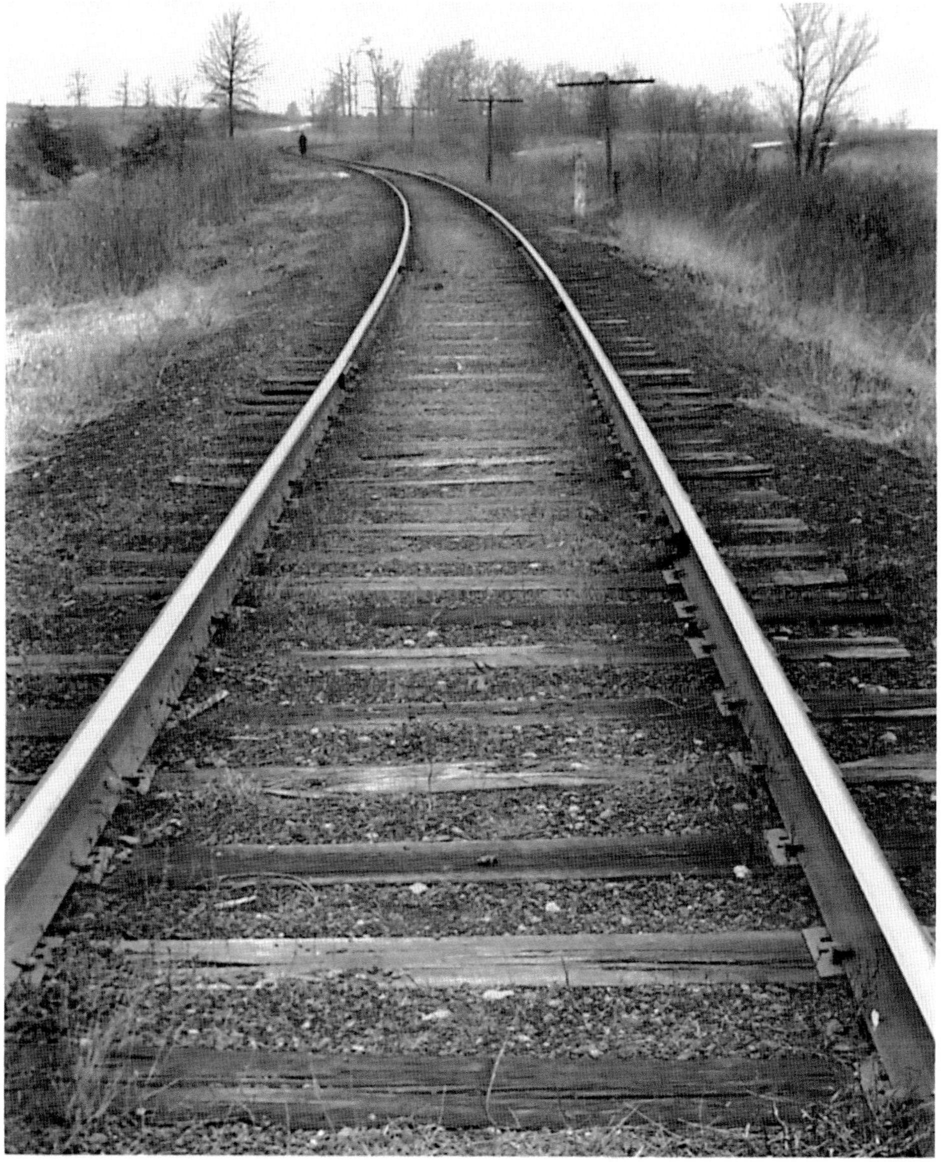

Railroad tracks.
Williamson County. January, 1939.
Arthur Rothstein

LIBRARY OF CONGRESS
NEGATIVE NUMBERS

LIBRARY OF CONGRESS NEGATIVE NUMBERS

3. LC-USF 34-60996-D
4. LC-USF 34-27030-D
5. LC-USF 34-27044-D
6. LC-USF 34-27017-D
7. LC-USF 34-27027-D
8. LC-USF 34-27010-D
9. LC-USZ 62-64492
10. LC-USF 34-10717-E
11. LC-USF 34-26912-D
12. LC-USF 34-60995-D
13. LC-USF 341-10205-B
14. LC-USF 341-10423-B
15. LC-USF 34-60986-D
16. LC-USF 34-60994-D
17. LC-USF 34-27066-D
18. LC-USF 34-64324-D
19. LC-USF 34-26785-D
20. LC-USF 34-26787-D
21. LC-USF 34-27037-D
22. LC-USF 34-60989-D
23. LC-USF 34-10275-E
24. LC-USF 33-11149-M3
25. LC-USF 33-611-M1
26. LC-USF 34-27053-D
27. LC-USF 34-60998-D
31. LC-USF 34-26989-D
32. LC-USF 34-26884-D
33. LC-USF 34-26839-D
34. LC-USF 34-26866-D
35. LC-USF 34-26981-D
36. LC-USF 34-26980-D
37. LC-USF 34-26962-D
38. LC-USF 34-26968-D
39. LC-USF 34-26972-D
40. LC-USF 34-26868-D
41. LC-USF 34-26852-D
42. LC-USF 33-2964-M4
43. LC-USF 34-26929-D
44. LC-USF 34-26829-D
45. LC-USF 34-26953-D

46. LC-USF 34-26921-D
47. LC-USF 34-26948-D
48. LC-USF 33-2991-M4
49. LC-USF 34-26933-D
50. LC-USF 34-26936-D
51. LC-USF 34-27056-D
52. LC-USF 33-2941-M3
53. LC-USF 34-26782-D
54. LC-USF 34-26783-D
55. LC-USF 33-3534-M3
56. LC-USF 33-3524-M5
57. LC-USF 33-3505-M5
58. LC-USF 34-14249E
61. LC-USF 33-3017-M4
62. LC-USF 33-3016-M4
63. LC-USF 33-3023-M1
64. LC-USF 341-10684-B
65. LC-USF 34-10731-E
66. LC-USF 34-10255-E
67. LC-USF 341-10664-B
68. LC-USF 34-10795-E
69. LC-USF 34-10793-E
70. LC-USF 34-10659-D
71. LC-USF 34-10646-D
72. LC-USF 34-10721-E
73. LC-USF 341-10678-B
74. LC-USF 341-10680-B
75. LC-USF 341-10677-B
76. LC-USF 341-10431-B
77. LC-USF 34-26784-D
78. LC-USF 33-1883-M3
79. LC-USW 3-31744-D
80. LC-USW 3-31794-E
81. LC-USW 3-31705-D
82. LC-USF 34-60963-D
85. LC-USF 33-2974-M5
86. LC-USF 34-26914-D
87. LC-USF 34-26875-D
88. LC-USF 34-26826-D
89. LC-USF 33-1885-M3
90. LC-USF 34-60939-D
91. LC-USF 34-27025-D
92. LC-USF 34-26926-D
93. LC-USF 34-64312-D
94. LC-USF 34-26825-D
95. LC-USF 34-26749-D
96. LC-USF 34-26744-D
97. LC-USF 34-64315-D
101. LC-USF 34-26915-D
102. LC-USF 33-2994-M2
103. LC-USF 34-26999-D
104. LC-USF 34-26923-D
105. LC-USF 34-26803-D
106. LC-USF 34-26801-D
107. LC-USF 33-2976-M3
108. LC-USF 33-3530-M5
109. LC-USF 33-2981-M4
110. LC-USF 34-14250-C
111. LC-USF 34-10274-E
112. LC-USF 33-3012-M4
113. LC-USF 33-3530-M1
114. LC-USF 34-26922-D
115. LC-USF 34-26797-D
116. LC-USF 33-1885-M1
117. LC-USF 34-26871-D
118. LC-USF 34-64305-D
119. LC-USF 33-3008-M5
120. LC-USF 34-26800-D
121. LC-USF 34-26988-D

HERBERT K. RUSSELL is Director of College Relations at John A. Logan College, Carterville, Illinois. A native Illinoisan, he received his Ph.D. degree in English from Southern Illinois University, where he taught the subject and subsequently served as Editorial Writer and Technical Editor at the university's Coal Research Center. He has published widely on the life and works of Edgar Lee Masters, most recently in the *Dictionary of Literary Biography.* Russell has also edited a new edition of Mary Tracy Earle's Civil War novel *The Flag on the Hilltop,* also published in the Shawnee Books series.

F. JACK HURLEY is Professor of History at Memphis State University in Memphis, Tennessee. He is the author of several books on photography in the 1930s including *Portrait of a Decade: Roy Stryker and the Development of Documentary Photography in the Thirties,* published by Louisiana State University Press in 1972, *Russell Lee: Photographer,* Morgan and Morgan, New York, 1978, and most recently *Marion Post Wolcott: A Photographic Journey,* which was brought out in 1989 by the University of New Mexico Press.

SHAWNEE BOOKS

Also available in this series . . .

The Next New Madrid Earthquake: A Survival Guide for the Midwest
WILLIAM ATKINSON

Forgetting and the Forgotten: A Thousand Years of Contested Histories in the Heartland
MICHAEL C. BATINSKI

Reckoning at Eagle Creek: The Secret Legacy of Coal in the Heartland
JEFF BIGGERS

History as They Lived It: A Social History of Prairie du Rocher, Illinois
MARGARET KIMBALL BROWN

Foothold on a Hillside: Memories of a Southern Illinoisan
CHARLESS CARAWAY

Growing Up in a Land Called Egypt: A Southern Illinois Family Biography
CLEO CARAWAY

Colonial Ste. Genevieve: An Adventure on the Mississippi Frontier
CARL J. EKBERG

Dawn's Light Woman & Nicholas Franchomme: Marriage and Law in the Illinois Country
CARL J. EKBERG AND SHARON K. PERSON

A Nickel's Worth of Skim Milk: A Boy's View of the Great Depression
ROBERT J. HASTINGS

A Penny's Worth of Minced Ham: Another Look at the Great Depression
ROBERT J. HASTINGS

Southern Illinois Coal: A Portfolio
C. WILLIAM HORRELL

Always of Home: A Southern Illinois Childhood
EDGAR ALLEN IMHOFF

Lives of Fort de Chartres: Commandants, Soldiers, and Civilians in French Illinois, 1720–1770
DAVID MACDONALD

Kaskaskia: The Lost Capital of Illinois
DAVID MACDONALD AND RAINE WATERS

20 Day Trips in and around the Shawnee National Forest
LARRY P. AND DONNA J. MAHAN

Land of Big Rivers: French and Indian Illinois, 1699–1778
M. J. MORGAN

America's Deadliest Twister: The Tri-State Tornado of 1925
GEOFF PARTLOW

Escape Betwixt Two Suns: A True Tale of the Underground Railroad in Illinois
CAROL PIRTLE

Fishing Southern Illinois
ART REID

All Anybody Ever Wanted of Me Was to Work: The Memoirs of Edith Bradley Rendleman
EDITH BRADLEY RENDLEMAN
EDITED BY JANE ADAMS

The Civilian Conservation Corps in Southern Illinois, 1933–1942
KAY RIPPELMEYER

Giant City State Park and the Civilian Conservation Corps: A History in Words and Pictures
KAY RIPPELMEYER

Fluorspar Mining: Photos from Illinois and Kentucky, 1905–1995
HERBERT K. RUSSELL

The State of Southern Illinois: An Illustrated History
HERBERT K. RUSSELL

Southern Illinois Fishing: A Comprehensive Guide for Anglers
COLBY SIMMS

Snake Road: A Field Guide to the Snakes of LaRue–Pine Hills
JOSHUA J. VOSSLER

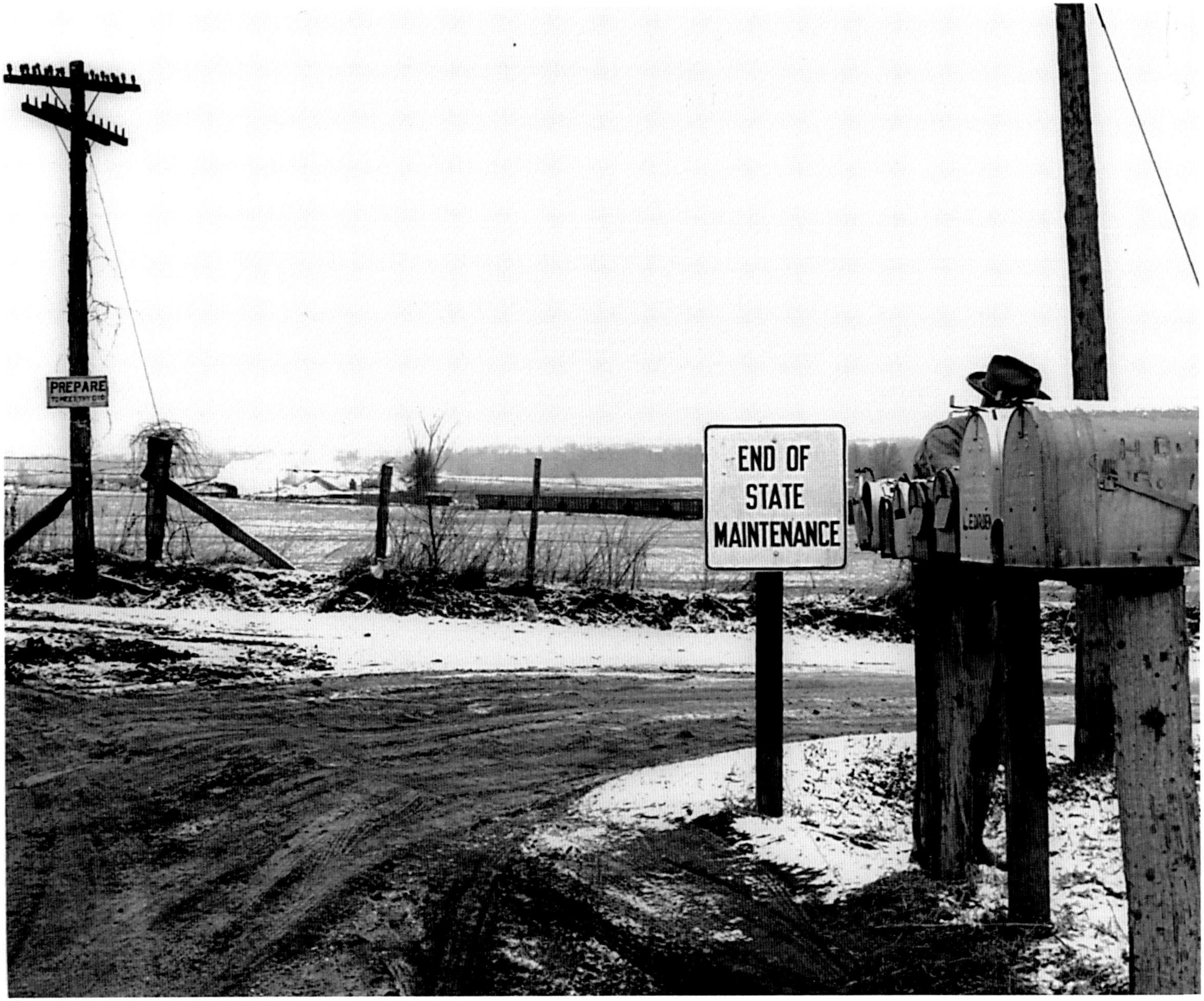
PREPARE
END OF
STATE
MAINTENANCE